THE DEATH OF THE OLD
AND THE BIRTH OF THE NEW

Program in Judaic Studies
Brown University
BROWN JUDAIC STUDIES

Edited by
Jacob Neusner,
Wendell S. Dietrich, Ernest S. Frerichs,
Calvin Goldscheider, Alan Zuckerman

Project Editors (Project)

David Blumenthal, Emory University (Approaches to Medieval Judaism)
William Brinner (Studies in Judaism and Islam)
Ernest S. Frerichs, Brown University (Dissertations and Monographs)
Lenn Evan Goodman, University of Hawaii (Studies in Medieval Judaism) (Studies in
Judaism and Islam)
William Scott Green, University of Rochester (Approaches to Ancient Judaism)
Ivan Marcus, Jewish Theological Seminary of America
(Texts and Studies in Medieval Judaism)
Marc L. Raphael, Ohio State University (Approaches to Judaism in Modern Times)
Norbert Samuelson, Temple University (Jewish Philosophy)
Jonathan Z. Smith, University of Chicago (Studia Philonica)

Number 71

THE DEATH OF THE OLD AND THE BIRTH OF THE NEW
The Framework of the Book of Numbers and the Pentateuch

by
Dennis T. Olson

THE DEATH OF THE OLD
AND THE BIRTH OF THE NEW
The Framework of the Book of Numbers and the Pentateuch

by
Dennis T. Olson

Scholars Press
Chico, California

THE DEATH OF THE OLD AND THE BIRTH OF THE NEW
The Framework of the Book of Numbers and the Pentateuch

by
Dennis T. Olson

Library of Congress Cataloging in Publication Data

Olson, Dennis T.
  The death of the old and the birth of the new.

  (Brown Judaic studies ; no. 71)
  Bibliography: p.
  Includes index.
  1. Bible. O.T. Numbers—Criticism, interpretation, etc.
  2. Bible. O.T. Pentateuch—Criticism, interpretation, etc.
  I. Title. II. Series.
  BS1265.2.047   1985   222'.1406   85–10738
  ISBN 0–89130–885–7 (alk. paper)
  ISBN 0–89130–886–5 (pbk. : alk. paper)

Printed in the United States of America
on acid-free paper

For Eric and Kristen,
the promise of a new generation

TABLE OF CONTENTS

INTRODUCTION

A major obstacle to the appreciation and interpretation of
any literary work is a perceived lack of coherence or organization.
If no structure is detected, the work collapses into a jumble of
unrelated fragments with no unifying purpose or meaning. Perhaps
more than any other book of the Bible, the book of Numbers has
evaded the search by modern scholars and commentators for a convincing and meaningful structure. The problem of its perceived
lack of coherence is all the more acute because the book remains
a part of the normative Scriptural tradition of Judaism and
Christianity. As such, the book of Numbers should be expected
to render a coherent message for its readers and hearers.

The problem extends beyond the book of Numbers to the entire
Pentateuch, the first five books of the Bible. College or seminary
courses on the Pentateuch tend to concentrate on the books of
Genesis and Exodus. The structure of these books is fairly clear
and straightforward. Often skipping lightly over Leviticus and
Numbers, courses continue with a more in-depth study of the book
of Deuteronomy with its unique issues and problems. The result
is that students rarely get a sense for the structure of the
whole Pentateuch. One jumps from the generation of those led out
of Egypt and wandering in the wilderness in the book of Exodus to
a new generation on the edge of the promised land in the book of
Deuteronomy. But what has happened in the meantime? Where and in
what way is the transition made from the old Exodus generation to
the new generation which we find in Deuteronomy? What is the
theological and hermeneutical significance of that transition and
its effect on interpreting the Pentateuch? Is there a defined and
intentional structure which has been built into the Torah, the
five books of Genesis-Deuteronomy? These are the questions with
which our study will wrestle.

It will be obvious that while we fully embrace and utilize
the tools of critical study, we are not primarily concerned with
dissecting the text into its component parts or layers. When the
evidence warrants it, such a procedure is certainly legitimate.
Our concern, however, is to use the tools of critical study in

such a way as to discern the definitive literary and theological
structure which now holds the book of Numbers and the entire
Pentateuch together as a coherent whole. As we will discover,
that definitive theological shaping for the book of Numbers did
not occur with the final stage of editing. Rather, the definitive
shaping of the book's structure occurred earlier than the final
form but was carried forward in its essentials and enriched by
successive editings until the book reached its present shape.

The purpose of this study, then, is to attempt to overcome
the obstacle of a perceived lack of structure for the book of
Numbers and the Pentateuch and thereby allow their theological
witness to be heard anew. We will begin by tracing the modern
study of the book of Numbers. We will establish the nature of
the major problem in the interpretation of Numbers and the reason
it arose (Part One). We will then suggest an alternative proposal
for the overarching structure of Numbers based on the two census
lists in Numbers 1 and 26. We will also present evidence for the
intentional formation of such a structure by the later editors of
Numbers and the way in which this structure provides the linchpin
for understanding the framework of the entire Pentateuch (Part
Two). This structure provides the basis for understanding the
unifying theological theme of Numbers as the death of the old
generation and the birth of the new generation of God's people,
a generation of hope and expectation on the boundary of the
promised land. The theological implications for the interpretation
of the book of Numbers and the Pentateuch will then be presented
(Part Three).

By proposing a means of overcoming the obstacle of a lack of
structure and coherence, we hope also to engage a larger hermeneutical issue. How does a normative religious tradition which has
been shaped in a distant past continue to address and involve
readers and hearers of future generations? Has the present structure of the book of Numbers been intentionally shaped by its
writers and editors in such a way that the story of a people of
the past can become the story of a people in the present? How
does the story of the Pentateuch continue to lay claim upon its
readers in succeeding generations? These larger questions will
be kept in mind as we proceed through our study of the problem
of the interpretation of Numbers, an alternative proposal to
overcome the problem, and the implications of such a proposal
for the book of Numbers and the Pentateuch.

ACKNOWLEDGEMENTS

The present work is a partially revised version of a doctoral dissertation submitted to the Department of Religious Studies of Yale University in New Haven, Connecticut. This work has benefited from the help and support of many people. I wish to thank Yale University for the financial support of its graduate study fellowships and for the use of its libraries and other resources. A word of appreciation is also extended to the Division for Theological Education and Ministry of the American Lutheran Church for its scholarship assistance.

I have benefited from the friendship and stimulation of my fellow graduate students in Religious Studies at Yale. I am also grateful to the faculty members of my dissertation committee, Professor Marvin Pope, Professor Robert R. Wilson, and most of all, to my dissertation advisor, Professor Brevard S. Childs, whose generous and unfailing interest, guidance and encouragement since the inception of the project have made the writing of this work a much more enjoyable experience than I could have ever hoped.

Throughout the process of writing, my wife Carol has been a constant source of loving support and encouragement. Finally, I wish to thank my son and daughter, Eric and Kristen, who along with this book were born at Yale and who provided much needed and much welcomed diversion from the tasks of research and writing. To these institutions and to these individuals whose interest, help and generosity have contributed so much, I extend my warmest thanks.

ABBREVIATIONS

AB	=	Anchor Bible
ATD	=	Das Alte Testament Deutsch
BA	=	Biblical Archaeologist
BeO	=	Bibbia e oriente
Bib	=	Biblica
BibLeb	=	Bibel und Leben
BR	=	Biblical Research
BZ	=	Biblische Zeitschrift
BZAW	=	Beihefte zur ZAW
CBQ	=	Catholic Biblical Quarterly
EncJud	=	Encyclopedia Judaica (1971)
HKAT	=	Handkommentar zum Alten Testament
HSM	=	Harvard Semitic Monographs
HTR	=	Harvard Theological Review
HUCA	=	Hebrew Union College Annual
IB	=	Interpreter's Bible
ICC	=	International Critical Commentary
IDB	=	G. A. Buttrick (ed.), Interpreter's Dictionary of the Bible
IDBSup	=	Supplementary volume to IDB
Int	=	Interpretation
JANESCU	=	Journal of the Ancient Near Eastern Society of Columbia University
JAOS	=	Journal of the American Oriental Society
JBC	=	R. E. Brown et al. (eds.), Jerome Biblical Commentary
JBL	=	Journal of Biblical Literature
JCS	=	Journal of Cuneiform Studies
JEA	=	Journal of Egyptian Archaeology
JPOS	=	Journal of the Palestine Oriental Society
JQR	=	Jewish Quarterly Review
JSOT	=	Journal for the Study of the Old Testament
JSS	=	Journal of Semitic Studies
KAT	=	E. Sellin (ed.), Kommentar zum Alten Testament
LCL	=	Loeb Classical Library

NCCHS	=	R. D. Fuller et al. (eds.), New Catholic Commentary on Holy Scripture
OTL	=	Old Testament Library
OTS	=	Oudtestamentische Studiën
PCB	=	M. Black and H. H. Rowley (eds.), Peake's Commentary on the Bible
PEQ	=	Palestine Exploration Quarterly
PJ	=	Palästina-Jahrbuch
RAC	=	Reallexicon für Antike und Christentum
RB	=	Revue Biblique
TDNT	=	G. Kittel and G. Friedrich (eds.), Theological Dictionary of the New Testament
UF	=	Ugartische Forschungen
VT	=	Vetus Testamentum
VTSup	=	Supplements to Vetus Testamentum
ZAW	=	Zeitschrift für die alttestamentliche Wissenschaft
ZDMG	=	Zeitschrift der deutschen morgenländischen Gesellschaft
ZDPV	=	Zeitschrift des deutschen Palästina-Vereins

PART I

THE BOOK OF NUMBERS: THE PROBLEM

CHAPTER ONE

A SURVEY OF THE MODERN STUDY
OF THE BOOK OF NUMBERS

MODERN COMMENTARIES ON NUMBERS

The book of Numbers is a collection of a great variety of
genres, literary styles, and subject matters. The book includes
narratives and laws, itineraries and census lists, lists of names
and lists of cultic regulations, battle reports and accounts of
legal disputes. This variety has lent itself to study from a number of different perspectives and methods in the modern period of
biblical research, all of which have in one way or another entered
into the discussion of the major commentaries on Numbers. In order
to gain a sense of the variety of approaches which have been employed
in the interpretations of the book and to assess the gains and
possible shortcomings of these approaches, we will present a survey
of major representative commentaries on Numbers in the last century
and a quarter of biblical scholarship. This first section of the
survey will treat each commentary in approximate chronological order,
beginning with the year 1861 and extending to the present. The
commentaries will be analyzed according to their general aim or goal,
their stance on historical-critical issues, and their views of the
theological value of the book of Numbers.

We will divide the survey into three broad chronological
periods, each roughly correlating with a shift in general method:
1) 1861-1912; 2) 1913-1965; and 3) 1966-1984. In Section Two of
this chapter, we will also briefly review the range of specialized
studies in recent biblical research which have had an impact on the
study of Numbers. Section Three will attempt to establish that one
of the central problems in past interpretations of Numbers is the
lack of consensus on the outline of the book of Numbers and the lack
of purposeful reflection on the structure of Numbers as a literary
unit.

Under the Shadow of Wellhausen, 1861-1912

The commentaries on the book of Numbers which derive from this
period were largely involved in an intense debate on the validity
of the so-called documentary hypothesis which posited the existence

of several written sources with diverse authorship within the Pentateuch. This, of course, was opposed to the traditional view of the
Mosaic authorship of the books of Genesis through Deuteronomy. The
critical theory of multiple sources within the Pentateuch was most
forcefully posed by Julius Wellhausen in his Die Composition des
Hexateuchs (1885) with its historical ramifications spelled out in
his Prolegomena to the History of Israel (1883).[1] The existence of
separate literary strata within the Pentateuch which had originated
in different periods of Israel's history had been recognized and
debated long before Wellhausen, but it was Wellhausen who gave the
source-critical theory its definitive shape. This was particularly
true in Wellhausen's placement of the Priestly source as the latest
of the literary strata within the Pentateuch, originating in the
post-exilic period.[2]

     The commentary by August Dillmann in 1886 was the first to
begin to reflect the growing critical concensus which had been
spearheaded by Wellhausen, Kuenen, Graf and others.[3] The Yahwist
and Elohist literary strands were now understood as the earliest
layers and the Priestly strand was the latest of the literary
sources. Furthermore, these literary sources were found not only
in the five books of Genesis through Deuteronomy but also in Joshua.
Thus, the traditional concept of the Pentateuch was replaced by the
critical notion of the Hexateuch, the first six books of the Bible,
as the correct context for interpretation. Dillmann's study was a
revision of August Knobel's earlier commentary in the same series.
Dillmann was likewise concerned in large part with dividing the
various literary sources and with discussing issues of historicity.[4]

     The year 1903 saw the advent of three significant and detailed
treatments of the book of Numbers. All three approached Numbers
from a critical perspective with emphasis on distinguishing the
literary sources of the Yahwist, Elohist and the later Priestly
writer. H. Holzinger (1903) combined a source-critical study of
Numbers with a careful text-critical analysis in his German commentary on Numbers.[5] Holzinger identified a considerable number of
secondary Priestly insertions into the basic Priestly document of
Numbers along with a series of redactional glosses from various
hands. The layers of the Yahwist and the Elohist, according to
Holzinger, were difficult to separate. In addition, they were so
broken in Numbers that no consistent theme could be obtained for
either literary layer. Thus, much of Holzinger's attention was
devoted to the primary and secondary layers of the Priestly
document. Holzinger concluded that the book of Numbers lacked any
sense of unity. One could detect no connection between the

narrative and the legal material within the book. The census lists
of the Israelites in Numbers 1 and 26 and the chronology of the
book were historically inaccurate and were purely literary constructions composed by the Priestly writer. Very little of a theology
of the book of Numbers was given. Primary emphasis was placed on a
description of the growth of the literature from various earlier
layers.

Even more than the commentary by Holzinger, the German critical
commentary by Bruno Baentsch was dominated by source-critical
divisions and analyses.[6] The text of Numbers was printed and
divided in minute detail with brackets and labels which assigned
every word of the text to a particular source, redactional layer or
gloss. The sigla employed for the sources illustrate the complexity
and detail involved: J, E, JE, R(J), R(E), R(JE), R(P), R(D), P,
Ps, Px, Pss, and others. Every verse or often part of a verse was
assigned to a source. Baentsch acknowledged that some reflections
of actual history may be found in Numbers but the details were not
reliable. The theology of Numbers was divided according to each of
the source-critical strands. God appeared in the J source as a God
of a people, not a universal God. J had little ethical interest.
The religious interest of the E source involved the cult of the
ancient folk religion and prophetic concerns. The P source was
concerned with the cult, sacrifice and the priestly hierarchy of
the post-exilic period. P was also dominated by the notion of God's
transcendent greatness and holiness.

The most formidable and thorough commentary written in English
on Numbers in the modern period was written by George B. Gray
(1903).[7] Gray viewed his work as in the same critical line as
Dillmann's earlier commentary. However, Gray significantly advanced
beyond Dillmann, particularly in the use of lexicography, textual
and literary criticism, archaeology and even modern anthropological
study. Gray basically followed Wellhausen's dating of the literary
sources of J, E, D and P rather than Dillmann's more idiosyncratic
view. Gray's work was a fresh and original synthesis of available
resources as they pertained to issues in Numbers. Gray also viewed
his work as a critical alternative to Keil's conservative commentary
which was the last to appear in English with any independent value
before Gray. Numbers, according to Gray, was not the work of Moses
or any contemporary of the events described. The book was the
result of the compilation of the literary sources of J, E and P.
Within the Priestly material, Gray distinguished three separate
layers (Pg, Px, Ps).

These sources were all written centuries later than the events
of the wilderness which they describe so that "the historical value
of Numbers consists largely in the evidence indirectly given by
these sources regarding the periods to which they belong."[8] Gray
admitted that some historical facts may underlie the Yahwist and
Elohist material and perhaps even the Priestly source. Such facts,
however, were difficult to reconstruct because they have had "only
too many opportunities of being distorted or placed in a wrong
light" as the stories were retold for centuries before J, E and P.[9]
Gray argued that most of the book of Numbers did not reflect the
actual conditions of the wilderness sojourn from Sinai to the plains
of Moab in the time of Moses. The numbers in the census lists, the
lists of names, the organization and duties of the priests and
Levites, the laws, and the chronological statements in the book all
seemed to be products of a later time with no real historical value.

Gray's description of the theology of Numbers was actually
more a history of Israelite religious development.

> The various parts of Numbers are products of many generations
> widely separated from one another in time, and in some respects
> sharply distinguished from one another in the matter of reli-
> gious belief and practice. The consequence is that Numbers
> is as lacking in unity of religious expression as in literary
> unity. It is therefore impossible to summarize the fundamen-
> tal ideas, or to point out in general terms the religious
> value of the book; for these are different in the different
> parts.[10]

Hence, the religious ideas of the JE literary material included
Yahweh's care of Israel, the simplicity of worship, an account of
the religious customs of the early monarchy, and Moses as the ideal
prophet of God. The main religious theme of the Priestly writer
from the period of the exile (seventh century B.C.) involved the
same issues of the book of Ezekiel: how can Yahweh, if he destroys
Israel, maintain a reputation for power among the nations? The
editorial passage from P in Numbers 14:12-24 addressed this same
question. Most of the Priestly material derived from the post-exilic
period which reflected the religious life and organization of the
post-exilic period. Yahweh's holiness or unapproachableness is
emphasized. "The spontaneity of religious life which so strongly
colored the earlier time is lost."[11] In short, Gray's commentary
remained one of the most detailed studies on Numbers available,
especially in the area of technical text-critical and lexical issues.
It did, however, suffer from a general lack of theological concern
and an absorption in the details of source-critical divisions.

The commentaries on Numbers by Baentsch, Gray and Holzinger
represented the epitome of a thoroughly source-critical method in

the study of the book of Numbers. The other commentaries in this
early period of the twentieth century possessed little independent
value.[12]

It is clear that by 1911 the source critics had won the day.
Even some conservative commentators were forced to acknowledge the
consensus which supported the source-critical view of the origin of
Numbers. Debate continued on the details of source divisions of
individual passages. The J and E sources were often difficult to
disentangle. The P source was not a unified layer in Numbers;
numerous layers of accretions were detected. But the method of
source criticism as a whole was firmly established. Since the
literary authors of JE and P were primarily responsible for
gathering and shaping their material for a particular end, scholars
described the theologies of JE and P as separate entities. Often
very little theological analysis entered into the commentaries at
all. When it did, descriptions of the theology tended to be superficial and not the result of a close reading of the text. Certainly
no detailed and convincing theology of the book of Numbers as a
whole was produced in this period.

Under the Shadow of Gunkel and Gressmann, 1913-1967

The methodology of source criticism continued to be used in
commentaries on Numbers. But some of its assumptions were altered
by the introduction of form criticism as a tool of biblical exegesis.
Hermann Gunkel was the pioneer of form criticism of the Bible, particularly as applied to the narratives of Genesis.[13] Hugo Gressmann
was a student of Gunkel. Gressmann sought to extend the method of
form criticism beyond Genesis to the narratives in Exodus, Leviticus,
Numbers and Deuteronomy in his book, Mose und seine Zeit, which was
published in 1913.[14] Gressmann was also the author of a commentary
on Numbers in 1914 which was the first thoroughly form-critical
treatment of the book to appear.[15] The method of form criticism
sought to isolate and reconstruct the original oral forms, functions
and sociological or historical settings of the narratives and ancient
poems which were embedded in the text of Numbers and which had been
reworked in the course of transmission. Source criticism had placed
emphasis on the importance of the later literary stage of compiling
and writing in providing the definitive shape and aim of the present
biblical material. Form criticism placed its emphasis on the importance of the earlier oral stage of the biblical material when it
functioned in certain stereotypical oral forms which corresponded
to definable sociological settings within the history of Israel.
Hence, the task of the form critic was to uncover and reconstruct

the original forms and sociological settings for the narratives and
poems of Numbers which had originated in a period early in Israel's
history.

Gressmann found vestiges or remnants of numerous sagas of
various types. Some of the sagas were originally connected to a
geographical place and explained the reason for its name. Mara,
Massa and Meriba in Num 20:1ff. were examples. Other stories were
originally cult sagas and explained the origin of a place of worship. Gressmann used Num 9:15ff. and 21:4ff. as examples of this
type. Some sagas originally explained the origin of certain
hierarchies or organizations. One could find this in the discussion
of the relationship of priests and Levites in Numbers 3. Gressmann
removed all the lists and numbers, the sacrificial ordinances, and
all other laws and secondary material from consideration. He was
left with 18 vestigal sagas whose original form he attempted to
reconstruct. Thus, Gressmann's commentary on Numbers was not the
usual verse-by-verse analysis but rather a study of 18 selected
portions of the book of Numbers which had been taken out of their
present literary context in Numbers and isolated for separate study.

Gressmann's work was the first entirely form-critical commentary on Numbers and it was the last. Subsequent commentaries used
the fruits of form criticism to a greater or lesser extent, but
always in dialog with source criticism and questions of historical
interest. The critical and exegetical task became more complex.
The commentary by L. Elliott Binns is an example.[16] Binns, an
Anglican scholar, attempted to bring together the developments of
source criticism and form criticism. Numbers was not just a mosaic
of different written documents as the source critics held. Many
different oral traditions which were carried by groups within
Israel's history and which preceded these documents also needed to
be taken into account. The task of dating the sources of J, E, D
and P, according to Binns, became more complicated:

> The four main sources then come from different ages in the
> history of the Hebrew people; and indeed since each of the
> documents is the production, not so much of an individual
> writer as of a school, the separate documents have a long
> and extensive history of their own. The dates which may be
> assigned to the sources are therefore approximate only. On
> the one hand much that is early in time may have been included
> in a late source, on the other much that is late may have been
> added by way of gloss or correction to an early source.[17]

Form criticism did indeed make an impact on the commentary's
presentation of the growth of the literature. But it had little
effect on the commentary's exposition of the theology of Numbers.
The smaller units produced by form-critical work did not provide

enough material from which to derive a theological viewpoint or
message. Thus, the only critical avenue by which to make any theological reflections remained with the documentary sources. Although
form criticism accentuated the variety of both written and oral
traditions, Binns focused on the written documents as the source of
any theological statements:

> Since Numbers is no unity but comes from different ages of the
> history of Israel, and from writers whose ideas about God,
> and the demands which He makes upon men, were very diverse,
> its religious value in the first place is not that of the
> book as a whole but of the different sources from which
> it has been compiled.[18]

And Binns had a clear idea of what he thought about the theologies
of the earlier and later written sources:

> For the lowest ideas about God we naturally turn to the
> oldest documents, but it must by no means be supposed that
> the later ones are free from superstitious and unworthy
> conceptions... In fact, it would be true to say of the
> whole priestly school, and of its religious outlook, that
> it had a pathetic desire to magnify God's holy name, and
> yet a quite inadequate idea of what holiness really was
> and of the methods by which it was to be attained.[19]

As in many of the previous commentaries, this one drew any theological statements from a rather superficial reading of the text on the
basis of the separated documents of JE and P. Thus, Binns continued
to use source criticism as a primary tool. Scholars in England like
Binns appeared to employ Gressmann's form-critical work only
sporadically with little grasp of the implications of the form-
critical program which emphasized the original oral stage as the
primary creative locus for shaping the tradition.

A number of commentaries on Numbers by Roman Catholic scholars
appeared in this period as Catholic scholarship began to appropriate,
at first cautiously and then more readily, the methods of historical-
critical exegesis. An early 1928 Italian commentary by B. Ubach
continued to reflect a traditional and conservative stance in the
interpretation of the narratives of Numbers.[20] After Ubach, three
German Catholic commentaries were published. Paul Heinisch and
Heinrich Schneider published separate expositions of the book of
Numbers which displayed careful exegesis which was critical and yet
cautious.[21] They admitted the hypothetical nature of many of the
source divisions of the text, and they tended to attribute more
historical value to the early traditions than many earlier source
critics. Form criticism showed its influence here. Heinisch, for
example, stated that many of the laws and narratives went back to
Moses himself but were reshaped in the course of transmission.

A third and more substantial German commentary by Karl F. Kramer came on the scene in 1955.[22] Kramer admitted gaps in our knowledge of the history of the wilderness period. Although not accurate in every historical detail, the book of Numbers rested on a solid core of historical events.

Two Roman Catholic commentaries on Numbers were also produced in France in this period. A combination of traditional and critical exegesis characterized the commentary by A. Clamer in La Sainte Bible which appeared in 1940.[23] Clamer used a traditional Roman Catholic perspective modified in part by a modern critical awareness of various levels within the text. He tended to list a range of possible interpretations from modern sources, the Church Fathers, and medieval commentaries with little integration or evaluation. Clamer was unable to bridge the gap between traditional exegesis and modern critical interpretation. His view of the theology of Numbers did not represent a close reading of the text nor did it reflect a careful analysis of the structure of the book itself.

H. Cazelles, another French Roman Catholic scholar, wrote his 157-page commentary on Numbers in 1952.[24] On critical issues, Cazelles contended that historical criticism and archaeology confirmed the traditions of Numbers as originating with Moses himself. The oracles of Balaam in Numbers 22-24, for example, may have been even older than Moses and part of the sources utilized by him. Traditions like the census lists of the twelve tribes in Israel in Numbers 1 and 26 reflected genuine early tribal tradition. This was confirmed, according to Cazelles, by extra-biblical parallels from Mari which had censuses of semi-nomadic tribes and the Ugaritic tablets which contained lists of names in the manner of a census. Perhaps the greatest fault of the commentary by Cazelles was its portrayal of the structure of Numbers around nine separate themes which were not related. Such a scheme left the book in fragments without any attempt to discern a coherent plan or unity.

A. Drubbel is a Dutch Catholic scholar whose commentary on Numbers appeared in 1963.[25] Historical-critical issues were touched very lightly. Drubbel commented at some length on the juxtaposition of laws and narratives in Numbers, a phenomenon which he understood as unique to Israel within the ancient Near East and as a very ancient tradition in Israel. Drubbel observed that the theology of Numbers was rich, but his own exposition of that theology was not exhaustive.

In general, Roman Catholic scholarship in this period experienced some movement toward critical exegesis. The papal encyclical Divino Afflante Spiritu in 1943 provided an official sanction for

Catholic scholars to engage in historical-critical research which
gave the movement some impetus.[26] And yet Roman Catholic commentaries on Numbers from the period even after the encyclical appeared
ambivalent and unable to hold together traditional interpretations
and critical exegesis in a compelling synthesis. For example, form
criticism was often used apologetically for the most part in attempting to undergird the Mosaic origins of much of the Pentateuch. Such
a move resulted in what appeared to be a return to a conservative
pre-Wellhausen view via a selected and often strained use of form
criticism.

     Jewish commentaries on the book of Numbers which were published
in this period adopted a quite different perspective from that of
Protestant or Roman Catholic studies of the book.[27] The most independent Jewish commentary on Numbers in this period was one done by
Julius Greenstone.[28] Greenstone combined traditional Jewish interpretations of texts with modern critical insights. Greenstone
seemed more aware of the issues of historical criticism than other
Jewish scholars of his time. He frequently cited Wellhausen,
Dillmann, Gray and Holzinger, and he also frequently disagreed with
them. Greenstone rejected the strictly orthodox view that every
work in the Pentateuch was written by Moses, but the bulk of Numbers
emanated from Moses himself and from the period in which he lived.
According to Greenstone, "whatever changes or emendations have been
made in later ages were in the spirit of and in harmony with the
original documents."[29] Hence, Greenstone used the results of critical exegesis when it supported the antiquity of a given passage.
At other points, he would simply set the opinions of critical scholars side by side with traditional Jewish interpretations without
deciding between the two.

     A number of Protestant Christian commentaries also appeared
in the latter part of this period in the 1950's and early 1960's.[30]
Although not strictly a commentary, B. D. Eerdmans wrote a lengthy
essay entitled "The Composition of Numbers" in 1949.[31] Eerdmans
went chapter by chapter through Numbers and raised objections to
the details of the theory of documentary sources within Numbers.
For example, the Priestly document was often best explained as containing both pre-exilic material and exilic or post-exilic material.
It did not contain only later post-exilic traditions. Furthermore,
many independent traditions had been added to the Priestly material
so that no coherent or unified Priestly document really existed.
Eerdmans showed a clear indebtedness to the results of form criticism and raised a direct refutation of a strictly source-critical
approach to the text.

The only two-volume commentary on Numbers which has been
written in the modern period was done by Willem Gispen, a conservative Dutch scholar.[32] Gispen's work was detailed and comprehensive,
although he emphasized text-critical and historical issues. He
defended the historicity of the text whenever possible: "Whoever
holds fast to the historicity of the narrated events in the book
has fastened himself to the great value of Numbers."[33] Several
sections of the book, he argued, came from Moses himself. He
criticized source critics like Gray and Baentsch and form critics
as well since their views gave little historical worth to the book
except as indirect evidence for the periods to which the layers of
the book belong. They also made it impossible to speak of Numbers
as a religious or literary unity. Yet Gispen was not reluctant to
use form-critical conclusions if they helped to bolster his view of
the historicity of some of the narratives (cf. his treatment of the
rebellion of Korah, Dathan and Abiram in Numbers 16-17). To this
same end, Gispen employed extra-biblical material as well. Using
the texts from Mari, he is the most recent commentator to support
the historicity of the census lists in Numbers 1 and 26 as genuine
records from the time of Israel's wandering in the wilderness before
the conquest of the land.

Gispen's commentary was essentially quite conservative. Yet
it differed substantially in tone from Keil's commentary which was
a conservative approach to Numbers from before the turn of the
century.[34] Keil's primary aim seemed to be to refute source criticism rather than to concentrate on interpreting the text. His
harshly polemical attacks on historical criticism tended to drown
out his theological exposition. Gispen's work was more balanced
in that he set forth the various options among source and form
critics as well as those who disagreed with them. He typically
would then proceed to his own theological interpretation of the
text which usually assumed the unit to be a cohesive whole with
roots in the early period of Israel's history. The difficulty
with Gispen was that he often failed to engage historical-critical
positions, being content to simply list the representative positions
without evaluating or incorporating their conclusions. The work
was detailed and comprehensive but provided no real creative or
convincing synthesis.

A brief and non-technical study of Numbers was done by James
L. Mays in the Layman's Bible Commentary series in 1963.[35] Mays
argued that the book of Numbers carried no independent meaning on
its own but was part of a larger Hexateuch which ran from Genesis
through Joshua. He did not understand the literary sources of

Numbers as the original inventors of the material as the earlier
source critics had tended to do. Rather, he understood the sources
of JE and P as earlier oral tradition which had been shaped and
reinterpreted into a literary form. He thereby incorporated the
results of form criticism into his study. The theology of Numbers
could not be reduced to a few ideas or categories, according to
Mays. Different passages had different vantage points and different
methods which may be appropriate to understanding them. Mays displayed a notable sensitivity to the theological significance of
individual texts. He made many insightful comments in spite of the
commentary's restricted size. He did not, however, find any overarching theological framework for the book of Numbers as a literary
unit.

By the end of this period in which the study of Numbers was
influenced by form criticism, several new trends had arisen. Compared to earlier source critics, one can discern a greater willing-
ness to acknowledge that many of the traditions were ancient and
deeply rooted in the past. This tendency even extended to the traditions associated with the Priestly source. The P source was not
merely a creation de novo from the post-exilic period; it too contained some genuine ancient traditions. There was also less assurance about dating the multifarious sources, layers and glosses
detected within the text. The results of form criticism tended to
complicate the pictue of the growth of the literature. A long history of oral traditon before material was committed to writing was
now assumed for many parts of Numbers. The separation of the Yahwist and the Elohist sources was seen as even more difficult than
before. Some of the multiple layers of Priestly material had roots
in the pre-exilic period, but precise dating was seen as difficult.
As for conservative scholars in this period, they tended to use the
results of form criticism selectively in order to support the historicity of laws or narratives within Numbers.

Interestingly, the main sources for purposes of theological
reflection among many scholars remained the documentary sources of
J and E (or often JE together) and the Priestly source. The much
smaller units of oral tradition which form criticism isolated were
perhaps not large enough blocks of material on which to base larger
theological conclusions. The present form of the biblical text was
rarely studied for its particular literary or theological structure
in this period. Another noteworthy trend was the frequent absence
of the traditonal view of the Mosaic authorship of all of Numbers
in some of the even relatively conservative or traditonal commentaries. Greenberg, Clamer and Gispen are examples of this tendency.

Although Gressmann's commentary in 1914 remained the only thoroughly
form-critical study of Numbers, his method had an important impact
on the continuing study of the book of Numbers.

Under the Shadow of Noth, 1966-1984

Martin Noth's important commentary on Numbers first appeared
in German in 1966 and then in English in 1968.[36] Noth's primary
aim was to trace the history of the growth of the literature through
the various oral and written stages. This reconstruction of the
history of traditions was based on his concept of the five basic
themes of the Pentateuch. These Pentateuchal themes were originally
separate oral traditions which were gradually filled out and linked
together to form the corpus of Genesis through Numbers. These
themes included "the exodus out of Egypt," "the conquest of the
land," "the promise to the patriarchs," "guidance in the wilderness," and "the revelation at Sinai."[37] From a tradition-historical
perspective, the significance of the book of Numbers was its conclusion of the theme of "the revelation at Sinai," its presentation of
the secondary theme of "guidance in the wilderness," and its introduction of the theme of the "conquest of the land." Noth held that
the book of Numbers"participates only marginally in the great themes
of the Pentateuchal tradition."[38] The main body of Numbers presents
the theme of "guidance in the wilderness" which is only a secondary
and artificial link between the two more basic themes which Numbers
only concludes and begins, "the Sinai revelation" and "the conquest."

Noth commended caution and restraint in the use of source
criticism in Numbers:

> If we compare Numbers with the other books of the Pentateuch,
> what strikes us most of all here is the lack of longer com-
> plexes... If we were to take the book of Numbers on its
> own, then we would think not so much of 'continuous sources'
> as of an unsystematic collection of innumerable pieces of
> tradition of very varied content, age and character ('Frag-
> ment Hypothesis')... It is certainly not practicable simply
> to proceed to a division of the textual material among the
> Pentateuchal sources J, E and P (and in any event, it would
> have to be a question of secondary forms of these tradi-
> tions).[39]

A substantial portion of Numbers consisted of secondary insertions
which were later than the various Pentateuchal sources. These insertions were primarily laws and other items which were read back into
the conclusion of the Sinai revelation of the conclusion of the life
of Moses from a late period in Israel's history in order to legitimate their authority.

> So, at a very late stage, but before the Pentateuch achieved
> canonical status, thereby becoming unalterable, all kinds of
> material were added in 5:1-9:14, material which can no longer
> be regarded as belonging to the various 'sources.' This mater-
> ial consists of numerous individual units, having no connec-
> tion with one another and in whose sequence no factual ar-
> rangement can be discerned. The simplest hypothesis is that
> in the course of time these units gradually became attached
> to each other.[40]

A similar situation obtained for Numbers 25-36:

> The remaining contents of the last eleven chapters of Numbers,
> apart from the above-mentioned four verses in chapter 32 (vv.
> 1, 16-19), comprise material from a later period which is not
> susceptible of division among the sources, and this, again,
> is to be explained by the position of these chapters within
> the Pentateuch as a whole.[41]

Noth's analysis of Numbers made the question of the growth of the
book considerably more complex. One now had to reckon not only with
three or more written sources (J, E, P) and with a long oral history
of tradition before the written sources. For the book of Numbers,
at least, one also had to take into account various substantial
additions which occurred after the completion and combination of the
written sources of J, E and P in Genesis-Numbers. It was not surprising, then, that Noth believed that "the book lacks unity, and
it is difficult to see any pattern in its construction."[42] He concluded that "we can scarcely speak of a specific significance peculiar to the book of Numbers."[43] Thus, Noth's commentary provided
virtually no consciously theological reflection on the book of
Numbers.

Noth's work on the Pentateuch in general and the book of Numbers in particular was certainly one of the most comprehensive and
significant contributions to the study of the growth of the literature in the more recent period. Noth's peculiar form of the tradition-historical method and his notion of free-floating Pentateuchal
"themes" have proven somewhat idiosyncratic and are not universally
accepted. Noth failed to establish any concrete sociological setting
within the history or traditions of Israel for his Pentateuchal
"themes." Therefore, these "themes" run the risk of being simply
modern artificial constructions with no actual sociological or historical setting within Israel. Yet Noth's work provided many important insights into the nature and development of the literature,
particularly in the possibility of secondary material in Numbers
which is later than and independent of the written sources of J,
E and P.

Not all commentaries in this later period followed Noth's
method, although many were influenced by his work. N. H. Snaith

produced a brief study of the book of Numbers in Peake's Commentary
on the Bible in 1962 and a full-length commentary in The Century
Bible series in 1967.[44] Snaith's work reflected a more customary
source-critical approach than Noth's commentary, but Snaith did
describe the sources as "broad traditions" which had solidified at
different periods of Israel's history rather than as written documents of individual authors. Thus, Snaith was more skeptical about
precise dating of the various Pentateuchal sources than earlier
source critics. Snaith saw the main thrust of Numbers to be the
Priestly editors' propogandistic attempt to project their post-
exilic institutions and ideas into the past.

   Some of the critical exegesis on Numbers done by Jewish scholars in this recent period showed a dependence on Noth's concept of
"tradition-themes" and the fragmentary character of Numbers. Arnold
Goldberg's German commentary (1970) was a short study of Numbers
which analyzed the book in broad strokes.[45] Goldberg adopted Noth's
terminology of "tradition-themes." His primary concern, however,
was the revision and editing of these themes and their literary
interconnections with other material in the Pentateuch. Goldberg
acknowledged the diversity and complexity of Numbers.

> That does not mean, however, that we have here only a poorly
> thought out attempt to create a unity. The redactors have
> probably never incorporated any tradition-theme without
> careful deliberation.[46]

Thus, in contrast to Noth, Goldberg believed that the final redactor
of this diverse material had given it some coherent and inclusive
point of view which was akin to the spirit of the books of Chronicles. Both were concerned with Israel as the people of God under
the sacred order of holiness. Contrary to Snaith, Goldberg did not
interpret Numbers as simply a Priestly work of propoganda which
projected its own utopian sacred order backward to the period of the
wilderness wandering. Goldberg offered a more positive theological
interpretation:

> The picture which the redactor of the book of Numbers pre-
> sents of this Israel which lives for a short time totally
> in the presence of God is a picture of redemption. For
> Jewish theology it is a prototype for future redemption,
> since also in the end time the people of God shall live in
> sacred perfection in the sight of God. For the Christian
> reader this book contains only the past, an epoch of
> salvation-history, an epoch of history which leads from
> Adam, the fallen man, to Jesus.[47]

Although Goldberg's insights were often suggestive and his general
approach to the text was commendable, his work lacked detail and a
closeness to the text. Goldberg's tendency to defend the

historicity of the text sometimes obstructed theological insights which could have been made.

Another brief treatment of Numbers by a Jewish scholar was an article by Baruch Levine in the supplementary volume of the Interpreter's Dictionary of the Bible.[48] Levine divided Numbers into Priestly and non-Priestly material and considered the historical and religious significance of each independently. The focus of Levine's emphasis was on the Priestly material and an analysis of the details and historical backgrounds of cultic terms and religious institutions. No comprehensive outline or interpretation of the book as a whole was offered.

A major liberal Jewish commentary on Numbers was recently produced by W. Gunther Plaut with the assistance of William W. Hallo in the volume entitled The Torah, A Modern Commentary (1981).[49] The commentary was open-ended in the sense that it stressed options in possible interpretations, derived from critical exegesis and from past Jewish interpreters and other commentators. Plaut acknowledged the existence of various layers and traditions which were embedded in the text, but their precise delineation did not play a major role in the commentary.

Although Jewish commentaries on Numbers in the most recent period reflected a spectrum from more liberal Reformed Judaism to Conservative Judaism, there were some basic features which Jewish scholarship on Numbers tended to share. One may note a greater appreciation of the theological insight of the later Priestly tradition and of later biblical redactors in general in their role of giving a final and meaningful shape to the material. Jewish scholars also tended to emphasize the early pre-exilic origins of much of the Priestly tradition. There was also a greater concern for the significance and background of the legal and cultic material and institutions as they appear in the book. Finally, a frequent feature of Jewish commentaries involved a tendency to set the results of critical exegesis side by side with traditional interpretations, allowing both to stand without significant synthesis.

Some of the more theologically sensitive commentaries on Numbers in the most recent period have been produced by Roman Catholic scholars.[50] Two full-length commentaries on Numbers by Roman Catholic scholars appeared in 1972, one in French and one in Italian. The French commentary by J. de Vaulx is perhaps the most notable among all modern commentaries on Numbers for its attempt to combine a rigorous historical-critical reading of the text along with a substantial theological interpretation.[51] The commentary also sought to summarize the history of the interpretation of the

texts of Numbers among traditional Jewish and Christian sources.
The literary layers of J, E and P were traditions which had been
gradually reworked and edited over a long period of time. They were
not written sources of single authors. The Priestly tradition makes
up most of Numbers. It contained both pre-exilic and post-exilic
material and was responsible for the final form of the book.

An important dimension of de Vaulx's work was his emphasis on
the theological concerns of the redactors of the book who sought
to actualize and relay past traditions to the present and to all
succeeding generations. Cultic and historical etymologies, laws
and rituals which commemorate particular events or commandments,
the notation of the date of great events, and the remodeling of
certain laws to adapt to new situations are all means by which the
text is shaped in order to address future generations of God's
people. "The successive redactors of the narratives and laws remind
each of their contemporaries that the sacred history applies to them
'today' so that they should do the will of God."[52] The march in the
wilderness which Numbers narrates moves along both a geographical
and a spiritual itinerary, according to de Vaulx. The itinerary
has some historical foundation, but it also has a religious or
moral dimension:

> The time of the desert is thus the time of decision and
> choice in response to the gracious offer of Yahweh. It
> allows one to make the decisive step of faith and of
> fidelity which gives access to the realization of the
> promises. . . The time passed in the desert, therefore,
> has no other goal than to provoke the moral conversion and
> the spiritual progress necessary for the people to attain
> their destiny.[53]

We will offer a more detailed evaluation of de Vaulx's view of the
theology of Numbers in our own treatment of the book's theology in
Part Three. In general, however, it can be said that de Vaulx was
not always successful in clearly bridging the gap between his
historical-critical reading of the text and his theological interpretations. They often remained sharply separated. His scheme of
the final redactional structure of the book, in our view, was
incorrect so that he missed the major theological theme of the
book which that structure entails. On the other hand, de Vaulx's
work was an important advance in critical scholarship insofar as
it took seriously the theological concern of the later redactors
to shape the material so that it was accessible to the generations
which followed.

The other full-length commentary by a Roman Catholic author
which appeared in 1972 was an Italian work by Giuseppe Bernini.[54]

Bernini was influenced in his depiction of the growth of the book
by Noth's concept of Pentateuchal themes. Bernini described three
major blocks of tradition which had been used to structure the work:
1) the traditions relating to the final period of Israel's stay at
Sinai--Num 1:1-10:10; 2) the traditions relating to the march in
the desert--Num 10:11-25:18; 3) the traditions relating to the
divine ordinances in the steppes of Moab--Num 25:19-36:13. Bernini
encountered the same problem as Noth in his concept of themes:
these traditions were given no sociological setting within any
group or tradition in Israel's history. According to Bernini, they
were simply arranged topically on the basis of a loose attachment
to a geographical location, either Sinai or the desert or the
steppes of Moab. Bernini also tended to be conservative in his
historical conclusions. For example, he stated that the census
numbers in Numbers 1 and 26 could not be post-exilic "for doctrinal
reasons" which seems a less than adequate basis for a historical
judgment.[55]

One of Bernini's important insights was the detection of
Num 25:19-36:13 as a major section in Numbers which portrayed "the
community of the new generation" which was about to receive the
promised land. Of the commentators surveyed, Bernini was the only
one to make a major structural break with the census list in
chapter 26, beginning in the Hebrew text with 25:19 (EVV 26:1).
However, Bernini did not fully exploit the theological and hermeneutical implications of this section nor did he, in our judgment,
correctly perceive its relation to the preceding material in Numbers.
Our assessment of Bernini will be expanded in Part Three of our
study.

Other commentaries written from a more conservative Protestant
viewpoint also emerged in this period. One example is the work by
Walter Riggans which is one of the most recent commentaries on
Numbers to appear.[56] The commentary was part of the Old Testament
companion series to William Barclay's New Testament series of
commentaries and shared its emphasis on homiletical reflections on
the text from a Christian perspective. Riggans concluded, however,
that Numbers had "only the poorest of literary or theological
structure" with an abundance of disjointed material which played
no role in the book's central theme, including the census lists and
many of the cultic and ritual ordinances.[57]

Finally, Gordon Wenham has published a non-technical treatment
of Numbers in the Tyndale Old Testament Commentaries series in
1981.[58] Wenham's portrayal of the growth of the literature was
much dependent on the model recently proposed by Rolf Rendtorff for

the book of Genesis.[59] Rendtorff argued that Genesis was composed
by joining end to end large blocks or cycles of originally separate
material (the Abraham cycle, the primeval history, the Jacob cycle).
The process of joining the cycles occurred relatively late in
Israel's history. This model attempted to replace the classical
source-critical view of the documentary sources as long and continuous strands which ran all through the books of Genesis through
Numbers and which had been knitted together to form the present
narrative.

     Rendtorff's proposal for the book of Genesis has been questioned
at several points.[60] The strength of his argument, however, lies
in the fact that the book of Genesis does seem to be made up of
fairly cohesive and self-contained blocks of material consisting of
the primeval history, the Abraham cycle, the Jacob cycle, and the
Joseph cycle. The question, of course, is whether the apparent
cohesiveness of these blocks of material is a result of later
editing of originally continuous strands of tradition which run all
through Genesis ("literary sources") or a result of the growth of
originally self-contained cycles which only later were joined end
to end. The debate on this issue for the book of Genesis will continue, and I will not attempt to address it here. However, it is
important to note that the same cohesiveness of the blocks of
material in Genesis does not seem to apply to the blocks of material
which Wenham tried to delineate in Numbers. These blocks of tradition, according to Wenham, included Num 1:1-10:10 ("Preparation to
Enter the Promised Land, the Conclusion of the Sinai Cycle"), Num
13:1-19:22 ("The Kadesh Cycle"), and Num 22:2-36:13 ("The Plains of
Moab Cycle"). These three blocks were in turn connected by short
travelogues in Num 10:11-12:16 ("From Sinai to Kadesh") and Num
20:1-22:1 ("From Kadesh to the Plains of Moab"). Wenham extended
this analysis of cycles to the entire Pentateuch. Genesis is a
prologue and Deuteronomy is an epilogue to the main section of
Exodus, Leviticus and Numbers. The material in Exodus-Numbers may
be represented diagrammatically as follows:[61]

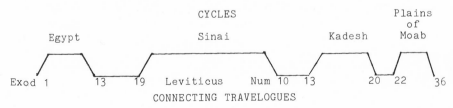

Wenham concluded that

> the structure of Numbers outlined above lends itself to the
> type of analysis proposed by Rendtorf for Genesis. Thus we
> may think of an editor bringing together a block of material
> dealing with Kadesh, a block dealing with the plains of Moab,
> and linking them to the Sinai material using short travelogues.
> This would avoid splitting up well-constructed units within
> these blocks (the spies, Balaam) into contradictory sources.[62]

We will not evaluate Wenham's proposal in detail, but four
major difficulties need to be mentioned. First of all as suggested
above, the cycles of material in Numbers do not have the same cohesiveness of subject matter as do the cycles in Genesis. In the
Abraham cycle in Genesis, for example, Abraham and his family are
closely tied to all the material within the cycle. If one removed
the figure of Abraham, one would destroy the coherence and intelligibility of the whole cycle. The same is not true for the blocks of
material in Numbers. The geographical locations which have been
assigned to these sections (Sinai, Kadesh, Plains of Moab) are very
loosely connected to the material with which they are now associated. Many of the laws and narratives would be perfectly coherent
and intelligible if one removed the geographical association or
placed their location somewhere else. Thus, these geographical
notations seem to be later and artificial redactional devices by
which to link varied material rather than an original and intrinsic
part of the laws and narratives to which they are now related.

Secondly, Wenham's proposal implies that the material in each
individual cycle of Numbers had a history of development which was
separate and distinct from the other cycles. The independent cycles
were simply joined end to end by short travelogues. Given this
reconstruction, Wenham is unable to explain the clear and substantial relationships among the cycles which the notion of sources or
continuous traditions of JE and P would better explain. For example,
the census list in Numbers 1 (the Sinai cycle) and the census list
in Numbers 26 (the Moab cycle) seem to be clearly related and to
have derived from one source or editor. Similarly, the clan list
in Numbers 26 seems clearly related to the one in Genesis 46. The
itinerary in Numbers 33 likewise seems to have a relationship to
the geographical notations all throughout Exodus, Leviticus and
Numbers. These examples suggest continuous strands or traditions
which run through the cycles which Wenham has attempted to isolate
as independent blocks.

Thirdly, Wenham argued that his reconstruction of the growth
of the literature in Numbers "would avoid splitting up well-con-
structed units within these blocks (the spies, Balaam) into con-
tradictory sources."[63] The spy story in Numbers 13-14 and the

Balaam cycle in Numbers 22-24 are indeed skillfully crafted literary
units in their present form. Yet the tensions and the redactional
seams which are still evident in the two units make it very probable
that two or more separate traditions have been interwoven in order
to form the present narratives. For example, the spy story contains
some tension and redundancy in the relationship of Joshua and Caleb
as well as in the specific parts of Canaan covered by the spies.[64]
The same is true of the Balaam episode which also contains apparent
doublets and other literary tensions, especially in Numbers 22.[65]
This is not to say that the spy story or the Balaam narrative cannot be read as skillfully crafted literary units in their present
forms. But one must still reckon with the evidence of a multi-
layered text if one wishes accurately to describe the history of the
growth of the literature. Wenham failed to factor this evidence of
more than one tradition into his view of the literature's development.

Fourthly, Wenham stated that "it is the final form of the text
that has canonical authority for the church, and that is the focus
of interest in the chapters that follow."[66] Yet his interpretation
of the final form of the text of Numbers ignored the present canonical division of the Pentateuch into the five separate books of
Genesis, Exodus, Leviticus, Numbers and Deuteronomy. Wenham separated Numbers 1-10 from the rest of Numbers and joined it with the
Sinai cycle which extends from Exodus 19 through Numbers 10. The
clear break between Leviticus and Numbers which is part of the final
form of the text was not registered in Wenham's interpretation of
the structure of Numbers. The importance of this separation of the
book of Numbers as a literary unit from what precedes and what
follows will be explored in Chapter Two of our study.

In summing up this latest period of commentaries on the book
of Numbers, Noth's portrayal of the history of the literature has
been very influential. It is now widely recognized that the formative shaping of the traditions which eventually came to make up
the present ofrm of Numbers occurred at several levels in the process
of the text's growth. The significant shaping of the material did
not only occur at the level of the written sources of individual
authors as the source critics believed. Nor did it primarily occur
only at the level of the oral tradition as the older form critics
held. One now must take into account a series of editings and
additions all along the route of the growth of the literature up
to its final canonical form. Furthermore, much of the material in
Numbers is difficult to date or place in any one historical
setting with any degree of precision.

There is a general tendency to retain the labels of the Yahwist, the Elohist and the Priestly work only as broad traditions rather than as individual literary sources. Some like Gordon Wenham would dismiss the existence of continuous sources entirely, following Rendtorff's model of separate cycles in his study of Genesis. As we have seen, such a model has difficulties when applied to Numbers and requires more thorough study and evidence if it is to be accepted as the key to the growth of the Pentateuch as a whole.

Another tendency is to focus more on the secondary additions or supplements which were inserted after the main Priestly material in Numbers had solidified. These supplements are often seen as largely arbitrary or haphazard interpolations. The only motive involved is a later editor's desire to include favorite traditions somewhere before the end of the Pentateuch. However, some of the latest commentators have attempted to give a more positive theological assessment of the work of later editors. Some have even set their goal as the interpretation of the final canonical form of the text, though the goal may not always be uniformly achieved.[67]

A greater theological sensitivity was displayed by some scholars in this latest period, especially among some of the Roman Catholic commentators (de Vaulx, Bernini). Yet one detects a general failure to bridge the gap convincingly between historical-critical exegesis and traditional religious interpretation. Critical commentators still often describe the separate theologies of the JE and P traditions (no longer written sources by only one author), but the existence of multiple layers within the individual traditions makes such an enterprise difficult, especially for the Priestly tradition. Furthermore, the presentation of the theologies of JE and P often depends to a large extent on the theologies as depicted in earlier parts of the Pentateuch. Thus, the book of Numbers often is not given a thorough analysis of its own theology as a separate literary entity within the Pentateuch. Sections on the theology of Numbers tend to be brief, general, and based on a broad topical analysis (presence of God, holiness of God, punishment of the people) which may not be entirely wrong. But the topics or concepts are often impressionistic and do not closely follow the structure of the book of Numbers itself.

One final observation worth noting is the way in which the lines between conservative and critical scholarship have blurred. The sharp polemics by conservatives on the Mosaic authorship and the historical value of Numbers of the earlier source-critical period have given way to a selective and widespread use of critical methodology by conservative scholars. The differences between

recent critical and conservative scholarship on the book of Numbers
do not center on the appropriate methods of study as much as on the
results derived from similar methods. Conservatives tend to date
material, particularly much of the Priestly tradition, earlier while
more critical scholars tend to date material later with a host of
variations between these extremes. The scholarship of Roman Catholic, Protestant and Jewish circles tends to retain some distinctiveness in flavor. Roman Catholic and Jewish commentaries, in particular, often attempt to retain traditional interpretations alongside
critical exegesis. But they often fail to engage the two in any
fresh synthesis. Yet the methods and approaches of these three
religious traditions have in many instances become very similar
when compared with earlier periods of scholarship in the last 120
years.

RECENT SPECIALIZED STUDIES RELATED TO THE BOOK OF NUMBERS

Apart from the commentaries which we have surveyed, recent
scholarship has involved a broad range of specialized studies on
topics related to the book of Numbers. A number of these studies
will be cited in later parts of our work, especially in Part Two
and Part Three. It may be helpful at this point, however, to present a selected overview of some of the recent subjects of research
associated with the book of Numbers. Important historical concerns
include the history of the Israelite priesthood and, in particular,
the role of the Levites,[68] the history of the tabernacle and aspects
of cult and sacrifice,[69] issues of geography and itinerary,[70] the
arrangement of the Israelite camp,[71] the conquest and settlement of
the east Jordan,[72] the role of the Midianites in relation to Israel,[73] and the social structure of pre-monarchical Israel.[74] Matters
of textual criticism and philology in parts of Numbers have also
been subjects for critical research.[75] Specialized studies on
source criticism,[76] form criticism,[77] and tradition history and its
relationship to the analysis of the composition of the Pentateuch[78]
have raised new questions and perspectives on the development of
Numbers and the Pentateuch as a whole. Structuralism has been used
as a tool for analyzing selected narratives in the book of Numbers.[79]
Methods and data from the social sciences such as sociology or
anthropology have been applied to some sections of Numbers, including the tribal lists and some of the ritual laws.[80] Interpretations
of some sections of Numbers from the perspectives of feminist
theology[81] and process theology[82] have also appeared on the contemporary scene of interpretation. All in all, the book of Numbers
has been studied from a wide variety of perspectives.

CHAPTER TWO

THE PROBLEM OF THE STRUCTURE
OF THE BOOK OF NUMBERS

The central problem in the interpretation of the book of Numbers, in our judgment, is the failure to detect a convincing and
meaningful structure for the book. Little systematic discussion of
the structure of Numbers can be found in the scholarly literature.
Commentaries often simply propose an outline with little or no comment or defense. Numerous interpreters lament the difficulty of
determining any coherent plan or outline. Martin Noth's observations are typical: "From the point of view of its contents, the
book lacks unity, and it is difficult to see any pattern in its
construction."[1] Furthermore, because of "the confusion and lack
of order in its contents," Noth concludes that "we can scarcely
speak of a specific significance peculiar to the book of Numbers."[2]
R. C. Dentan is even more explicit when he writes that "since the
book has no real unity and was not composed in accordance with any
logical, predetermined plan, whatever outline may be imposed upon
it will have to be recognized as largely subjective and arbitrary."[3]

THE DIVERSITY OF PROPOSED OUTLINES FOR THE STRUCTURE OF NUMBERS
    The importance of the problem of determining a structure for
Numbers is strikingly underscored when one examines the various
outlines which commentators have actually suggested over the last
120 years. Among the 46 commentaries which we have surveyed, 24
substantially different proposals for the outline or structure of
Numbers have been made. In addition, five other outlines have been
suggested which are also different from any other proposals but in
less significant ways.[4]
    The wide range of differences in the proposed outlines and the
lack of any clear consensus on the book's structure may be illustrated in a number of ways. Among all the various proposals, the
two most common are the following:

1) I.   Num 1:1-10:10   2) I.   Num 1:1-10:10
   II. Num 10:11-22:1   II. Num 10:11-20:13
   III. Num 22:2-36:13   III. Num 20:14-36:13

The first outline is suggested by 12 of the 46 commentaries. The
second is proposed by 7 of the 46 commentaries. The two individual

31

sections within Numbers which are most frequently suggested include
Num 1:1-10:10 (37 out of 46 commentaries) and Num 22:2-36:13 (16 out
of 46 commentaries).

The suggested number of major sections, however, varies enor-
mously from two and three sections to four, five and even nine sections. The most common number of sections is three, but no agreement exists on where these major sections begin. Proposals for the
beginning of major sections in the outline of Numbers have been
suggested for all the following verses in Numbers:

Numbers	1:1	11:1	22:1
	5:1	13:1	22:2
	7:1	15:1	25:1
	9:1	20:1	25:19 (EVV 26:1)
	9:15	20:14	28:1
	10:11	21:1	31:1
	10:29	21:10	32:1
			33:1

Obviously, there is no agreement on where the major sections within
Numbers begin and end.

Some interpreters even include two different outlines for the
book of Numbers within the same commentary. The commentary by John
J. Owens presents one form of the outline of Numbers on page 75
which breaks the book into three sections. Another form of the
outline is given on pages 80-83 which divides the book into four
entirely different sections. No explanation is given for the two
different outlines in the same commentary.[5] Likewise, the entry on
Numbers in the Jewish Encyclopedia presents one outline in the first
half of the article and an entirely different outline in the second
half. Two different authors are involved, but it is significant
that no attempt is made to bring agreement between the two authors
on the outline of Numbers within the same article.[6] Walter Riggans
also presents two different outlines for Numbers in the same commentary, one based on geographical locations within Numbers and the
other based on thematic divisions.[7] He attempts to weave the two
outlines together which results in a strained view of the structure
of the book.

Another important factor in the disarray surrounding the analysis of the structure of Numbers is that several commentaries ignore
the present boundaries of the book as a separate literary unit
within the five-fold division of the Pentateuch. A significant section of Numbers, usually Num 1:1-10:10, is separated from the rest
of the book and attached to material in Exodus and Leviticus as a
block. This is most explicitly the case in the commentaries by
Dillmann, Baentsch and Mays, and in some ways Gray, Noth and
Wenham.[8] Gray, for example, maintains that

the first section of Numbers (1:1-10:10) may be regarded as
an appendix to the books of Exodus and Leviticus. The arrival
of the Israelites in the wilderness of Sinai is recorded in
Ex. 19:1, their departure therefrom in Num. 10:11f.; and
thus the scene of all that lies between these two passages
is the same. . . Exodus, Leviticus and Numbers might have
been much more suitably, though very unequally, divided as
follows: (1) Ex. 1-18: The Exodus from Egypt to Sinai;
(2) Ex. 19-Num. 10:10: Sinai; (3) Num. 10:11-36:13: From
Sinai to the Jordan. . . The book of Numbers is a section
somewhat mechanically cut out of the whole of which it forms
a part; the result is that it possesses no unity of subject.[9]

Similar sentiments are expressed by a number of other scholars.[10]
Disagreement also exists among these same scholars as to the correct
wider context in which Numbers is to be interpreted, whether the
Pentateuch of the five books of Genesis-Deuteronomy or the Hexateuch
of Genesis-Joshua or the Tetrateuch of Genesis-Numbers.

THE REASON FOR THE LACK OF AGREEMENT ON THE STRUCTURE OF NUMBERS

The reasons for this absence of consensus on the structure of
the book of Numbers and its proper interpretive context are many.
It is certainly true that the book of Numbers is a collection of
material which is very diverse in form, age and original function.
Early oral or literary layers have been woven together in various
ways with later traditions, and the flow of the material is often
less than entirely smooth. Combined with this is the great variety
in scholarly methods and approaches in the study of Numbers as our
survey above demonstrated. Interests range from historical to
literary and theological questions. Orientations differ from
Christian to Jewish, Roman Catholic to Protestant, critical to conservative. The surprising fact is that even among those who share
similar methods or orientations, absolutely no agreement is discernible on the question of the structure of the book.

We believe, however, that the _primary_ reason for this lack of
unanimity on the structure of Numbers is that previous scholars have
used the wrong foundations on which to build their proposals for the
framework of the book. The chronological notations in Numbers, the
geographical notations of movement by the Israelites from one place
to another, major tradition-historical "themes," and the detection
of different documentary sources have all been used as the basis
for suggested outlines for the book. We will now briefly review
these attempts to delineate the structure of Numbers and the reasons
for their inadequacy.

Some scholars have used the chronology of the book as a possible unifying framework.[11] The book of Numbers does indeed contain
a sequence of chronological indicators. Using the month of the
first Passover in Egypt as its starting point (cf. Exod 12:2), the

book lists the year, the month and usually the day of the time
elapsed since the first Passover at several points in the narrative
(1:1; 9:1; 9:5; 10:11; 20:1; 33:3; 33:38). The book begins "on the
first day of the second month, in the second year after they had
come out of the land of Egypt" (1:1). Num 9:1 and 9:5 indicate the
date on which Israel celebrated the second Passover in commemoration
of the first Passover a year before. In Num 10:11, the date is
given for the inauguration of the march of Israel after being constituted as the holy people of God. A juncture occurs in 20:1 in
which the only indication of time given is the month ("in the first
month") with no year or day stated. Num 33:3 and 33:38 are both in
an itinerary which recapitulates the stages of Israel's journey
from the first Passover in Egypt (33:3) through the wilderness wandering to the plains of Moab, including the date when Aaron died at
Mount Hor (33:38).

These chronological indicators do sometimes function as
bracketing devices in the narrative, but they do not represent the
core of the structural or conceptual framework of the book. The
omission of the chronological information in 20:1 which represents
a somewhat significant transition, the lack of chronological information for the forty years from 10:11 to 20:22 (cf. 33:38), and the
unrealistic nature of the length of some of the periods[12] demonstrate
that the chief element in the thematic structure of Numbers is not
its record of chronology. The dates in the book of Numbers do seem
to function as signals of important events: the census (1:1), the
celebration of the Passover (9:1,5); the inauguration of the march
(10:11); the arrival at Kadesh and the death of Miriam (20:1); the
remembrance of the first Passover in Egypt (33:3); and the remembrance of the death of Aaron (33:38). These highlighted portions
of the narrative do form part of the larger structural framework of
Numbers, as we shall see below. However, the chronological indicators by themselves do not represent a coherent or unifying structure
of the book.

The majority of scholars divide the book of Numbers into its
major structural divisions on the basis of the geographical indicators or Israel's movement from place to place in the wilderness.[13]
Typically, the book is divided into three major sections. Some
examples include the three outlines listed below.[14]

  1) I.   Num 1:1-10:10---In the Wilderness of Sinai
     II.   Num 10:11-22:1--From Sinai to Kadesh
     III. Num 22:2-36:13--On the Plains of Moab

  2) I.   Num 1:1-10:10---In the Wilderness of Sinai
     II.   Num 10:11-20:13-From Sinai to Kadesh
     III. Num 20:14-36:13-From Kadesh to the Plains of Moab

3) I.   Num 1:1-10:10---The Wilderness of Sinai
   II.   Num 10:11-21:19-North of Sinai; West of the Arabah
                         (Jordan Valley)
   III. Num 21:10-36:13-East of the Arabah (Jordan Valley)

One of the major difficulties of this scheme is the end of the
second unit. The location of the major break in this second section
of Numbers differs greatly among scholars. A number of indications
of Israel's geographical movement from place to place occur at the
end of this section (Kadesh, Edom, Mount Hor, Moab), but no one
geographical indicator compels more obvious significance than
another. In fact, among the 33 commentators who based their suggested outlines of Numbers on its geographical notations, 18 significantly different proposals were presented. A judgment on the
thematic structure of the book on the basis of geographical indicators alone leads to a somewhat arbitrary division of the book at
crucial points. Furthermore, it is unlikely that the essential
thematic concern of Numbers was perceived by its later redactors as
simply a record of the geography of Israel's wandering from Sinai
to the plains of Moab.

It should also be noted that many more geographical references
to Israel's movement or location are present in Numbers than the
typical three-part scheme suggests. Besides the two itineraries in
Numbers 21 and 33, there are at least 35 other verses which record
some geographical movement from one place to another.[15] We would
agree that the geographical indicators do often signal an important
transition or emphasize the significance of an action. But the
determination of which of these transitions represent the major
structural divisions must be made on the basis of other criteria
than geographical indicators alone. We will have more to say on
the role of geographical notations in the structure of Numbers and
in the structure of the entire Pentateuch in connection with our
discussion of the redactional framework of the Priestly tradition
in Part Two.

One might conceivably use the existence of different documentary sources as a criterion of division of the material in Numbers.
Most scholars agree that the three major Pentateuchal strands of
the Yahwist, Elohist and Priestly traditions are evident in the
book of Numbers. Roughly speaking, one may divide the book on
source-critical grounds in the following way with some variations
among scholars:[16]

     Num 1:1-10:28----All Priestly material
     Num 10:29-25:18--A composite of J, E and P
     Num 26:1-36:13---All Priestly or later material with the
                      exception of Numbers 32 which is composite

Diether Kellermann has used these source-critical divisions as

justification for isolating Num 1:1-10:10 as a separate unit of
study.[17] Although the Priestly material serves as an inclusio of
sorts for the book in that it surrounds the chapters which are a
composite of literary sources (10:29-25:18), it is improbable that
the bare delineation of the various sources could provide the fundamental starting point for the structure of the book as it was read
and handed down in its present form. On the other hand, these rough
divisions may be helpful in determining some of the major redactional
transitions in the book when used in conjunction with a more probable unifying theme or structure.

Some commentators have used the various tradition-historical
themes which they have detected in Numbers as a possible narrative
framework. Noth, Bernini and Wenham have all used this approach.
Noth describes the book of Numbers as involving the merger of three
"themes" which play a role in the shape of the Pentateuchal material.
Num 1:1-10:10 is the conclusion of the theme of the "revelation at
Sinai" which begins with Exodus 19. Another theme in Numbers is
"guidance through the wilderness" which occupies the bulk of the
material in Numbers. Noth also detects the beginnings of the theme
of the conquest or "guidance into the land" in chapters 21 and 32.[18]
Bernini also uses the notion of tradition-historical themes in
analyzing the structure of Numbers, but his divisions differ from
those of Noth. Bernini divides the material into the theme of "the
organization of the people" (Num 1:1-10:10), "the march in the
desert" (Num 10:11-25:18), and "ordinances relating to the entrance
into Canaan" (Num 25:19-36:13).[19] Wenham also bases his conception
of the structure of Numbers on tradition-historical themes, but he
has yet another alternative. Wenham divides the book on the basis
of three major blocks of tradition which are tied to geographical
themes. Num 1:1-10:10 is the conclusion of the Sinai complex which
begins at Exodus 19. Num 13:1-19:22 is the Kadesh complex, and
Num 22:2-36:13 is the Plains of Moab complex. These three major
blocks of tradition are then connected by two short travelogues:
Num 10:11-12:16 (From Sinai to Kadesh) and Num 20:1-22:1 (From
Kadesh to the Plains of Moab).[20]

Without embarking on a discussion of the soundness of the
concept of tradition-historical "themes" and the lack of any clear
grounding of the themes in a sociological setting in the history of
Israel, one need only note that dividing the book in this way simply
tears the book asunder. It does not allow the book to function
under any sort of unifying conceptual framework. Moreover, the
clear differences in the outlines proposed by the three commentators
demonstrate the subjectivity and lack of agreement on what

constitutes a "theme" from a tradition-historical perspective. The
criteria for determining the boundaries of a given "theme" are
unclear.

Most importantly, such an approach tends to ignore the present
form of the book of Numbers as a separate literary unit within the
Pentateuch. Even if Num 1:1-10:10 was originally part of the
"Sinai theme" in the history of the growth of the literature, it
has now been cut off from what precedes and has been joined to the
rest of the material in Numbers to form a separate literary entity.
Thus, a proper method must begin with the present form of Numbers
and ease into the later stages of redaction and on into the rest of
the history of the growth of the literature as far as the evidence
allows. Otherwise, we are left to conclude, with Noth, that "we
can scarcely speak of a specific significance peculiar to the book
of Numbers."[21] Again, however, the results of tradition-historical
research may help us in better defining the structure of the book
insofar as it provides evidence of divisions in the text which
elucidate the structure which the book defines for itself.

CONCLUSION TO PART ONE

Attempts to analyze the structure of the book of Numbers on the basis of chronology, geography, source criticism and tradition history do not in themselves provide an adequate basis from which to determine the unifying framework of the book. Chronological and geographical indicators lack consistency and significance of content. Source criticism and tradition-historical work are inadequate for the task in that they seek to define the structure of the work on a more diachronic level, that is, "underneath" the present form of the text. They fail to seek the conceptual unity of the book itself after the book's later definitive redaction and emerging acceptance as scripture.

Each of these criteria by which to analyze the book, however, can at times be helpful in uncovering the unifying structure of Numbers as the later definitive redactors defined it for future readers. Historical-critical work on Numbers has done much to help account for the book's diversity and unevenness as the product of a long oral and literary history. Such study helps to answer modern questions of historicity and the development of the literature which may get in the way of hearing the text if these questions are not addressed. Having wrestled with such issues and having come to some understanding of the pre-history of the text in its diverse units and layers, one must move on. One needs to discern the results of historical-critical work which are appropriate and valuable in understanding more clearly the final form of the text. One must also use the primary evidence which the present form of the book itself provides in order to fit the pieces back together and to gain some understanding of the way the text as a whole is to be comprehended by the reader.

Our survey of commentaries on Numbers in the last 120 years has shown that both critical and conservative scholars have tended to concentrate maximum effort on the question of the historical referentiality of the text. Conservative scholars have tended to defend the historicity and antiquity of the text. Because of this emphasis, they have often failed to recognize fully the multi-layered quality of the text. Often ignored is the fact that material in Numbers may function now in its present form in a way which is quite different from its original function. Critical scholars, while correctly perceiving the multi-layered dimension of the text, have often

39

failed to emphasize the religious or theological factors which gave rise to the various layers of the book. This is especially true in the stages of the later definitive shaping and editing of the book which led to its present form.

PART II

THE FRAMEWORK OF NUMBERS: AN ALTERNATIVE PROPOSAL

CHAPTER THREE

THE CASE FOR THE BOOK OF NUMBERS
AS A LITERARY UNIT

The present form of Numbers is a book, a separate literary
entity within the Pentateuch. Numbers is certainly not an entirely
independent entity for it is an integral part of the broader context
of the five books of Genesis through Deuteronomy. Yet the book
forms a distinct literary division. The crucial question which
must be asked before we proceed to our proposal for the structure
of Numbers is this: Is the form of Numbers as a separate book
merely a late and arbitrary division or is it an exegetically meaningful and significant datum for the book's interpretation?

Many commentators explicitly ignore the present form of the
book of Numbers as a separate literary unit in their outlines of
the structure of the book.[1] Scholars like Guthrie simply reject
any attempt to read the book of Numbers as a unit at any stage of
its literary history:

> Neither in its final form nor in any of the sources underlying
> it is Numbers a separate unit. It is part of a larger unit
> the division of which is largely arbitrary.[2]

This sentiment is shared by R. C. Dentan:

> The material in the book is of the most heterogeneous charac-
> ter and its arrangement, at least as respects the non-narra-
> tive elements, is largely fortuitous. Since any unity one
> may attribute to Numbers must be artificially imposed upon it,
> it is better not to think of it as a book so much as a more
> or less arbitrary division in the larger structure of the
> Pentateuch.[3]

Several scholars detach Num 1:1-10:10 from the book and join it to
a section which extends from Exodus 19 through Leviticus and on to
Num 10:10. This section is typically termed the Sinai complex.
Such an exegetical move, however, makes irrelevant the present division of Numbers as a literary unit. Is such a procedure proper?

In contrast to the positions above, we will argue that the
present form of the book of Numbers invites the reader to interpret
it as a meaningful literary unit in its own right. The present
five-fold division of the Pentateuch is, in fact, an ancient tradition. This division has been built into the final redactional form
of the book of Numbers and needs to be assumed as an important

datum in the book's interpretation. This division into five books
has meaningful exegetical significance and is not just a matter of
arbitrary division or convenience.

EXTERNAL EVIDENCE FOR NUMBERS AS A LITERARY UNIT

Evidence from outside the book of Numbers itself that the book
is to be understood as a separate literary entity derives principally from three sources: the rabbinic tradition, the Hebrew textual
tradition, and the Greek textual tradition. Each set of evidence
supports the antiquity and unanimity of the tradition of the division of the Pentateuch into five separate books.

The rabbinic tradition often makes reference to the five books
of the Torah. In the Jerusalem Talmud, Megilla 1:7, 70d contains
the phrase, "the five books of the Torah" (חמשת ספרי תורה). Sotah
5:8, 20d in the Jerusalem Talmud also refers to the "five books of
the Torah" (חמשה סיפרי תורה). In the Babylonian Talmud, Sanhedrin
44a and Hagigah 14a use the phrase, "the five fifths of the Torah"
(חמשה חומשי תורה). The same designation is also used in the
Jerusalem Talmud in Sanhedrin 10:1, 28a. Similar references to the
five-fold division of the Torah appear frequently throughout the
rabbinic corpus.[4]

The book of Numbers, the fourth of the five books, is often
designated in the early rabbinic tradition as "The Fifth of the
Musterings" (חומש הפקודים), that is, the one of the five books which
deals with the mustering or census of the people. The early traditions of the Mishnah,[5] the Tosefta,[6] and the early midrashic collec-
tions[7] attest to the widespread use of this phrase for Numbers.[8]
Other Hebrew titles for the book include וידבר ("And he said"), the
first word in the book, or במדבר ("In the wilderness"), the fifth
word of the first verse of the book.

Flavius Josephus (ca. 37-107 A.D.) is also an early Jewish
witness to the Scriptural canon of first century Palestine. In the
treatise _Against Apion I_, paragraphs 38-39, Josephus writes:

> Our books, those which are justly accredited, are but two
> and twenty, and contain the record of all time. Of these,
> five are the books of Moses, comprising the laws and the
> traditional history of man down to the death of the law
> giver.[9]

Mention should also be made of the Talmudic regulation which states
that "between the books in a Torah scroll a vacant space of four
lines must be left."[10] This rabbinic ordinance further corroborates
the tenacity of the tradition of five books within the Pentateuch.
It can be safely said that Jewish tradition is unanimous in the
matter of dividing the Torah into five individual books.

This tradition of a Torah of five books is also supported by
the witness of the Hebrew textual tradition. All Massoretic Hebrew
manuscripts attest to the division of the Torah into five books.[11]
Important evidence involving a Hebrew text is also provided by the
Samaritan Pentateuch. Recent studies have shown that the Samaritan
Pentateuch branched off from an earlier Palestinian Hebrew text-type
early in the first century B.C. This breach between the Samaritan
and other Palestinian texts gives further evidence of two important
points: the Samaritan Pentateuch shows that the Pentateuch could
be and was treated as a separate collection which the Samaritans
used apart from the other books of the Prophets and Writings, and
it shows that the Torah was divided into five individual books at
this early date.[12]

Perhaps the most compelling external evidence of the antiquity
of the tradition of the five books of the Pentateuch derives from
the Greek or Septuagintal textual tradition. All extant Greek manuscripts of the Old Testament clearly divide the five books of the
Pentateuch in their present form.[13] For example, the facsimile of
Codex Alexandrinus, a fifth century A.D. Greek uncial codex, makes
clear divisions between each of the five books of the Pentateuch
with a line, the title of the preceding book and a large blank
space in the column between the books.[14] Moreover, the codex marks
a major separation between the five books of the Pentateuch and the
books which follow by leaving an entire page blank between the
books of Deuteronomy and Joshua.

The Hebrew designation of the Torah as "the five fifths of the
Law" was mentioned above in our discussion of the rabbinic tradition.
The Greek textual tradition used a similar phrase. Otto Eissfeldt
wrote in his Old Testament, An Introduction:

> Admittedly the description corresponding to this five-fold
> division, "the five fifths of the Law," is first to be found
> in Talmudic times. But it is clearly older. For the term
> hē pentateuchos (bíblos), "the book consisting of five books,"
> which is probably to be understood as a translation of the
> Hebrew name, already appears in the second century A.D., and
> its Latin form pentateuchas (liber) soon after. Our entitling
> of the five books of Moses as the Pentateuch corresponds to
> the Latin.[15]

This further supports the antiquity of the tradition of the five-
fold Torah. The received division and order of Genesis, Exodus,
Leviticus, Numbers and Deuteronomy is also corroborated by all the
patristic canonical lists of the Eastern and Western churches with
three minor exceptions in which Numbers and Leviticus are simply
interchanged and one exception which involves an unintentional
scribal error.[16]

The most important document, however, associated with the Greek
translation of the Hebrew Torah which we call the Septuagint is the
Letter of Aristeas. The letter purports to explain the process by
which "the book of the Law of the Jews" was translated from Hebrew
to Greek in the Jewish center of Alexandria in Egypt. Although the
letter seems to contain some legendary and improbable features, most
scholars agree that certain accurate historical facts can be derived
from the letter. They include the fact that Egypt is the probable
origin of the Septuagintal tradition. The Pentateuch or the Torah
was the first section of the Scriptures to be translated into Greek.
And finally, the translation of the Pentateuch in its present form
can be dated to the third century B.C.[17] This third century B.C.
date provides strong evidence of the ancient character of the five-
fold division of the Pentateuch. If one combines the evidence which
we have cited above with the early attestations of the canonical
authority of the Torah in the Apocrypha and Pseudepigrapha[18] as well
as in the Qumran literature,[19] one is led to assume at least a
fourth century B.C. date for the present form of the Torah with its
division into five books. The conclusion made by Otto Kaiser in
his _Introduction_ _to_ _the_ _Old_ _Testament_ is on the mark:

> At present we can do no more than draw the conclusion, on the
> basis of the general considerations about the earlier history
> of different forms of the text about the beginnings of the
> Septuagint translation, that the Pentateuch reached its posi-
> tion of special dignity at the latest in the fourth century.[20]

Some have argued for the possibility that the Torah reached canonical status in its present form already in the time of Ezra and
Nehemiah in the fifth century B.C.[21] This remains a possibility,
but the external evidence alone can only support a date as early as
the fourth century B.C.

INTERNAL EVIDENCE FOR NUMBERS AS A LITERARY UNIT

Given the fact that the external evidence for the division of
the Pentateuch into five books is a very old tradition, one needs
to ask whether this ancient tradition is supported by the internal
evidence of the books themselves. Are there clear editorial introductions and conclusions to the five books of the Pentateuch as
well as other redactional devices which separate each of the books
as a literary unit? Our primary interest, of course, is on the
book of Numbers, but the other Pentateuchal books may also be
profitably considered.

We will begin by listing the first and last verses of each of
the five books to determine whether they may function as redactional
introductions or conclusions to the books.

Gen 1:1   "In the beginning God created the heavens and
the earth. . ."

Gen 50:26   "So Joseph died, being a hundred and ten years
old; and they embalmed him, and he was put in a
coffin in Egypt."

— — — — — — — — — — — — — — — — —

Exod 1:1-7   "These are the names of the sons of Israel who
came to Egypt with Jacob, each with his house-
hold: Reuben, Simeon, Levi, and Judah, Issachar,
Zebulun, and Benjamin, Dan and Naphtali, Gad and
Asher. All the offspring of Jacob were seventy
persons; Joseph was already in Egypt. Then
Joseph died, and all his brothers, and all that
generation. But the descendants of Israel were
fruitful and increased greatly; they multiplied
and grew exceedingly strong; so that the land
was filled with them."

Exod 40:38   "For throughout all their journeys the cloud of
the LORD was upon the tabernacle by day, and fire
was in it by night, in the sight of all the house
of Israel."

— — — — — — — — — — — — — — — — —

Lev 1:1-2   "The LORD called Moses, and spoke to him from
the tent of meeting, saying, 'Speak to the people
of Israel and say to them, When any man of you
brings an offering to the LORD, you shall bring
your offering of cattle from the herd or from
the flock. . .'"

Lev 27:34   "These are the commandments which the LORD
commanded Moses for the people of Israel on
Mount Sinai."

— — — — — — — — — — — — — — — — —

Num 1:1   "The LORD spoke to Moses in the wilderness of
Sinai, in the tent of meeting, on the first day
of the second month, in the second year after
they had come out of the land of Egypt, saying,
'Take a census. . .'"

Num 36:13   "These are the commandments and the ordinances
which the LORD commanded by Moses to the people
of Israel in the plains of Moab by the Jordan
at Jericho."

— — — — — — — — — — — — — — — — —

Deut 1:1   "These are the words which Moses spoke to all
Israel beyond the Jordan in the wilderness, in
the Arabah over against Suph, between Paran and
Tophel, Laban, Hazeroth, and Dizahab. . ."

Deut 34:9-12 (After recounting the death of Moses) "And there
has not arisen a prophet since in Israel like
Moses, whom the LORD knew face to face, none like
him for all the signs and wonders which the LORD
sent him to do in the land of Egypt, to Pharaoh
and to all his servants and to all his land, and
for all the mighty power and terrible deeds which
Moses did in the sight of all Israel."

— — — — — — — — — — — — — — — — —

Josh 1:1   "After the death of Moses the servant of the
LORD, the LORD said to Joshua son of Nun, Moses'
minister. . ."

The first and final verses of each of the books of the Pentateuch do in fact serve to mark major transitions from one book to
another. The book of Genesis recounts the primeval history from
the beginnings of the heavens and the earth through the stories of
the patriarchs. The last verse of Genesis narrates the death of
the last patriarch and the end of his generation. Then Exodus
begins with the story of the next generation and marks a decisive
break with Genesis. Exodus tells of the deliverance from Egypt,
the giving of the commandments at Sinai, and the building of the
tabernacle which ends the book. The book of Leviticus is set off
from Exodus by its introduction and by its content and structure
which consists almost entirely of ritual and priestly law.[22]

The demarcation of the end of Leviticus and the beginning of
Numbers is an important one for our purposes. As we have seen, it
is this break between Leviticus and Numbers which scholars most
often ignore. The book of Leviticus is often connected with Num
1:1-10:10 and with Exodus 19-40 as a unified complex which disre-
gards the traditional boundaries of the books. This block of
material is often called "the Sinai tradition." Now it must be
admitted that the division between Leviticus and Numbers is the
least obvious of all the books of the Pentateuch. Genesis and
Deuteronomy exhibit much more evidence of being books with independent integrity.

However, a close examination reveals that a failure to divide
between Leviticus and Numbers ignores the present editorial indices
which do in fact separate the two books. The conclusion to Leviticus, "These are the commandments which the LORD commanded Moses for
the people of Israel on Mount Sinai," provides the theological context for the whole book of Leviticus. This conclusion designates
Leviticus as part of the normative revelation of God to Moses on
Mount Sinai. The introduction to Numbers, on the other hand, represents an entirely different context, both geographically and theologically. The action has moved from Mount Sinai to the wilderness
of Sinai. God no longer speaks from the top of the mountain but he
now speaks in Numbers from the portable tent of meeting. The commands in Leviticus are basically enduring legal precepts; the command to take a census which begins the book of Numbers, on the other
hand, applies only to the one time in the wilderness.

Those scholars who refer to the material in Exodus 19-40, all
of Leviticus, and Numbers 1-10 as a unified block of the Sinai
tradition do so on the basis of the reference to the Israelites
arriving at the "wilderness of Sinai in Exod 19:1-2 and leaving the
"wilderness of Sinai" in Num 10:11. However, the dynamic of the

material in its present form involves a major break between the
events and laws connected with Mount Sinai and the events and laws
connected with the wilderness of Sinai. After the references in
Exod 19:1-2, all references to Sinai in Exodus and all through
Leviticus are to the mountain of Sinai.[23] Only at Num 1:1 and
following do we again read of events and laws in the wilderness
of Sinai, not the mountain of Sinai. At the beginning of Numbers,
the elevated and stationary site of God's revelation on the mountain
has been transferred in a decisive transition to a moveable site of
revelation in the midst of the people in the wilderness. Hence,
the beginning of Numbers provides clear evidence of an editorial
intention to separate the end of Leviticus and the beginning of
Numbers.

    The books of Numbers and Deuteronomy are obviously divided.
Deuteronomy is clearly structured as an independent literary unit
with its own distinctive vocabulary and style. The book of Numbers
concludes with these words, "These are the commandments and ordinances which the LORD commanded by Moses to the people of Israel in
the plains of Moab by the Jordan at Jericho." Deuteronomy follows
with a clearly distinguishable introductory formula, "These are
the words which Moses spoke to all Israel beyond the Jordan in the
wilderness, in the Arabah, over against Suph, between Paran and
Tophel, Laban, Hazeroth, and Dizahab." Deuteronomy also has a clear
conclusion with the account of the death of Moses and his uniqueness
as a prophet in Israel.

    Thus, every book of the Pentateuch provides its own internal
evidence of an intentional editorial structure which provides each
book with a clear introduction and conclusion. Each book is given
a level of its own literary integrity apart from the other books of
the Pentateuch which may precede or follow it. The significance
for the interpretation of the book of Numbers is that, in its
present form, it is intended to be read as a literary unit with its
own integrity.

THE TRADITION RESPONSIBLE FOR EDITING THE BOOKS
    The suggestion that the present form of Numbers as a separate
book is to be taken seriously is not meant to imply that the division of the Pentateuch into five parts was an original part of the
literary pre-history of the text. It was more probably a result
of later editing. The determination of the editor or editors who
were responsible for making Numbers one of the five individual books
of the Pentateuch is a more difficult issue for the conclusion of
Numbers than for the beginning of Numbers. Since the earliest

literary critics, scholars have generally assigned the conclusion
of Leviticus and the introduction of Numbers to some level of the
Priestly tradition. Since the tradition-historical work of Martin
Noth[24] and Ivan Engnell,[25] the notion of an originally independent
Priestly Tetrateuch which encompassed the books of Genesis through
Numbers and an originally separate Deuteronomistic History which
encompassed the books of Deuteronomy through Kings has gained much
support. Thus, the Priestly tradition would be viewed as responsible for the present shape of Genesis through Numbers.

Frank Cross has argued that the introductions to the books of
Exodus, Leviticus and Numbers are "Priestly headings which have
been drawn from a tangible Priestly document."[26] Rudolf Smend
concurs in his discussion of the final editing of the Pentateuchal
books. The division of the books was done at least in the spirit
of the Priestly tradition. The final verse in Leviticus (27:34)
was intended by the Priestly editors as a conclusion to the book
which separates it from the beginning of Numbers.[27] Finally,
Diether Kellermann's careful literary and redactional analysis of
the opening section of Numbers confirms the Priestly character of
the introductory material.[28]

The question of who is responsible for the concluding section
of Numbers is a more disputed matter. Literary critics have typically assigned the end of Numbers to a later level of Priestly supplements to the original Priestly source.[29] Martin Noth described
the latter part of Numbers as the result of several secondary additions of unknown origin. The chapters were added to the already
completed narrative rather than to the Priestly source alone as
earlier source critics had maintained. Noth argued that these
secondary insertions had been made after the Deuteronomistic History
had been attached to the Priestly Tetrateuch of Genesis through
Numbers.[30] Rudolf Smend altered Noth's view by suggesting that the
pre-Priestly Tetrateuch was linked by a Deuteronomistic editor with
the Deuteronomistic History. Subsequently, a later Priestly redaction gave the Pentateuch its present shape and was responsible for
dividing the Pentateuch into five books with introductions and conclusions to each book. Thus, the conclusion of Numbers reflects
the spirit of the Priestly tradition.[31]

Rolf Rendtorff has emphasized the affinities of the last chapters of Numbers with parts of the Deuteronomistic History and concludes that a Deuteronomistic editor was responsible for these
later chapters as well as other editorial links in Genesis through
Numbers. Thus, he rejects Noth's almost complete separation of
Genesis through Numbers and the Deuteronomistic History.[32]

Finally, A. Graeme Auld has provided a useful summary and
evaluation of issues relating to the final chapters of Numbers and
their relationship to the material in the Deuteronomistic History,
especially the book of Joshua.[33] Auld acknowledges the affinities
of the last chapters of Numbers with material in the Deuteronomistic
History which Rendtorff observes. However, Auld's study draws a
different conclusion. The end of Numbers was the work of Priestly
redactors who knew the text of the Deuteronomistic History at a late
stage in its development and incorporated some of its material in
their own work. This explains why the structure of the chapters in
Numbers is not Deuteronomistic but thoroughly Priestly in character,
although affinities in content and language with Deuteronomistic
material is evident. Auld concludes that the lines of influence run
in only one direction. The Priestly tradition incorporated the
material at the end of Numbers from the book of Joshua which was
available at a late stage as a text which was no longer confined
only to the Deuteronomistic tradition. Auld's objections to
Rendtorff's position are significant, but the issues will surely
continue to be debated.[34]

The three available options, therefore, as to who was responsible for the concluding section of Numbers include the Priestly
tradition (Smend, Auld and most literary critics), the Deuteronomistic tradition (Rendtorff), or an unknown redactor (Noth). We would
argue that a later stage of the Priestly tradition is perhaps the
best option, at least for the question of who was responsible for
the last verse in Numbers (36:13) which marks the conclusion of the
book and sets it off as a literary entity. The affinity of this
verse with the conclusion of Leviticus (27:34) which is typically
ascribed to the Priestly tradition provides some additional support
to such a position. However, the Priestly tradition itself appears
to contain several layers, many of which are difficult to date
absolutely or relatively. Any attempt to be more precise in identi-
fying the editor or editors who gave the book of Numbers its present
shape as a literary unit would be speculative.

THE SIGNIFICANCE OF THE DIVISION OF THE PENTATEUCH INTO FIVE BOOKS

We have sought to demonstrate that the division of the five-
fold Pentateuch is a very ancient tradition which is built into the
redactional structure of the books themselves. In particular, we
have shown that the book of Numbers has a clear introduction and
conclusion and is distinguished from the book of Leviticus which
precedes it and the book of Deuteronomy which follows it. We now
must consider the significance of the delimitation of Numbers as a

"book."

Some would argue that the present division was due purely to
accident or matters of convenience. In his commentary on Numbers,
Arnold Goldberg writes:

> The book of Numbers, the fourth of the five books of the
> Pentateuch, was never an independent literary work. Its
> existence as a book is due to a division of the Pentateuch
> into books which was occasioned by a purely practical
> necessity: the handling of the Torah scrolls.[35]

Nahum Sarna adopts a similar position. The Torah, he assumes, was
first fixed only for liturgical purposes and was originally written
as a whole and undivided on one single scroll.

> With the widespread dissemination of the Torah in the genera-
> tions following the activities of Ezra and Nehemiah, it
> became customary, for strictly nonliturgical purposes and
> for convenience of handling, to transcribe the work on five
> separate scrolls: hence the Greek name hē pentateuchos
> (bíblos), "the five-volumed (book)," which has passed into
> English as Pentateuch.[36]

Josef Oesch has recently argued for an alternative view of the
significance of the five-fold division of the Pentateuch.[37] He argues that the individual books of the Torah are not later than the
Torah itself in its present form. As evidence, Oesch cites the
total agreement of the tradition on the number and order of the five
books, the early witness of the Septuagint and other good textual
exemplars, the rabbinic instructions for leaving blank lines between
each of the five books in ceremonial Torah scrolls, and the conservative tendency in the handing down of sacred texts. Perhaps the
most important of Oesch's observations is directed against the contention of Goldberg and Sarna that the content of the Torah was
divided into five books or scrolls of similar length for practical
purposes. Such is not the case, according to Oesch. The book of
Genesis, for example, contains almost twice as many verses as
Leviticus. Even among the closely related books of Exodus, Leviticus
and Numbers, the division of the books is not at all even since
Leviticus contains only two-thirds of the verses in Exodus or Numbers.[38] Thus, the five books of the Pentateuch were not the result
of a purely mechanical and arbitrary division into equal segments
for reasons of convenience.

The division into five books, according to Oesch, may best be
explained as the product of an intentional redactional shaping of
the Pentateuch into five separate books. Our discussion of the
evidence of Priestly redaction of Numbers as a separate literary
entity would further buttress Oesch's conclusions. Therefore, the
ancient and unanimous tradition of Numbers as a separate book within

the Pentateuch has a positive exegetical significance. Now that
we have established the parameters and significance of Numbers as a
literary unit, we must turn to an examination of the internal
literary structure of the present form of the book of Numbers.

CHAPTER FOUR

MODERN INTERPRETATIONS OF NUMBERS 1 AND 26

Given the assumption that the book of Numbers is to be treated
as a literary unit, we move on to consider the possibility that the
book contains some sort of intelligible structure or framework.
The central problem in the interpretation of Numbers is the lack of
scholarly agreement on the book's structure. The primary reason
for this lack of consensus was that scholars have attempted to use
the wrong foundations on which to construct their proposed outlines.
We believe that the two census lists of the twelve tribes of Israel
in Numbers 1 and 26 provide the major structural edifice on which
the organization of the book as a whole stands. The primary argu-
mentation for this position will be presented in Chapter Five.

The purpose of this chapter is to delineate and evaluate the
significant lines of recent research on the census lists of Numbers
1 and 26. We hope thereby to indicate the manner in which our
interpretation of the census lists both incorporates and advances
beyond past attempts to understand the significance of the census
lists in Numbers 1 and 26. Two separate but related issues are
involved with the census lists in Numbers: 1) the interpretation
of the lists of the names of the twelve tribes of Israel in the
census lists, and 2) the interpretation of the numerical census
figures which are connected to the list of tribal names. We will
first consider these two issues independently and then attempt to
draw them together in order to formulate our own conclusions
regarding the history and interpretation of the census lists.

THE LISTS OF THE NAMES OF THE TWELVE TRIBES OF ISRAEL

The Data
Since much of the debate on the tribal lists has centered on
the questions of relative dating and literary dependence of one
list upon another, we will begin with a table of the Israelite
tribal lists as they appear in the book of Numbers. These lists
represent the order of the tribes as they appear in the Massoretic
text.[1]

Num 1:5-15	Num 1:20-43	Num 2:3-31
(Tribal leaders chosen to carry out the census)	(The account of the actual census)	(The 12 tribes arranged into four marching groups)
Reuben	Reuben	Judah
Simeon	Simeon	Issachar (EAST)
Judah	Gad	Zebulun
Issachar	Judah	Reuben
Zebulun	Issachar	Simeon (SOUTH)
Ephraim	Zebulun	Gad
Manasseh	Ephraim	Ephraim
Benjamin	Manasseh	Manasseh (WEST)
Dan	Benjamin	Benjamin
Asher	Dan	Dan
Gad	Asher	Asher (NORTH)
Naphtali	Naphtali	Naphtali

Num 7:12-83	Num 10:14-28	Num 13:4-15
(Tribal leaders give offerings at dedication of altar)	(The order of the tribes setting out from Sinai)	(One man from each tribe sent to spy out the land)
Judah	Judah	Reuben
Issachar	Issachar	Simeon
Zebulun	Zebulun	Judah
Reuben	Reuben	Issachar
Simeon	Simeon	Ephraim
Gad	Gad	Benjamin
Ephraim	Ephraim	Zebulun
Manasseh	Manasseh	Manasseh
Benjamin	Benjamin	Dan
Dan	Dan	Asher
Asher	Asher	Naphtali
Naphtali	Naphtali	Gad

Num 26:5-51	Num 34:16-29
(The second census of the 12 tribes, with an expanded genealogy for each tribe)	(One man from each tribe chosen to divide the land)
Reuben	Judah
Simeon	Simeon
Gad	Benjamin
Judah	Dan
Issachar	Manasseh
Zebulun	Ephraim
Manasseh	Zebulun
Ephraim	Issachar
Benjamin	Asher
Dan	Naphtali
Asher	(Reuben, Gad and the half-tribe of
Naphtali	Manasseh had already settled in
	Trans-Jordan)

All scholars tend to agree that the tribal lists in Numbers are related in some way to the twelve-tribe genealogies and lists which occur in earlier sections of the Pentateuch, especially in Genesis and the beginning of Exodus. The following are the tribal lists which are frequently cited in this connection.

Gen 29:31-30:24
(J's genealogy of the
sons of Jacob within
a narrative context)

LEAH'S SONS
  Reuben
  Simeon
  Levi
  Judah
SONS OF BILHAH,
RACHEL'S MAID
  Dan
  Naphtali
SONS OF ZILPAH,
LEAH'S MAID
  Gad
  Asher
LEAH'S SONS
  Issachar
  Zebulun
RACHEL'S SONS
  Joseph
  (Benjamin--Gen
  35:16-20)

Gen 35:22-26
(Priestly genealogy
of the sons of
Jacob)

LEAH'S SONS
  Reuben
  Simeon
  Levi
  Judah
  Issachar
  Zebulun
RACHEL'S SONS
  Joseph
  Benjamin
SONS OF BILHAH,
RACHEL'S MAID
  Dan
  Naphtali
SONS OF ZILPAH,
LEAH'S MAID
  Gad
  Asher

Gen 46:8-27
(Expanded Priestly
genealogy of the
sons of Jacob and
their offspring)

Reuben
Simeon
Levi
Judah
Issachar
Zebulun
Gad
Asher
Joseph
  Manasseh
  Ephraim
Benjamin
Dan
Naphtali

Gen 49:3-27
(Jacob's blessing
of his sons--J?)

Reuben
Simeon
Levi
Judah
Zebulun
Issachar
Dan
Gad
Asher
Naphtali
Joseph
Benjamin

Exod 1:1-5
(The sons of Israel
who came into Egypt
with Jacob)

Reuben
Simeon
Levi
Judah
Issachar
Zebulun
Benjamin
Dan
Naphtali
Gad
Asher
(Joseph was already
in Egypt)

Exod 6:14-26
(A genealogy which
begins with Reuben
and Simeon but ends
with and focuses on
the sons of Levi,
especially Moses
and Aaron)

Reuben
Simeon
Levi
(with the sons of
Levi and their
descendants, includ-
ing Moses and Aaron
and the offspring
of Aaron)

The Interpretation of the Data

Martin Noth's proposal of the twelve-tribe amphictyonic league
which was based on his study of the twelve-tribe lists has been the
generating force for much of the later discussion of the tribal
lists in the Old Testament.[2]   Our analysis will be largely confined
to the effect which this discussion has had on the understanding of
the lists in Numbers 1 and 26.   Noth argued that the tribal lists
in Genesis 49 and Numbers 26 are the most important and most original groupings of the tribes.   All the lists which include Levi as
one of the twelve Israelite tribes (Deut 27:12-13; Deut 33; Exod 1:
2-5; Ezek 48:31-34; 1 Chr 12:25-38; 1 Chr 27:16-22) ultimately
derive from the list in Genesis 49.

All the lists which do not include Levi as one of the twelve
Israelite tribes (Num 1:20-43; Num 2:3-31; Num 7:12-83; Num 10:14-
28; Num 13:4-15) derive either from Num 1:5-15 (so the lists in
Num 1:20-43; 2; 7; and 10) or from Num 26:5-51 (so the list in
Num 13:4-15).[3] Since Levi is not included in these two lists in
Num 1:5-15 and Num 26:5-51, the twelve-tribe structure is retained
by dividing the Joseph tribe into two tribes, Ephraim and Manasseh,
but in different order. Num 1:5-15 presents the order Ephraim-
Manasseh while Num 26:5-51 has the order Manasseh-Ephraim. Noth
evaluates the order in Num 26:5-51 as older on the basis of the
blessing by Jacob of these two sons of Joseph in Genesis 48. The
blessing expresses the rising superiority of Ephraim over the once
superior Manasseh. Hence, the old order of Manasseh-Ephraim (Num
26:5-51) was replaced by the later order of Ephraim-Manasseh (Num
1:5-15).[4] Thus, Noth concludes that the whole list in Num 26:5-51
is the more original.

As for the relative dating of the lists in Genesis 49 and
Numbers 26, Noth argues that Genesis 49 is an earlier list since it
contains the tribe of Levi as a "secular" tribe on an equal basis
with the other Israelite tribes. Noth believes that this reflects
an earlier stage of Israelite history than that reflected in the
list in Numbers 26 which does not include Levi among the twelve
tribes.[5] This assumption is based on Noth's interpretation of
Genesis 49 which he understands as portraying Levi as a "secular"
tribe. The exclusion of Levi as a landless priestly tribe represents a later historical development.

An absolute dating for the lists, according to Noth, can be
determined from Numbers 26. Since the list in Numbers 26 refers to
the tribe of Manasseh, it must come from a time later than the Song
of Deborah in Judges 5 where Manasseh has not yet achieved the status of an independent tribe. Since none of the great and well-
known Canaanite city-states of the plains of Palestine are mentioned
in Numbers 26, the list must come from a time before the Canaanite
city-states of the plains had been incorporated into Israel by David.
Thus, the list of tribal names derives from a time in the second
half of the period of the judges before the time of David and after
the Song of Deborah.[6] While the list in Genesis 49 in its present
form comes from the time of David or Solomon, it originates ultimately in the early period of the judges. Noth then uses these
lists as evidence of the existence of an Israelite twelve-tribe
amphictyony in the period of the judges. The two lists reflect the
slight changes in structure from an earlier to a later stage in the
premonarchical period.

A. D. H. Mayes has offered a thorough summary and critique of Noth's view of the lists of the twelve tribes.[7] In contrast to Noth, Mayes argues that Num 1:5-15 represents the original tribal list from which all the other lists which exclude Levi derive (Num 1:20-43; Num 2:3-31; 7:12-83; 10:14-28; 13:4-15; 26:5-51). Mayes rejects Noth's position that the story of the blessing by Jacob of Ephraim and Manasseh in Genesis 48 which exalts Ephraim presupposes an earlier historical period when Manasseh was superior to Ephraim. The narrative simply uses the motif of Manasseh as the first-born as a literary device to accentuate the exaltation of Ephraim. It cannot be used to reconstruct a historical sequence of development. Therefore, it cannot be used to assign historical priority to the list which gives Manasseh first place (Num 26:5-51) as Noth attempted to do.[8]

Mayes also discusses the one other difference among the various lists which exclude Levi, namely, the position assigned to the tribe of Gad. Noth maintained that three different forms of the twelve-tribe system may be reconstructed on the basis of the biblical evidence and the shifting position of Gad in the lists. The first form of the twelve-tribe list had Levi in the third position as a "secular" tribe (Reuben, Simeon, Levi, Judah, . . .) with Gad toward the end of the list. Noth suggested that this sequence was subsequently altered when Levi disappeared as a "secular" tribe and became a landless priestly tribe. This suggestion is based on his interpretation of Gen 49:5-7:

> Simeon and Levi are brothers
> Weapons of violence are their swords. . .
> Cursed be their anger, for it is fierce;
> And their wrath, for it is cruel.
> I will divide them in Jacob and scatter them in Israel.

Noth understands these verses as indicating that Levi was once a "secular" tribe on an equal standing with the other tribes. Later Levi became a priestly tribe, lost its land and was excluded from its position in the tribal list. Levi's position was taken by Gad and the number of twelve tribes was retained by dividing Joseph into Ephraim and Manasseh.

The third and latest stage, according to Noth, is represented by Num 1:5-15 in its present form where Gad occupies a position near the end of the list. Thus, the chronological progression may be presented as follows: 1) Gen 49:3-27 (original form of the list--Levi and Joseph included); 2) Num 26:5-51 (later form of the list--Levi deleted and Joseph divided into Manasseh and Ephraim); and 3) Num 1:5-15 (latest form of the list).[9]

Mayes rejects Noth's sequence of lists and suggests Num 1:5-15 is actually the original tribal list from which the other lists which do not include Levi (including Numbers 26) derive. The date which Mayes proposes for this form of the list is sometime after the battle against Sisera as celebrated in the Song of Deborah in Judges 5 since the tribe of Manasseh is not mentioned in the Song. Its absence indicates it did not yet exist as a tribe in that period. And the list must come from a time before the fall of the northern kingdom (722 B.C.)

The lists which do include Levi (such as Genesis 49) stem from an independent form of the tradition. In their present form, these lists may be dated to the time of Solomon, but their date of origin is only a matter of speculation. They probably originated after the event celebrated in the Song of Deborah in Judges 5, that is, the latter half of the period of the judges.[10]

Mayes offers several contentions against Noth's reconstruction of the sequence of the tribal lists. First of all, Mayes points out that Gen 49:5-7 does not conclusively prove that Levi was a secular tribe in an earlier period. The verses simply refer to a loss of land and so remain ambiguous as to whether Levi was originally a secular or a priestly tribe. Mayes understands these verses as literary reflections of Genesis 34 rather than as a historical expression of Levi as a once secular tribe. The passage cannot prove that Levi was originally a secular tribe and only later became a priestly tribe.[11]

Secondly, Noth argued that Joseph was the original tribe which was subsequently divided after the settlement in Palestine into the two tribes of Ephraim and Manasseh. Joseph does not appear in the Song of Ephraim while Ephraim does. Thus, the list which included Joseph (Genesis 49) could be dated to the time before the Song of Deborah (the early period of the judges). Moreover, the lists which included Ephraim-Manasseh (Numbers 1 and 26) could be dated after the Song of Deborah.

The major difficulty of this view, however, is that Ephraim appears in the Song of Deborah but Manasseh does not. If Joseph was the original tribe which later split into Ephraim and Manasseh, it is strange that both do not appear together in the Song of Deborah. Mayes thinks the evidence is better interpreted if Joseph is taken as a collective designation which came into use only after the stabilization of tribal relationships which resulted in the emergence of Manasseh as a brother-tribe to Ephraim. However, this does not necessarily mean that the list in Genesis 49 which includes Joseph is later than the list in Numbers 1 which does not. A long period of fluidity may be presupposed in the use of these names.[12]

Thirdly, Noth maintained that the tribal list which included Levi in third position (Genesis 49) was the original form. When Levi was dropped as a secular tribe, Gad was moved into the third position vacated by Levi (so Numbers 26). Mayes rejected Noth's contention that the list which included Levi was original. Is there then another explanation for Gad's position as the third tribe in the lists in Num 26:5-51 and Num 1:20-43?

Mayes believes such an explanation can be found in the literary context of the Priestly writer rather than in the historical tribal relationships within Israel. Mayes contends that Num 1:5-15 is the original list. Numbers 2 recounts the division of the tribes into a camp of four groups with three tribes in each group. Each group is assigned to one of the four cardinal points (east, south, west, north). If the division had strictly followed the original list in Num 1:5-15, the division would have created the following groups:

Reuben	Issachar	Manasseh	Asher
Simeon	Zebulun	Benjamin	Gad
Judah	Ephraim	Dan	Naphtali

The placement of Judah in an inferior position in the group headed by Reuben would not have been tolerated by the Priestly traditon which had its origins in Judah. Hence, the division of the tribes in Num 2:3-31 was altered by the Priestly writer by placing Judah at the head of one group and using Gad to fill in the slot in the Reuben group.

Gad may have been chosen because Reuben and Gad may have been historically associated. This gave rise to the arrangement of the present form of the text in Numbers 2:

Judah	Reuben	Ephraim	Dan
Issachar	Simeon	Manasseh	Asher
Zebulun	Gad	Benjamin	Naphtali

The lists in Num 1:20-43 and Num 26:5-51 then use this form of the list, except that the Reuben group is placed before the Judah group. Gad is then found in the third position of the list: Reuben, Simeon, Gad, Judah, Issachar, Zebulun, Ephraim, Manasseh, Benjamin, Dan, Asher, Naphtali.[13]

In sum, Mayes has raised considerable doubt regarding Noth's date of the origin of the twelve-tribe lists as early in the first half of the period of the judges as well as Noth's scheme of rela-tive dating among the various tribal lists. None of the twelve-tribe lists gives evidence of existing before the event celebrated in the Song of Deborah. Any more precise dating is difficult to substantiate. Mayes has also shown that some important differences

among the lists can be explained on the basis of _literary_ reworking
rather than on the basis of changing _historical_ relationships among
the tribes.

Norman Gottwald has attempted a more precise dating of the
origin of the twelve-tribe lists.[14] While the lists indicate
rootage in some form of premonarchic intertribal association,
Gottwald contends that the present form of the twelve-tribe lists
was developed by David for administrative purposes. The lists were
used to recruit the citizen army and possibly also to levy taxes or
labor from the citizenry. This twelve-tribe scheme served to
solidify David's kingdom on the foundation of the old Yahwistic
intertribal association. Gottwald assumes that the lists in Num
1:20-43 and Num 26:5-51 represent the form of the list which David
originated: Reuben, Simeon, Gad, Judah, Issachar, Zebulun, Ephraim,
Manasseh, Benjamin, Dan, Asher, Naphtali. The number of Israelite
tribes in David's time was made to correspond to the number of
months into which the militia would be divided for reserve service.

Gottwald's evidence is primarily negative in nature: there is
no conclusive evidence that any of the twelve-tribe lists derive
from the period before the monarchy, since the earliest literary
source (the Yahwist) is dated to the period of the united monarchy.
Gottwald agrees with Mayes in rejecting Noth's contention that the
lists which include Levi and Joseph are demonstrably earlier than
the lists which do not include Levi and substitute Ephraim-Manasseh
for Joseph.

However, in contrast to Mayes' reluctance to date precisely
or relatively these two sets of tribal lists, Gottwald maintains
that the Levi-Joseph lists originate in the Solomonic period when
the Davidic twelve-tribe system had lost its administrative political
function due to Solomon's redistricting and was used instead in a
religious function to symbolize Israel's inclusive unity. The
inclusion of Levi created a list of thirteen tribes, however, so
that Ephraim and Manasseh were reduced to one tribe which was represented as their common father, Joseph, a tradition which had a
sound basis in the traditional memory of the Israelites.

Gottwald's analysis may be questioned at several points. First
of all, Gottwald acknowledges that David used the twelve-tribe
schema in order to appease the traditional tribal order. Would it
then not be more probable that the twelve-tribe schema in some way
closely approximated the traditonal tribal order of the pre-Davidic
period rather than represent an original innovation on David's part?
Gottwald's own analysis here seems to suggest a _pre_-Davidic origin
for the twelve-tribe list which was then carried into the Davidic

era. If so, the question of the dating of the lists is again thrown open to sometime in the premonarchic period after the event celebrated in Judges 5.

Secondly, Gottwald's assumption that Num 1:20-43 and Num 26:5-51 are the original Davidic creations of the tribal lists ignores Mayes' contention that Num 1:5-15 is the more original list and that the alterations in the sequence of the other lists in Numbers (including Num 1:20-43 and Num 26:5-51) can best be explained as literary reworking of this basic list in Num 1:5-15. Gottwald's position is unable to account as satisfactorily for these alterations.

Thirdly, the assumption that the Levi-Joseph form of the list comes from the Solomonic period presupposes at least two things. It presupposes Gottwald's earlier contention that no twelve-tribe list existed before David. We would not, however, be prepared to rule this out as a possibility since the evidence for this position is primarily negative and Gottwald's own analysis would seem to imply a pre-Davidic origin.

Gottwald's assumption also presupposes a knowledge that the tribe of Levi was never considered a "secular" tribe on a par with the other tribes before the Solomonic period. Gottwald has his own interpretations of the Levites and their role in Israel, but the question of the nature and historical function of the tribe of Levi is still a much debated one with no clear consensus. The evidence which involves the interpretation of Gen 49:5-7 and Genesis 34 remains ambiguous. A fact which is often neglected is that the narrative contexts of the lists which do not include Levi and which Gottwald suggests are the original lists, Num 1:20-43 and Num 26:5-51, include the Levites in a separate census but in close association with the other twelve tribes. This suggests again the possibility that an earlier pre-Solomonic form of the tradition which included Levi in the tribal roster may have circulated. Given the present state of our knowledge of the Levites, it seems preferable to withhold judgment and leave the question of the exact dating open as Mayes has argued. In regard to the conflation of Manasseh and Ephraim into the one tribe of Joseph as a secondary development, Gottwald admits that this association had a sound basis in the traditonal memory of the Israelites. This again opens the possibility of an earlier pre-Solomonic form of the list which included Joseph. We would conclude that Gottwald's attempt at a precise dating of the tribal lists offers one possible option among others, but the evidence is lacking to evaluate his attempt as more than a possibility.

The detailed study of the genealogies of the Old Testament in
the light of modern anthropological and ancient Near Eastern parallels by Robert R. Wilson has served to place the biblical genealogies
and tribal lists into a broader interpretive context.[15] Wilson's
outline of the development of the twelve-tribe lists and genealogies
includes several stages. First, the names in the twelve-tribe lists
would represent independent traditions of the eponymous ancestors
of the various Israelite tribes.

In the course of the history of transmission, these names were
collected into a traditional list of twelve tribes and joined with
the Jacob-Laban narratives. There the tribal names were distributed
among the wives and maids in the stories as the sons of Jacob.
Whatever the original rationale for the distribution of the names,
the present form and context of the tribal genealogy which is found
in the earliest Pentateuchal source in Gen 29:31-30:24 (J) portrays
Benjamin and, above all, Joseph as superior to the other sons. They
are the offspring of Jacob's favored wife, Rachel. As a result,
this form of the genealogy represents a time in the history of
Israel when the Joseph tribes were politically superior. It was
also a time when the Judah tribe, which rose to power with the rise
of the Davidic monarchy, was still subordinate. Wilson suggests a
date which fits this exalted position of the Joseph tribe as one
at the end of the period of the judges before the rise of the monarchy and a centralized government when segmented genealogies of this
kind no longer had a political function.[16]

The tribal genealogy was then taken into the religious sphere
and functioned as an expression of the ideal Israel. This new
religious function no longer required the genealogy to be fluid in
form as was the case when it functioned politically. Therefore, it
was frozen in the form found in the Yahwist's narrative of Gen 29:31-
30:24. A later Priestly writer or editor maintained the same division of tribes among the wives and maids of the Yahwist's Jacob-
Laban narrative but placed the groups of tribes in a different and
perhaps more logical sequence, once they were divorced from their
narrative context in Gen 29:31-30:24. This is apparent when we com-
pare the Yahwist's sequence in Genesis 29-30 and the Priestly
writer's sequence in Gen 35:22-26. Thus, it seems probable that the
later Priestly writer or editor was dependent upon the genealogical
information provided in the genealogy in Gen 29:31-30:24. One cannot, however, rule out the possibility of an independent tradition
for the two versions of the genealogy.

In their present contexts, the political status differences
expressed in the genealogies of the Yahwist and the Priestly writer

or editor in the book of Genesis have no clear function. As Wilson
states, they now have distinct literary and theological functions.

> For the Yahwist, the genealogies not only introduce and relate
> some of the people mentioned in his later narratives but also
> make the eponymous ancestors of the tribes the inheritors of
> the promise given to Abraham, Isaac and Jacob. Similarly,
> the Priestly writer uses the genealogy in Gen. 35:22-26 to
> mark the conclusion of the Jacob narratives, and he may intend
> to relate the twelve tribes to the promise, which is repeated
> in Gen. 35:9-12. P may also use Gen. 46:8-27 to express the
> theological dogma that all of the tribes went down into Egypt
> and so ultimately shared in the Exodus.[17]

Therefore, genealogical material which once had a political function
in premonarchic Israel has now been used by the Yahwist and Priestly
writer in the book of Genesis to perform a literary and theological
role within a narrative context.

Wilson's treatment of the tribal lists in the book of Numbers
agrees in large measure with the analysis given by Mayes. Wilson
argues that at least an equal possibility exists that the tribal
list in Num 1:5-15 derives from the Priestly twelve-tribe genealogy
in Gen 35:22-26 as that it derives from another independent tradition. Likewise, at least an equal possibility exists that the other
tribal lists in the book of Numbers ultimately derive from the basic
list in Num 1:5-15 as that they derive from independent traditions.
Wilson's proposed development of the tribal genealogies may be
represented schematically in the following manner.

> Independent traditions of ancestors of various tribes
>
> A traditional twelve-tribe list---Jacob-Laban narratives
>
> A twelve-tribe genealogical narrative portraying the
> superiority of the Joseph tribes (exercising a political
> function of unifying a society without a centralized
> government--near the end of the period of the judges)
>
> Twelve-tribe list loses its political function with the
> rise of the centralized monarchy and is taken into the
> religious sphere to express the ideal Israel
>
> Twelve-tribe list is incorporated into the Yahwist's
> literary-theological work--Gen 29:31-30:24
>
> The literary and theological functions of the twelve-tribe
> lists is incorporated by the Priestly writer or editor
> as he reworks the Yahwist's material--Gen 35:22-26 and
> Gen 46:8-27

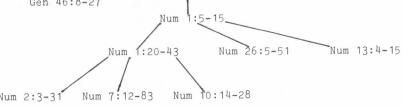

Wilson correctly exercises caution in assigning any degree of high probability to every stage of this reconstruction of the oral and literary development of the tribal genealogies and lists. One set of relationships among these various lists which may be deemed highly probable is the relationship of Num 1:20-43 as the basis for the three identical lists in Num 2:3-31, Num 7:12-83, and Num 10:14-28. Wilson provides an alternate explanation to the one provided by Mayes for this development but the conclusion reached is similar.[18] We would evaluate Wilson's analysis of the function and development of the tribal genealogies and lists as the most comprehensive and well grounded proposal among those we have surveyed. His careful use of anthropological and Near Eastern parallels provides the necessary precision as well as important safeguards in the study of these complex phenomena.

One important task remains in our study of the tribal lists in the book of Numbers. We need to examine the history and interpretation of the expanded segmented genealogy of the twelve tribes in Num 26:5-51. These genealogies exhibit a depth of three to seven generations while the other lists in Numbers have a depth of no more than two generations. This expanded form of the genealogy is unique in the book of Numbers, although there is a clear relationship between it and other expanded segmented genealogies in Gen 46:8-27, Exod 6:14-27, and 1 Chr 2-8. Scholars generally agree that the lists in Exod 6:14-27 and 1 Chr 2-8 are secondary developments and expansions. No clear consensus is evident, however, in the relationship between Gen 46:8-27 and Num 26:5-51.

A comparison of the two lists in Genesis 46 and Numbers 26 reveals striking similarities with a general tendency for the list in Numbers 26 to extend the names of the various sons or clans of each tribe mentioned in Genesis 46 to one more generation. For example, the tribe of Gad is listed in Genesis 46 as having seven sons. These same seven sons are listed in Numbers 26 along with the names of the clans of the next generation which belong to these seven sons.

Genesis 46		Numbers 26	
Gad		Gad	
sons of Gad:	Ziphion	sons of Gad:	Ziphion--Zephonites
	Haggi		Haggi----Haggites
	Shuni		Shuni----Shunites
	Ezbon		Ozni-----Oznites
	Evi		Eri------Erites
	Arodi		Arod-----Arodites
	Areli		Areli----Arelites

There are deviations from this pattern, some of which derive from textual corruptions, previous narratives which have an impact on the genealogical progression within a given tribe (e.g., the members of the tribe of Reuben in Numbers 26, especially Dathan and Abiram), or other factors which are not immediately apparent.[19] But the bulk of the material in Numbers 26 is related to Genesis 46 in the way which we have noted above.

The conclusions reached by scholars on the relative dating of these two expanded lists of clans and family groups seems to depend largely on their views of the relative dating of the twelve-tribe lists of the sons of Jacob. Thus, Noth argues that the twelve-tribe list of Numbers 26 and hence also the list of clans and sub-clans are prior to and provide the basis for the list in Genesis 46 which turned the list into a purely genealogical scheme.[20] The original clan list in Numbers 26, according to Noth, originated after the conquest and before the monarchy. Noth acknowledges that a number of interpolations have been added to the original list of clans and sub-clans in Numbers 26. Some derive from topographical lists and others from previous narratives.[21] The analyses of Genesis 46 by John Skinner, E. A. Speiser, and Gerhard von Rad result in the same conclusion as to the priority of Numbers 26.[22] Although all these commentators are agreed that both of the lists in Genesis 46 and Numbers 26 are Priestly material, they argue for a two-stage development within the Priestly tradition and assume an earlier and a later Priestly redaction.

Gottwald makes no explicit judgment on the dependence of one list of clans on the other. He focuses his attention on the list in Numbers 26, however, and describes the list of the names of the clans as a

> puzzling mishmash apparently drawn from diverse sources. Some of them are well known legendary figures whose role in the narrative traditions are sometimes commented on by the traditionist. Many more are found only in this list, or only here and by repetition in Chronicles. Some are place names; Hepher, Hoglah, Shechem, Shemida, and Tirzah are recognized cities in Manasseh, and Shimron was a city in Zebulun (here credited to Issachar). . . The apparent census list is actually constructed as a pseudo-genealogy (cf. Gen. 46:8-26) in which each named entry is both a "son" of one of the eponymous tribal fathers and himself the "father" of a social collectivity called a mishpāḥāh.[23]

Other commentators such as B. Baentsch and O. Procksch argue for the relative priority of the list of clans in Genesis 46 over the list in Numbers 26 since the list in Numbers 26 exhibits a greater elaboration of material than the list in Genesis 46.[24] We would suggest that either sequence of priority between the two lists is possible: Genesis 46 may well represent a more original list which was secondarily elaborated in Numbers 26, or the more complex

list in Numbers 26 may have been secondarily simplified and used in
Genesis 46. In any case, Noth's position that the list of the
twelve sons in Numbers 26 is more original cannot be used as conclusive evidence that the list of clans attached to the twelve-tribe
list in Numbers 26 is likewise more original. The two sets of
material must be treated separately in appraising their historical
development. We have, in fact, seen above that the twelve-tribe
list in Numbers 26 is quite probably a secondary development from
Num 1:5-15 which in turn is probably dependent on more original
twelve-tribe lists in Genesis.

Noth and Gottwald correctly observe that the list in Numbers
26 is a compilation of material from different sources which reflect
discernible differences in relative dating and character. Some of
the names can be understood as drawn from biblical sources while
the significance of other names is entirely lost to us. We can say,
with some assurance, that the list of clans in Numbers 26 in its
present form is the product of the Priestly tradition.

The important question remains, however, as to the function of
this expanded segmented genealogy in Numbers 26 in the present shape
of the book. We would argue that the enumeration of the clans and
sub-clans for each of the twelve tribes illustrates the dawn of a
new generation as a sign of the partial fulfillment of the patriarchal promises in Genesis which speak of innumerable generations of
descendants. The juxtaposition of the simple Priestly twelve-tribe
genealogy in Gen 35:22-26 with the expanded segmented Priestly
genealogy in Gen 46:8-27 seems to function in a similar manner as
the juxtaposition of the census list in Numbers 1 with the expanded
segmented genealogy in Numbers 26. Both mark the succession of
another generation.

Results and Prospects

Our survey of recent research on the lists of the twelve tribes
of Israel in Numbers 1 and 26 and the list of clans and sub-clans
in Numbers 26 leads to some important conclusions. On the one hand,
our analysis makes clear that this material had a long and complex
history as it developed from probable functions in the social or
political sphere of Israelite life to functions in the religious
sphere of Israelite faith and literature. On the other hand, we
have discerned the necessity for caution in dating this material to
precise historical events or periods. The evidence for dating the
origin of the twelve-tribe lists, for example, is ambiguous since
we know so little about the premonarchic period in the life of
Israel.

Although the interpretation of the origin and history of the
twelve-tribe lists in Numbers has been treated in some detail by
past scholarship and commentators, little has been done in studying
the literary and theological function which the twelve-tribe lists
play in the book of Numbers itself. Given the fact that commentators have often observed that genealogies and tribal lists have
important literary and theological functions in forming the structure of the book of Genesis for both the Yahwist and the Priestly
writer or editor, one would not be surprised if the same were true
in the book of Numbers. Yet modern commentators of the book of
Numbers almost universally structure the book on the basis of geographical or chronological indicators. For example, Frank M. Cross
discusses the primary sources used by the Priestly editor to structure his material. In Genesis, the genealogical formulae derived
from an earlier "Book of Generations" which provided the major
framework for structuring the narrative. However,

> a new framing device was taken up in Exodus-Leviticus-Numbers
> by the Priestly tradent. He apportioned his Epic and Priestly
> tradition in blocks, according to the stations of Israel in
> the journey from Egypt to the Plains of Moab.[25]

It is certainly true that the geographical indicators in the narrative provide an important linking device to give some narrational
cohesion and continuity among the disparate materials in Exodus-
Leviticus-Numbers as well as a sense of narrative action and movement in reflecting the traditional escape and journey from Egypt
toward the land of Canaan. At least in the book of Numbers, however,
we would argue that the twelve-tribe lists and particularly the
census lists in Numbers 1 and 26 provide the primary unifying narrative framework for the book of Numbers as a literary unit in its
present form.

Although the lists in Numbers display a somewhat altered form
from the genealogies and tribal lists of the book of Genesis, they
perform similar literary and theological functions. They mark major
structural divisions. They make a theological claim about the
continuity of the covenantal promises and laws given to the patriarchs for each succeeding generation. They make a theological claim
for the inclusiveness of the covenant promises and laws for all
Israel. Furthermore, the expanded segmented genealogies of Numbers
26 suggest a partial fulfillment of the promise of an abundance of
descendants which was given to the patriarchs in the Genesis narratives. This function is paralleled in the two Priestly genealogies
in Gen 35:22-26 and the expanded version in Gen 46:8-27. The full
argument for our position and its implications will be given in

the following chapter. But we have tried to illustrate the fact
that work is needed in studying the important literary and theological role which the tribal lists and especially the census lists
perform within the book of Numbers. We turn now to a brief survey
of modern scholarship on the interpretation of the list of actual
numbers given in the census lists in Numbers 1 and 26.

THE HIGH NUMBERS OF THE CENSUS LISTS OF THE TRIBES OF ISRAEL

The Data

Moses is commanded by the LORD to take a census of the tribes
of Israel at two separate occasions in the book of Numbers. The
results of these censuses are given in Numbers 1 and 26. All twelve
tribes are listed with a numerical total for each tribe. The order
of the tribal names is identical in both chapters. A grand total
for all twelve tribes is given at the end of each census list. The
numbers for the tribes and the total from each census are given
below.

	Numbers 1	Numbers 26
Reuben	46,500	43,730
Simeon	59,300	22,200
Gad	45,650	40,500
Judah	74,600	76,500
Issachar	54,400	64,300
Zebulun	57,400	60,500
Ephraim	40,500	32,500
Manasseh	32,200	52,700
Benjamin	35,400	45,600
Dan	62,700	64,400
Asher	41,500	53,400
Naphtali	53,400	45,400
Totals	603,550	601,730

Other biblical passages and numbers which may be relevant to the
interpretation of these numbers include the following:

Gen 46:26-27 (following a Priestly genealogy)
    All the persons belonging to Jacob who came into Egypt,
    who were his own offspring, not including Jacob's sons'
    wives, were sixty-six persons in all; and the sons of
    Joseph, who were born to him in Egypt, were two; all
    the persons of the house of Jacob, that came into Egypt,
    were seventy.

Exod 1:1-7 (P)
    These are the names of the sons of Israel who came to
    Egypt with Jacob, each with his household: Reuben,
    Simeon, Levi, and Judah, Issachar, Zebulun, and Benjamin,
    Dan and Naphtali, Gad and Asher. All the offspring of
    Jacob were seventy persons; Joseph was already in Egypt.
    Then Joseph died, and all his brothers, and all that
    generation. But the descendants of Israel were fruit-
    ful and increased greatly; they multiplied and grew
    exceedingly strong; so that the land was filled with
    them.

Exod 12:37-38 (J?)
> And the people of Israel journeyed from Ramses to
> Succoth, about six hundred thousand men on foot, besides
> women and children. A mixed multitude also went up with
> them, and very many cattle, both flocks and herds.

Exod 24:1, 9
> And he said to Moses, "Come up to the LORD, you and
> Aaron, Nadab, and Abihu, and seventy of the elders of
> Israel and worship afar off. . . Then Moses and Aaron,
> Nadab, and Abihu, and seventy of the elders of Israel
> went up.

Exod 38:24-26
> All the gold that was used for the work, in all the
> construction of the sanctuary, the gold from the offer-
> ing, was twenty-nine talents and seven hundred and
> thirty shekels, by the shekel of the sanctuary. And
> the silver from those of the congregations who were
> numbered was a hundred talents and a thousand seven
> hundred and seventy-five shekels, by the shekel of the
> sanctuary, a beka a head (that is, half a shekel, by the
> shekel of the sanctuary), for every one who was numbered
> in the census, from twenty years old and upward, for
> six hundred and three thousand, five hundred and fifty
> men.

Num 10:35-36
> And whenever the ark set out, Moses said, "Arise, O
> LORD, and let thy enemies be scattered; and let them
> that hate thee flee before thee." And when it rested,
> he said, "Return, O LORD, to the ten thousand thousands
> of Israel."

Num 11:21 (J?)
> But Moses said, "The people among whom I am number six
> hundred thousand on foot; and thou hast said, 'I will
> give them meat, that they may eat a whole month.'"

As we shall see, some scholars have also suggested a connection
between the census lists in Numbers and the Davidic census in
2 Samuel 24 with its parallel in 1 Chronicles 21.

The Interpretation of the Data

The enormous size of the numbers in the census lists in Numbers
1 and 26 has invariably struck commentators as amazing or incredible.
How could one small clan of seventy persons increase to such an
extent in the course of a few hundred years? Jerome, for example,
held the numbers to be mysterious.[26] John Calvin took note of the
enormous size of the numbers by disparaging any who would deny God's
miraculous ability so to increase his people from one family to over
600,000 within a period of 250 years.[27] As might be expected,
Julius Wellhausen dismissed the figures as historically untenable:

> To this first census, chapter 26 adds another at the close
> of the forty years, in which the various detailed figures
> are different, but the total is about the same. This total,
> 600,000 warriors, comes from the oldest tradition, but is
> proved to be quite worthless by the fact that in a really
> authentic document the levy of Israel in the time of Deborah

is stated to be 40,000 strong. Still, the Priestly Code is
entitled to the credit of having made the total a little less
round, and of having broken it up into artificial component
parts.[28]

Numerous commentators on Numbers have echoed Wellhausen's negative
view of the historicity of the numerical figures as they now stand
in the text.[29]

Sir Flinders Petrie was the first in the modern period to argue
that the numbers in the census lists actually reflected a historical
census, that is, if one assumed that the word ʾelef did not originally mean "thousand" but a subsection of a tribe or a tent-group.[30]
For example, Num 1:21 would have originally read: "Reuben: forty-
six tent groups, five hundred people" (וְרָאוּבֵן שִׁשָּׁה וְאַרְבָּעִים אֶלֶף). In
other words, the tribe of Reuben contained 46 tent-groups with a
total population figure for the whole tribe of 500 people. This
would significantly reduce the census numbers for all the tribes.
Sir Flinders Petrie assumed that the two census lists were products
of the Mosaic period.

William F. Albright among others rejected Petrie's suggestion
as having an inadequate philological basis as well as rendering an
"absurdly small" figure for a nation "which was to conquer all
Palestine."[31] Instead, Albright argued that "garbled versions of
the Davidic census" of the whole population of the Davidic empire
are preserved in Numbers 1 and 26. These census lists contain numbers which "cannot be explained solely as priestly speculations on
the principle of gematria."[32]

Claus Schedl has responded to Albright's position. Schedl's
conclusion is that Numbers 1 and 26 reflect a census of available
military manpower in the time of David, not the whole population in
the time of David as Albright maintained.[33] Contrary to Albright,
Schedl argued that the census numbers could not be taken as they
now stand. They should be interpreted in a way which is a variant
of the earlier suggestion by Sir Flinders Petrie. It is at this
point that Schedl's work is heavily indebted to the work of George
Mendenhall. Mendenhall's article on the census lists in Numbers 1
and 26 in 1958 has become the pivot point for much of the subsequent
work on the census lists.[34]

Mendenhall summarizes his findings in regard to the census
lists thusly:

1) The census lists of Numbers 1 and 26 represent an old
   tradition of tribal quotas committed for war on specific
   occasions.

2) ʾElef originally referred to a subsection of a tribe.
   The term was then carried over to designate the contingent
   of troops under its own leader which the subsection

contributed to the army of the Federation.

3) The old Federation system broke down early in the Monarchy if not before. The royal army included units of approximately a thousand men under the command of an officer appointed by the king. This system was naturally read back into the census lists of the federation period, yielding impossibly high figures.

4) Since every detail of the organization, the size of the units, and the total size of the army are all entirely in harmony with what we know of military and social organization of the Middle Bronze and Late Bronze Ages, there is no cogent reason for denying that the lists are authentic, but were misunderstood in post-Exilic times.[35]

Much of the strength of Mendenhall's thesis is based on his citation of parallels in census taking among tribal groups for military purposes in the ancient Near Eastern literature from the Middle and Late Bronze Ages. In particular, parallel census texts and texts of tribal mustering of troops from Mari, Alalakh, and Ugarit are cited to substantiate the claim that when the census numbers in Numbers 1 and 26 are read as signifying a given number of tribal subsections (e.g., Reuben: 46 tribal subsections or ʾalāphīm) and a round total of men able to go to war (e.g., 500), they accurately portray the historical reality of the Israelite tribal mustering of the Middle or Late Bronze Age. Scholars have long had access to census lists from ancient Egypt and Babylon, but it is only with the appearance of the Mari texts especially that one has any parallels of census lists of available military manpower among tribal groups rather than only among centralized administrative districts.[36]

Mendenhall also supports his hypothesis of the historicity of the census lists on the basis of the random character of the numerical figures in Numbers 1 and 26.

The numbers are so random that no pattern can be seen underlying them--historical reality is the best foundation for their interpretation. . . . Again, it must be emphasized that the very chaotic and unsystematic nature of this list is its best guarantee of historicity.[37]

As for a date for the census lists in the book of Numbers, Mendenhall suggests that "the Philistine crisis shortly after the time of Gideon would seem to be the best date for the lists of Numbers 1 and 26, which certainly cannot be very far apart in time."[38] In a later article, Mendenhall apparently amended his position to a date near the rise of Saul and the Israelite monarchy.[39]

The implications of this alleged historical basis of the census lists in the late premonarchical period is used by Mendenhall to support his peasant revolt model for the Israelite conquest of Palestine. He first assumes that the biblical tradition of 70 persons for Israel at the beginning of their stay in Egypt approximates

historical reality. He then reconstructs the total population of
Israel in Palestine in the late premonarchical period on the basis
of the census lists in Numbers 1 and 26 and arrives at a figure of
about 250,000 people. Mendenhall notes the phenomenal increase
from 70 to 250,000 people and concludes that the only way to account
for the increase is that the Israelites in Palestine drew a large
proportion of their numbers from indigenous peasants among the
Canaanite population. These peasants rose up in revolt along with
the Israelites against the Canaanite city-states. Natural propoga-
tion among the Israelites alone could never produce such a large
population increase over such a short period of time.[40]

Norman Gottwald has accepted Mendenhall's hypothesis and incorporated it into his own study of premonarchical Israel.[41] Gottwald
uses the numerical information in the census lists of Numbers 1 and
26 as evidence of a premonarchical Israelite military roster. From
this he concludes that the term mishpāḥāh and 'eleph refer to the
same secondary social division within the Israelite tribal system.
The numbers in the lists in Numbers 1 and 26 yield an approximate
average of fifty 'alāphīm per tribe, according to Gottwald's calculations. Thus, Gottwald has gone a step further than Mendenhall by
attempting to reconstruct some details of early Israelite social
structure on the basis of the lists.[42]

Although the hypothesis of Mendenhall and Gottwald may initially appear to make some sense of these difficult texts, it has several important weaknesses. First of all, the present shape of the
text speaks against the interpretation of the term 'eleph as a
tribal subgroup. The present text clearly assumes 'eleph to be a
straightforward designation of the numeral "thousand." Although
Noth is one who accepts a variation of Mendenhall's position, he
recognizes that this interpretation disrupts the meaning of the
present text:

> We must be clear that in this we are departing from the text,
> for as it stands 'eleph is meant to be taken in the sense of
> 'thousand,' as we can see from the total given in v. 46 and
> also from the regular reçurrence of "and" between the thou-
> sands and the hundreds.[43]

Of course, Mendenhall explains this as a result of the Priestly
writer's misunderstanding of the source material which he used and
adapted from a post-Exilic perspective. Yet it must be remembered
that the similar figure of 600,000 for the number of the people of
Israel is found in at least two sections which are typically
assigned to the Yahwist (Exod 12:37; Num 11:21) which Mendenhall
and Gottwald take to be from the Solomonic period. Did the Yahwist
already in the early monarchical period misunderstand a tribal

roster which had come from a short time before the rise of the monarchy? Mendenhall could respond that the Priestly writer corrected
the original numbers in Exod 12:37 and Num 11:21 to his own numbers
in Numbers 1 and 26. Such a conjecture, however, remains a highly
speculative and undemonstrated possibility which only begs the
question.

Secondly, Mendenhall's use of the Mari and Alalakh texts for
much of his support could only show that the projected size of the
Israelite tribal military subunits was historically possible in the
Middle and Late Bronze Age. Such parallel evidence cannot demonstrate any significant probability that Israel in a given period
levied troops in such a fashion. Given the ubiquity of census lists
and tribal musters in the ancient Near East in all periods of its
history as Mendenhall points out, there is no incontestable warrant
for locating the census lists in Numbers 1 and 26 in any one period,
whether the Middle or Late Bronze Age or any period thereafter.

Thirdly, a more important objection is that the conditions of
census taking in the ancient Near Eastern material and the censuses
in Numbers 1 and 26 are not clearly parallel. Every case of the
comparative ancient Near Eastern material involves a centralized
monarchical government as the agent of the census taking. This is
certainly evident in the Egyptian and Babylonian material. But it
is also true with the texts from Mari, Alalakh, and Ugarit.
Although a census of villages (Alalakh) and tribes (Mari) is
involved, it is the centralized governmental structure which is
responsible for the commission of the census. By their nature,
censuses require some amount of centralized bureaucracy. Our knowledge of social structures in premonarchical Israel is very limited.
But the structure of Israelite society probably did not reach the
level of governmental centralization of the level of Mari or Alalakh
or Ugarit until the rise of the monarchy. We would concede that a
census of the available military manpower of several of the Israelite tribes is a historical possibility, but the inexact nature of
the parallels from ancient Near Eastern texts gives little added
support to the possibility.

Fourthly, Mendenhall's position on the date and development of
the Israelite twelve-tribe lists to which the census numbers are
attached in Numbers 1 and 26 is not clearly spelled out, but he
seems to concede that a full twelve-tribe union did not arise much
before the time of Saul.[44] As we have seen, Gottwald is quite
explicit in separating the twelve-tribe lists and the census numbers.
The census numbers reflect a tribal muster in the premonarchical
period; the twelve-tribe lists are a product of the Davidic period

since no full union of twelve tribes existed before the monarchy.
If this is true, then an important question is left unanswered: to
what were these numbers in Numbers 1 and 26 originally attached if
no twelve-tribe lists existed at a time much before the monarchy?
Was it a shorter list of only six or ten tribes? Are some of the
tribal numbers fabrications from a later time used only to fill out
the list? These unanswered questions tend to cast some doubt on the
hypothesis.

Fifthly, nearly every attempt to solve the historical problem
of the census lists in Numbers 1 and 26 also flounders on the censuses of the Levites which follow both accounts. If one assumes
that the numbers in chapters 1 and 26 have some historical validity,
then one is forced to reckon with the fact that the Levitical censuses in chapters 3, 4 and 26 are based on an entirely different
population base which does not correspond to the numbers of the censuses of the twelve tribes. The number of Levites which is based
on the number of the first-born of all Israelites is not proportional
to the census numbers of all the twelve tribes. Gottwald and
Mendenhall fail to address this incongruity.

Sixthly, Mendenhall and Gottwald are agreed in emphasizing
that the random character of the numbers in Numbers 1 and 26 is the
best guarantee of their original historicity. Certainly if this
characteristic were challenged, a major blow would be dealt to
Mendenhall's reconstruction. Suggestions that the numbers are the
result of gematria have been made in the past as we noted above.
They, however, have not received much scholarly approval because of
the inexact knowledge of the phenomenon and the element of coinci-
dence rather than intentionality which enters into the picture.

A major challenge to the random character of the numerical
figures in the census lists which is based on a different foundation
has been made recently in two lengthy essays by M. Barnouin.[45]
Barnouin argues that the numbers in the census lists in Numbers 1
and 26 have no historical basis in early Israelite society. They
derive from some form of Babylonian mathematical and astronomical
lists which were accessible to and used by the Priestly writer to
formulate the census lists as they now stand in the text. Explicitly
rejected is the notion that the numbers are random and chaotic. The
preference for certain numerals over others (the numerals 2, 3, 4,
5 and 6 are used much more often than 0, 1, 7, 8 and 9) and certain
mathematical properties of addition, divisibility and squares of
numbers reflect a numerical system based on units of six rather
than on units of ten as we use. Such a system was in wide use among
Babylonian mathematicians. Numerous affinities also exist for the

numbers of the individual tribes and numbers from lists associated
with various planetary periods and other celestial movements which
have been found in Babylonian texts. Affinities of several of the
numbers with numbers connected with various periods of the lunar
calendar of Babylon are also evident.

Barnouin admits that he cannot trace the development of every
number in the two census lists. He also admits that it is very
difficult to determine whether the Priestly writer had any knowledge
of the significance of these lists or whether the numbers were
simply incorporated by the Priestly writer from one or more Babylonian lists without any intentional significance derived from their
mathematical or astronomical associations. The present shape of
the text surely gives no explicit indication that any such significance is intended. The figures appear simply as raw numbers in a
list.

In general, Barnouin understands the process to have begun
with the basic number of 600,000 (or 6,000) which we have noted is
found in passages often assigned to the older Yahwist source:

> When comparing the other passages of the Pentateuch with the
> totals of the two census lists in the book of Numbers (603,550
> and 601,730), one is led to consider them as two variations
> which have arisen from the more simple and basic number of
> 600,000 which is prior. Or rather, it would be in the form
> of the number 6000, a factor of general multiplication by
> 100 having subsequently intervened.[46]

The individual totals for the twelve tribes were then drawn from
one or more numerical lists in such a way that when added together,
they produced the given totals of 603,550 and 601,730.

Barnouin's analysis may best be evaluated not as conclusive
but as at least suggestive.[47] It represents one possible rebuttal
to the claim that the random and arbitrary nature of the numbers in
Numbers 1 and 26 is their best guarantee of historicity. Thus,
another question mark is placed over the reconstructions offered
by Mendenhall and Gottwald on the basis of the census lists in
Numbers.

Finally, the alleged random quality of the census numbers may
be questioned from another perspective. The relationship of the
relative status of the tribes and the relative size of the census
figures for each tribe suggest that the census numbers are not as
completely random as Mendenhall and Gottwald propose. The numbers
seem to play a literary and theological role within the context of
the narrative in Numbers, apart from the question of their reflection of genuine historical realia.

For example, the total number for the two censuses in chapters
1 and 26 approximates 600,000 which is equal to 12 x 50,000 or

50,000 per each of the twelve tribes. In both lists, exactly six
tribes have numbers above 50,000 and six tribes have numbers below
50,000.[48] Furthermore, the tribe of Judah has the largest number
in both census lists which corresponds to its preeminence as the
leader of the camp of Israel on the march in the wilderness. Judah
occupies the favored position in Israel's camp which is to the east,
the direction which the opening of the tent of meeting faces and
which parallels the favored position of the Aaronic priesthood in
the inner circle of the camp.[49] The book of Numbers begins in
chapter 1 and 2 with Reuben, the first-born of Jacob, as the preemi-
nent tribe in first position. Then the census takes place and Judah
is given the most favored position at the head of the tribes in
chapter 2.

     This change in status between Reuben and Judah is also apparent
when the census numbers in chapter 1 are compared with those in
chapter 26. Judah remains the most numerous tribe and increases
from 74,600 in Numbers 1 to 76,500 in Numbers 26. Reuben, on the
other hand, decreases in size from 46,500 to 43,730 which corresponds
to that tribe's demotion in status relative to Judah. The narrative
in Numbers 16 involving the rebellion of Dathan and Abiram who were
members of the tribe of Reuben may also reflect this lowering of
status in relation to Judah on a literary level.[50]

     The most dramatic decrease among all the tribes is that of
Simeon, from 59,300 in Numbers 1 to 22,200 in Numbers 26. This
"demotion" may reflect the narrative in Numbers 25 in which the
head of a Simeonite clan committed a grave sin against the LORD
which caused a severe plague among the people. The special census
for the Levites is another literary device which signals the special
position of this tribe in relation to the other tribal groups.
Although not all of the numbers can be shown to have a particular
literary significance within the narrative in Numbers, the presence
of at least some signs of a literary shaping of the numbers suggests
that they may not be entirely historical in nature. Mendenhall fails
to incorporate this element into his reconstruction.[51]

Results and Prospects

     We have sought to outline the major lines of research on the
interpretation of the numbers of the census lists in Numbers 1 and
26. We have seen that the possibility that the numbers represent
an actual census in early Israelite society cannot be denied, but
the several objections which we have raised indicate that such a
hypothesis cannot be deemed as anything more than a remote possibility. Several pieces of evidence speak against its probability.

Barnouin's recent attempts to account for the numbers in the census
lists are interesting, but the evidence is too scattered to trace
step by step the development of the numbers from their origins to
their present position in the text.

Are we then left at an impasse? Can we go no further in the
interpretation of the significance of the census numbers in Numbers
1 and 26? We believe one can indeed proceed forward to what is a
very important and more accessible interpretation of the numbers in
the census lists, namely, their function in the present literary
context and structure of the book of Numbers. Apparently because
of the incredibly large size of these numbers in the census lists,
any discussion of their role in the present form of the text has
been almost totally neglected in favor of the historical referents
in early Israelite society to which these lists of numbers may or
may not allude. The question of the historical basis for the census
numbers is by no means unnecessary, but we have seen that the
answers to that question yield only limited results. We need to
move on to consider the function of the numbers in their present
literary and redactional setting.

As a preliminary step in this direction, we would propose the
following observations. First of all, the census totals for the
twelve tribes at the end of Numbers 1 (603,550) and Numbers 26
(601,730) cannot be interpreted without reference to the number
600,000 which is used in sections attributed by many scholars to
the Yahwist (Exod 12:37; Num 11:21) for the number of Israelites
who came out of Egypt.[52] The number 600,000 may be a number which
is firmly fixed in early tradition whose origin is difficult to
uncover. It must be intended as the number 600,000 in these verses
and not as 600 'alaphim (tribal subgroups) as the context makes
especially clear in Exod 12:37: "And the people of Israel journeyed
from Rameses to Succoth, about six hundred thousand men on foot,
besides women and children." Whether the number was originally
6,000 as Barnouin suggests is difficult to determine. As it now
stands, the number appears to express the gracious extent of God's
blessing of Israel in multiplying Israel's descendants to such large
numbers and strength.

The stylized and symbolic quality of the number 600,000 is also
evident from the fact that it is a multiple of twelve for the twelve
tribes of Israel (12 x 50,000). The numbers of the individual tribes
in Numbers 1 and 26 do not usually stray very far from the range of
forty to sixty thousand or an average of 50,000. In both lists,
six of the tribes are above 50,000 and six of the tribes are below
50,000.

Secondly, the census numbers in Numbers 1 and 26 cannot be interpreted without reference to the number 70 which occurs at important transition points at the end of Genesis and the beginning of Exodus. It is used for the number of Jacob's descendants who went into Egypt with him from Canaan. Particularly important is the fact that the book of Exodus, like the book of Numbers, begins with a census of the twelve sons or tribes of Jacob/Israel. After a list of the names of the sons of Jacob, Exod 1:5-7 reads:

> All the offspring of Jacob were seventy persons; Joseph was already in Egypt. Then Joseph died, and all his brothers, and all that generation. But the descendants of Israel were fruitful and increased greatly; they multiplied and grew exceedingly strong; so that the land was filled with them.

This multiplication of Israel's descendants in a new generation after the death of the old generation seems to be what is in part expressed by the large numbers in Numbers 1 and 26.[53] Furthermore, the theme of the death of the old generation and the beginning of a new generation which begins the book of Exodus plays a major role in relationship to the census lists in Numbers 1 and 26 as they function as the unifying narrative framework for the book of Numbers.

Thirdly, the numbers in the census lists cannot be interpreted without reference to the divine promises extended to the patriarchs in the book of Genesis which included innumerable descendants and a great nation (e.g., Gen 12:1-3; Gen 15:5; Gen 17:4-8; etc.). Although the use of the census may indicate that the number of descendants is still capable of being counted so that the promises are not yet entirely fulfilled, the large numbers of the census lists indicate that God has indeed brought his promises to a partial fulfillment. Thus, Israel continues to live in a time between promise and final fulfillment.

The census lists in Numbers 1 and 26 have been variously interpreted in modern scholarship. Nearly all these interpretations have sought to uncover the historical development of the numbers attributed to the tribes in the census lists which led up to their present context. But scholars have generally failed to analyze the function of the twelve-tribe lists and the census numbers in their present context in the book of Numbers. It is at this level of the later redaction of the book that the interpretation of the function of the census lists may be most accessible and most fruitful. On the basis of our analysis, we have determined that both the twelve-tribe lists and the numerical figures associated with the census lists have a long pre-history. They most likely originated in spheres which are outside their present context and functioned in ways, political or otherwise, which are quite different from the

literary and theological functions which they have in their present
form in the book of Numbers. The census lists in Numbers 1 and 26
have been subjected to a theological reinterpretation which past
scholars in modern times have not fully studied. The study of this
literary and theological function of the census lists in Numbers
may yield a fresh appreciation for the interpretation of the book.
In the following chapter, we will consider the arguments for the
census lists in Numbers 1 and 26 as the overarching literary and
theological structure of the book of Numbers.

CHAPTER FIVE

THE CENSUS LISTS AS THE UNIFYING FRAMEWORK
OF NUMBERS

George B. Gray has observed that "as indicative of the contents
of the book the title Numbers is not aptly chosen; for it is only a
small part of the book (ch. 1-4, 26) that is concerned with the
numbers of the Israelites."[1] It is true that the census lists do
not constitute the bulk of the book, but it is our contention that
the two sets of census lists provide the key to the book's major
structure. Numbers may thus be considered an appropriate title for
the book. The census lists in Numbers 1 and 26 serve to divide the
book of Numbers into two separate generations of God's holy people
on the march. One generation ends in failure and death in the
wilderness (Numbers 1-25). A second generation arises whose end
is not yet determined but whose perspective is one which is poised
on the edge of the promised land (Numbers 26-36). This overarching
framework of the two census lists in Numbers provides the unifying
theme for the book in its present form: "the death of the old and
the birth of the new."

The primary author of this redactional structuring of the book
is most probably one or more levels of the Priestly tradition which
is relatively late in the oral and literary growth of the book. We
have seen in preceding chapters that the census lists themselves as
well as much of the other material in Numbers have experienced a
long history of development and shaping. At some point, one or more
writers have given this disparate material a coherent and definitive
structure. We need not assume that it was necessarily the last or
final editing of the book which provided this definitive structure.
As our discussion below will suggest, we should allow at least for
the possibility of some subsequent editing and later additions at
some point after the definitive structural editing of the book which
involved the census lists. This is particularly true in the second
half of Numbers. The definitive structures based on the census
lists, however, was retained in the course of these later editings.

The central aim of this chapter is to show in what ways the
book of Numbers itself gives evidence that the census lists form
its basic structure. We will provide three forms of evidence:
formal indicators within the book, the themes and content of the

83

book, and the signs of intentional editorial shaping within the
context of the larger Priestly editing of Genesis through Numbers.
Finally, we will present a complete outline of the book and discuss
several of the major subdivisions within the outline.

FORMAL INDICATORS

Formal indicators that the census lists in Numbers 1 and 26
constitute significant divisions within the book include the chronological notations of Israel's movement on the march in the wilderness which precede both lists. The chronology of Numbers is based
on the month of the first Passover in Egypt as its starting point
(Exod 12:2). These chronological notations do not run consistently
through Numbers. They occur sporadically to highlight important
events. Chronological notes accompany the census (Num 1:1), the
celebration of the Passover (Num 9:1,5), the inauguration of the
march (Num 10:11), the arrival at Kadesh and the death of Miriam
(Num 20:1), the remembrance of the first Passover in Egypt (Num
33:3), and the remembrance of the death of Aaron (Num 33:38). Num
1:1 contains a chronological note which introduces the first census,
"on the first day of the second month, in the second year after they
had come out of the land of Egypt." Likewise, the second census in
Numbers 26 begins with a significant time indication, "after the
plague" (ויהי אחרי המגפה) in 26:1. In light of the understanding
of the second census as the catalog of an entirely new generation,
this chronological note makes it clear that the plague in Numbers
25 is to be understood as the death of the last remaining members
of the first generation who had survived the previous series of
plagues. The phrase, "after the plague," is thus to be taken as
meaning, "after the death of the rest of the first generation."

A number of descriptions of Israel's geographical movements
from place to place occur in Numbers. Like the chronological statements, these geographical notations often signal an important transition or emphasize the significance of an action. Num 1:1 begins
"in the wilderness of Sinai, in the tent of meeting." The geographical note emphasizes the transition from God's stationary revelation
on Mount Sinai at the end of Leviticus (Lev 27:34) to the organization and inauguration of the march of God's people in the wilderness
of Sinai with the mobile sanctuary and the presence of God in their
midst. It is at this important point that the first census is taken.

An important geographical notice is also evident at the beginning of chapter 26 which introduces the second census of an entirely
new generation. The second census is taken "in the plains of Moab
by the Jordan at Jericho" (26:3). This new generation does not

begin in the wilderness as the first generation did; rather, they
now stand at the edge of the promised land "in the plains of Moab."
This is the scene for the remainder of Numbers, and it is at this
location that the book ends (36:13).

Other formal indications of the importance of the census lists
for the structure of Numbers are the strategic positions of the
two lists within the narrative and their symmetrical or parallel
construction. The most obvious formal evidence of the significance
of the censuses in Numbers is the fact that the first numbering of
the people occurs at the very beginning of the book. The census is
no incidental matter in that the census of the twelve tribes and of
the first-born and of the Levites occupies most of the first four
chapters of the book. The census functions to mark a new beginning
in the life of the generation which had experienced the Exodus and
the Sinai revelation. The census is linked with the organization
of the people into a holy camp with the tent of meeting in the
middle and the priests and Levites and people encircling it in
concentric circles of holiness. The census represents the consti-
tution of the people under the guidance of the LORD as a holy people
in preparation for the march through the wilderness toward the
promised land.

The census in Numbers 1 is the first census of the people
since leaving Egypt. The only previous full-scale census of the
twelve tribes of Jacob in the Pentateuch comes at the end of Genesis
46 and lists the sons of Jacob and their immediate offspring as
numbering 70 persons. The book of Exodus itself begins by reiterat-
ing this list of Jacob's sons and the number of their offspring as
70 persons. Exod 1:6-7 then reports that

> Joseph died, and all his brothers and all that generation.
> But the descendants of Israel were fruitful and increased
> greatly. . . so that the land was filled with them.

Thus, this census at the beginning of Exodus marks a whole new
generation as well as a major transition from a state of blessing
and prosperity to a state of bondage and oppression: "Now there
arose a new king over Egypt, who did not know Joseph" (Exod 1:8).
This oppression in Egypt was said to have lasted 400 years (Gen
15:13; Exod 12:40).

Similarly, the census in Numbers 1 introduces an important
transition in the life of Israel as the people prepare for the march
as a holy assembly. The Israelite generation who came out of Egypt
is taking its first step as it puts into practice its commission
as a holy people before the LORD. The generation lasts forty years
in the wilderness and ultimately fails in its commission. The

conclusion of the spy story in Numbers 14 records God's judgment
on the first generation:

> But as for you, your dead bodies shall fall in this wilder-
> ness. And your children shall be shepherds in the wilderness
> forty years, and shall suffer for your faithlessness, until
> the last of your dead bodies lies in the wilderness (Num
> 14:32-3).

As the narrative moves from the first census in Numbers 1 to the
second census in Numbers 26, the recurring cycle involves the con-
stitution of the people as a holy congregation under the LORD's
leadership, the rebellion of the people, the death of some members
of that generation to plague or military defeat, atonement and the
reconstitution of the people as a holy congregation. Immediately
following the eschatological promises of the Balaam oracles which
are directed to a more distant future and so point to a later generation (Num 24:17-18), the apostasy of the Israelites concerning the
worship of Baal Peor is the final act of the first generation. The
plague which afflicts the people apparently represents the elimina-
tion of the last vestiges of the first generation. Numbers 26
immediately commences with a second census "after the plague."
This second census involves an entirely new generation when compared
 with the generation of the first census (Num 26:63-65). Thus, the
strategic locations of the census lists at the beginning of the book
(Numbers 1) and at the precise point of transition between the death
of the previous generation and the appearance of the new generation
(Numbers 26) indicate the major structural divisions of the book in
its present form.

The symmetrical or parallel construction of the two census
lists also suggests that they are intended to function together as
the pillars of the framework of Numbers. The LORD's command to
count the people in Numbers 26 is cast in the same form as the
command in Numbers 1 with some minor abbreviation:

> Take a census (שְׂאוּ אֵת רֹאשׁ) of all the congregation of the
> people of Israel, by families, by fathers' houses, according
> to the number of names, every male, head by head, from twenty
> years old and upward, all in Israel who are able to go forth
> to war (Num 1:2-3).

> Take a census (שְׂאוּ אֵת רֹאשׁ) of all the congregation of the
> people of Israel, from twenty years old and upward, by their
> fathers' houses, all in Israel who are able to go forth to
> war (Num 26:2).

The list of the twelve tribes in chapter 26 is presented in exactly
the same order as in Numbers 1 except for a minor reversal in the
order of the two Joseph tribes, Manasseh and Ephraim.[2] Chapters 3
and 4 include a census of the Levites following the census of the

twelve tribes in chapter 1. The same sequence again occurs in
Numbers 26. A census of the Levites is taken after the twelve-tribe
census.

One significant difference between the two lists is that the
census in Numbers 26 records not only the name of the tribe and the
number of its members as in Numbers 1. Numbers 26 supplements the
list with an enumeration of the various sub-clans within each tribe.
Whatever the original function of this elaboration of the groups
within the tribes, its function within the present narrative and
in relation to Numbers 1 is to express the further development of
the tribal families into a new generation which now has branched
out into various sub-clans. This point is made particularly well
insofar as the names of the leaders of the tribe or clan in Numbers
26 are not attested in the earlier census list in Numbers 1 nor in
any of the other previous lists of clan leaders (1:5-15; 2:3-31)
or the spies who represented their tribes in their foray into
Canaan (13:4-15).[3] Thus, the addition of the elaborated sub-clan
structure as well as the newness of the names which are listed in
Numbers 26 enhances the impression of the second census as a second
and totally new generation when compared with the census in Numbers
1. Thus, the structure and symmetry of the two census lists in
chapters 1 and 26 provide further formal evidence that they operate
as the introduction of the two halves of the book.

Another formal element in discerning the major divisions of
Numbers is the series of parallels between the two halves, Numbers
1-25 and Numbers 26-36. Both halves of the book begin with a census
of the twelve tribes followed by a census of the Levites (Numbers
1-4 and 26). Numerous events or laws in Numbers 1-25 are in some
way recapitulated in the second half in Numbers 26-36. A legal
discourse involving women in chapter 5 follows the Levitical census.
Likewise, a legal discourse involving women in a different situation
(the daughters of Zelophehad) in Numbers 27 follows the second
Levitical census in chapter 26. The laws concerning vows in
chapter 6 are paralleled by the laws concerning vows in chapter 30.
The provisions for the Levites in Num 18:21-32 find an echo in the
provision for the Levitical cities in Numbers 35. The list of
offerings given by each tribe for the dedication of the altar in
chapter 7 and the laws concerning offerings in chapter 15 have a
parallel in the list of offerings to be given at the appointed
feasts and holy days in chapters 28 and 29. The celebration of the
Passover in Numbers 9 finds a parallel in Num 28:16-25 where details
are given of how the feast is to be celebrated in the future. The
passage in Numbers 9 records a one-time event of the first

generation's observance of the Passover "in the first month of the
second year after they had come out of the land of Egypt" (9:1).
The laws concerning Passover in chapter 28, on the other hand,
establish in more detail supplementary guidelines which are to
govern the celebration of the Passover for the next and each
succeeding generation. The one is a past event; the other is
intended as an on-going guide to future generations.

Another parallel is the list of spies from each of the twelve
tribes in Numbers 13 and the list of tribal leaders chosen to divide
the land of Canaan in Numbers 34. The stages of Israel's wilderness
journey which make up a large part of the narrative in the first
half of Numbers are recapitulated in Numbers 33 which also includes
recollections of Aaron's death at Mount Hor (20:27-29) and the
defeat of the Canaanite king of Arad (21:1-3). An important recapitulation involves the story of the spies and the consequent rebellion of the people which led to their death in the wilderness
(Numbers 13-14). This event is recalled and used as a lesson for
the new generation in Num 32:6-15.

The last act of the first generation was the Israelites'
apostasy in connection with the Midianites. The story ends with
God's command to Moses to "harass the Midianites, and smite them,
for they have harassed you with their wiles" (Num 25:17-18). This
command to avenge the Midianites is successfully carried out only
by the second generation in Numbers 31 in a holy war. In the battle,
the trumpets of alarm are carried by the priests (31:6) in accordance with the law given to the first generation in Numbers 10:

> And the sons of Aaron, the priests, shall blow the trumpets.
> The trumpets shall be to you for a perpetual statute through-
> out your generations. And when you go to war in your land
> against the adversary who oppresses you, then you shall sound
> an alarm with the trumpets, that you may be remembered before
> the LORD your God, and you shall be saved from your enemies
> (Num 10:8-9).

The booty from the battle with the Midianites is dedicated "as a
memorial for the people of Israel before the LORD" (31:54). The
second generation thereby remembers the sin and fate of the prior
generation.

Finally, another formal indication that the census lists in
chapters 1 and 26 demarcate the two halves of the book is the cohesiveness of the two sections. The first half begins with the census
and organization of the holy people of God on the march in the
wilderness in Numbers 1-10. After all these preparations and as
the march begins, however, the people immediately fall into rebellion (Numbers 11-12) which climaxes in the spy episode (Numbers 13-

14). The members of that first generation in Numbers are then condemned to die. Much of the rest of the section up through chapter 25 recounts further rebellions and plagues and deaths (chapters 16, 17, 20, 21 and 25). Some glimmers of hope shine through along the way with the regulations for when the people properly enter the promised land (Numbers 15) and the military victories over the king of Arad and Sihon and Og (Numbers 21). A final crescendo of hope and promise is sounded in the Balaam oracles (Numbers 22-24) which look forward to a more distant generation. The first generation ends with the final rebellion of the people and the death of the remainder of the first generation (Numbers 25).

The second half of Numbers also contains signs of editorial cohesiveness. Again, the census list begins the section. The second half is bracketed by an inclusio in chapters 27 and 36 which both deal with the daughters of Zelophehad and the inheritance of property. The legal issue at stake is resolved in both cases which sets a positive and hopeful tone for the entire second half. In contrast to the death of a whole generation in a series of rebellions and judgments in the first half, the second half of Numbers does not record the death of any Israelite. The Israelites are victorious in their first military engagement against the Midianites (Numbers 31). Potential crises do not turn into rebellions but are successfully negotiated and resolved (27:1-11; 31:14-15; 32:1-42). Numerous laws are given which look forward to the future residence in the promised land (Numbers 27, 34-36). The second half of Numbers, therefore, is uniformly hopeful and positive in tone.

In short, numerous formal indicators suggest that the census lists in Numbers 1 and 26 provide the major framework for the structure of the book. These indicators include the chronological and geographical indicators, the symmetry of the two census lists and their strategic locations within the narrative, the parallels between the two halves of the book, and the cohesiveness within each half of the book. We are not suggesting, however, that all of these formal indicators necessarily stem from one writer or editor. For example, it is quite possible that the writer who was responsible for constructing the census lists and for placing them in their present positions within the narrative (perhaps the early stage of the Priestly tradition) was not the same writer or editor who formulated the geographical or chronological indicators which preceded the census lists (perhaps a later stage of the Priestly tradition or other editor).[4] But these various formal indicators do seem to complement each other. Any later editors appear to have been sympathetic with and in many ways enhanced the earlier

definitive structuring of the book which was based on the census
lists. We will discuss the issue of editorial intentionality in
more detail below. First, however, we will examine the evidence
of themes and content in relation to the structure of the book.

THEMATIC OR CONTENT INDICATORS

We have suggested that various formal features are present in
Numbers which substantiate the function of the census lists in
Numbers 1 and 26 as the primary framework for the book in its
present form. Equally important is the role of the content or
themes of the book which also underscore the importance of the
census lists and the theme of the death of the old and the birth
of the new in Numbers. Three major passages explicitly announce
and develop the unifying theme of the book. The purpose of the
census in Numbers 1 is to count all the men "who are able to go
forth to war" (Num 1:3). The tribes are then organized into a holy
camp as an army marching toward the promised land (Numbers 2).[5]
The first military action of the tribes of Israel which is recorded
in Numbers is the spy story in Numbers 13-14. Israel has marched
to the southern border of Canaan, the promised land. The LORD
commands Moses to send twelve spies, one from each tribe to spy out
the land and bring back a report. The spies go out for forty days
and return. All but two, Caleb and Joshua, report that the inhabitants of Canaan are too powerful for them to conquer. Only Caleb
and Joshua urge the people to trust in the LORD and proceed to
enter and conquer Canaan. The people are afraid and so refuse to
go. Their refusal constitutes a rebellion against the LORD, and
the LORD decides to destroy the people and disinherit them. Moses
pleads for the LORD to pardon the people, whereupon the LORD respond
to Moses:

> Then the LORD said, "I have pardoned, according to your word;
> but truly as I live, and as all the earth shall be filled
> with the glory of the LORD, none of the men who have seen
> my glory and my signs which I wrought in Egypt and in the
> wilderness, and yet have put me to the proof these ten times
> and have not hearkened to my voice, shall see the land which
> I swore to give to their fathers; and one of those who despised
> me shall see it. But my servant Caleb, because he has a dif-
> ferent spirit and has followed me fully, I will bring into the
> land in which he went, and his descendants shall possess it"
> (Num 14:20-24).

The LORD then speaks again, now to Moses and Aaron, and instructs
them on what they shall say to the people.

> "Say to them, 'As I live,' says the LORD, 'what you have said
> in my hearing I will do to you: your dead bodies shall fall
> in this wilderness; and of all your number, numbered from

twenty years old and upward, who have murmured against me,
not one shall come into the land where I swore that I would
make you dwell, except Caleb the son of Jephuneh and Joshua
the son of Nun. But your little ones, who you said would
become a prey, I will bring in, and they shall know the land
which you have despised. But as for you, your dead bodies
shall fall in this wilderness. And your children shall be
shepherds in the wilderness forty years, and shall suffer
for your faithlessness, until the last of your dead bodies
lies in the wilderness" (Num 14:26-33).

Then, the fate of the entire people is foreshadowed by the death of
the spies themselves which follows immediately:

And the men whom Moses sent to spy out the land and who
returned and made all the congregation to murmur against
him by bring up an evil report against the land, the men
who brought up an evil report of the land, died by plague
before the LORD (Num 14:36-37).

A note of promise and hope, however, is struck in the following
verse:

But Joshua the son of Nun and Caleb the son of Jephuneh
remained alive, of those men who went to spy out the land
(Num 14:38).

These verses clearly express the central theme of the death of the
old generation and the birth of a new generation to whom the promise
is given. The theme is explicitly tied to the census list of
Numbers 1 by the phrase in Num 14:29: "And of all your number,
numbered from twenty years old and upward, who have murmured against
me." Thus, the narrative looks back to the census at the beginning
of the book and includes all of those numbered there in the judgment.
No tribe was exempt among all the twelve tribes.

And yet the story does not end here. The reader looks ahead.
On the one hand, the gradual death of the whole generation which
began the book lies ahead. On the other hand, the birth of a whole
new generation which is full of hope and promise and which is foreshadowed by the figures of Caleb and Joshua is yet to come. Therefore, the present shape and content of the spy narrative in Numbers
13-14 explicitly establishes for the first time the overarching
theme of the book.

The second major passage in Numbers which specifically picks
up the theme of the death of the old and the birth of the new occurs
precisely at the point one would expect it. The second census of
the twelve tribes of Israel in Numbers 26 concludes with these
words:

These were those numbered by Moses and Eleazar the priest,
who numbered the people of Israel in the plains of Moab by
the Jordan at Jericho. But among these there was not a man
of those numbered by Moses and Aaron the priest, who had

numbered the people of Israel in the wilderness of Sinai.
For the LORD had said of them, "They shall die in the wilderness." There was not left a man of them, except Caleb
the son of Jephuneh and Joshua the son of Nun (Num 26:63-65).

The theme of the spy narrative in Numbers 13-14 is here clearly
taken up and applied to the second census. The new census of Israel
involves an entirely different set of numbers for each of the tribes.
The enumeration of sub-clans in the extended segmented genealogy
in Numbers 26, as we have seen, also expresses the appearance of
another generation. An entirely new generation has now arisen to
take the place of the old. This text represents a programmatic
summary of the structure of the book of Numbers.[6]

A third major passage which explicitly develops the theme of
Numbers is found in Numbers 32. The new generation of Israelites
have just been successful in avening the Midianites in a military
campaign and have conquered the area of the Transjordan. Members
of the tribes of Reuben and Gad speak to Moses and request that they
be allowed to settle in the Transjordan rather than in Canaan.
Moses interprets this as an unwillingness to help the other tribes
in the conquest of Canaan. Moses fears that this may again discourage the people from attempting to enter the land. Moses speaks
to the tribes of Gad and Reuben:

> "Shall your brethern go to the war while you sit here? Why
> will you discourage the heart of the people of Israel from
> going over into the land which the LORD has given them? Thus
> did your fathers, when I sent them from Kadesh-barnea to see
> the land. For when they went up to the Valley of Eschol, and
> saw the land, they discouraged the heart of the people of
> Israel from going into the land which the LORD had given
> them. And the LORD's anger was kindled on that day, and he
> swore, saying, 'Surely none of the men who came up out of
> Egypt, from twenty years old and upward, shall see the land
> which I swore to give to Abraham, to Isaac, and to Jacob,
> because they have not wholly followed me; none except Caleb
> the son of Jephuneh the Kenizzite and Joshua the son of Nun,
> for they have wholly followed the LORD.' And the LORD's
> anger was kindled against Israel, and he made them wander
> in the wilderness forty years, until all the generation that
> had done evil in the sight of the LORD was consumed" (Num
> 32:6-13).

Standing now again on the edge of the promised land as he had done
a generation ago, Moses applies the lesson of the past to the new
generation in a stern warning. The new generation may itself
suffer the fate of the last generation:

> "And behold, you have arisen in your father's stead, a brood
> of sinful men, to increase still more the fierce anger of
> the LORD against Israel! For if you turn away from following
> him, he will again abandon them in the wilderness; and you
> will destroy all this people" (Num 32:14-15).

Fortunately, a compromise is reached whereby Reuben and Gad agree to help the other tribes conquer Canaan in exchange for which they will receive the Transjordan as their inheritance. Thereby, the promise and hope of the new generation, though momentarily threatened, remains intact. The theme of the narrative in Numbers 32 is clearly linked to the spy narrative of Numbers 13-14 as well as the census lists in Numbers 1 and 26. This is evident in Num 32:8, 11, 13, and 14. Thus, the content of these three key passages in Numbers 14, 26 and 32 very clearly develop the unifying theme of the book, the death of the old and the birth of the new. The passages also clearly support the claim that the census lists in chapters 1 and 26 provide the overarching framework for the book as a whole.

We need to keep two things in mind. This central theme and structure is a product of the reworking and editing of earlier material. In addition, some of the material in Numbers may be a result of supplements which were added at an even later date than that of the overarching structure of the book. As a result, not every part of Numbers is as clearly and closely related to the programmatic theme and overarching structure of the book as other parts. Some sections of Numbers retain a greater degree of independence than others. Nevertheless, the redactional framework and theme provides a sense of unity and coherence in the narrational movement of the entire book, even while it tolerates a degree of diversity and independence among some of the individual parts.

Numerous other passages in the book in some way support or advance the theme of the death of the old and the birth of the new. One motif which is central to the section dealing with the first generation is the death of its leadership and the concern for succession into a new generation. The death of Miriam (20:1), the threat of death to Moses and Aaron (20:12), the death of Aaron and the succession of the priesthood to Eleazar (20:22ff.), and the further succession of the priesthood to Phinehas (25:10ff.) all reflect a consciousness of one generation passing away and a new generation arising. The deaths which occurred after the various rebellions in this first generation can all be subsumed under this one idea.

In the first generation, leaders from each of the twelve tribes are chosen to spy out the land. The list of the spies is given in Numbers 13 and includes Caleb and Joshua. In the second generation, a list of tribal leaders is also named. According to Numbers 34, the leaders are delegated to supervise the division of the promised land. Although Caleb and Joshua are again included in this list of

the leaders of the second generation, all the other names in the
list in Numbers 34 are different from any of the preceding lists in
Numbers. The old generation has passed away, and a new generation
of leadership has emerged.

The discontinuity between the two generations is sharp, but it
is not complete. The members of the second generation are descendants of the same twelve tribes of Israel. In the section dealing
with the census of the tribe of Reuben in Numbers 26, Korah, Dathan,
and Abiram are mentioned as having died. Their death constitutes
a warning to this new generation. But the text also adds a note
of promise: "Notwithstanding, the sons of Korah did not die" (26:10-
11). Moses continues for a time as leader of this new generation
along with Eleazar the priest (not Aaron) as the new census is
taken (26:1). After the census, Moses adjudicates a legal case
involving the preservation of the inheritance of a lineage line
through daughters if there is no son (27:1-11). Moses then commissions a successor to his office of leadership in Joshua (27:12ff.).
Along with Eleazar the priest, Joshua is assigned to oversee the
division of the promised land, a land Moses will only see and not
enter (34:17; cf. 27:13).

Caleb, like Joshua, is paradigmatic of the continuity and discontinuity of the first and second generations. The figure of
Caleb functions as both a figure of promise and a figure of warning
to the members of the second generation. Unlike the other spies,
Caleb was faithful to the LORD in giving a positive spy report of
the land of Canaan. Thus, he was chosen to live on with the second
generation of wilderness wanderers with the promise of seeing the
land. Caleb is one of the tribal leaders chosen to supervise the
division of the promised land (34:19).

But the mention of Caleb's name is almost always accompaned by
the remembrance of the unfaithfulness of the spies of the first
generation and of their annihilation by the LORD's plague (14:24,
30, 38; 26:65; 32:12; 34:19). Continuity exists in the person of
Caleb, but the discontinuity is stressed in the recollection of the
fate of the unfaithful spies. Thus, some measure of continuity
links these two generations: the promises and warnings of the first
generation belong also to the second generation. The laws of the
first generation are to extend to succeeding generations. But there
is also discontinuity and hence the hope that the fate of the second
generation may be something other than the ultimate failure of the
first.

Another important section in Numbers which can be understood
within the theme of the death of the old and the birth of the new

is the Balaam cycle in Numbers 22-24. Balak, the king of Moab,
fears the might of Israel and so employs Balaam, a professional
diviner, to curse Israel and so bring about their destruction. In
some ways, Balak's desire to destroy Israel is a paradigm of the
curse of rebellion and the judgment of destruction which this first
generation of Israelites has experienced since the inauguration of
their march in the wilderness (Numbers 11-20). The whole theme of
the Balaam cycle which is developed in various ways is the relent-
less desire and ability of God to bless his people Israel against
all odds.

In his own way, God will overcome the obstacles which oppose
the fruition of God's promises, whether they be in the form of
Balak's attempt to curse Israel or Israel's own rebellion and lack
of faith. Just as God replaced the desired curse of Balak with the
blessing of Balaam, so God will replace the rebellion and death of
one generation with the hope and promise of a new generation. Will
God allow his people to be cursed and destroyed by the death of
this first generation? The Balaam story answers with a resounding
answer, "No!" God's blessing and promises to his people remain.
The new generation now carries the promise. The placement of the
Balaam cycle with its oracles of blessing and promise at the end
of the first generation looks ahead to a hopeful future after the
final rebellion and death of the first generation in Numbers 25.[7]
The census in Numbers 26 marks the emergence of this new generation
of the people of God.

Other themes and motifs which advance the notion of the death
of one generation and the birth of a new generation are scattered
throughout Numbers. The place-name associations which give etymologies of certain geographical locations in Numbers, for example,
usually occur in relation to the cult or to events in the history
of the people (Num 11:3, 34; 13:24; 20:13; 21:3). These place-name
associations serve to render the events of the past as contemporary
to those of a succeeding generation who may visit them or speak
their names with the knowledge of what occurred there and the lesson
it teaches to future generations.[8]

The chronological indicators which carefully mark the dates of
certain key events throughout Numbers have a similar function (Num
1:1; 9:11; 10:11; 33:3; 33:38). According to A. Jaubert, these
important dates fall almost always on Wednesdays or Fridays in
accordance with the calendar which was used at the time the
chronological notes were added to the text. Wednesdays and Fridays
are the liturgical feast days in the calendar of the time. This
suggests the possibility that these chronological notes functioned

as a means by which future generations could remember the important events of the past and what they meant for their own day.[9] This movement from a specific punctiliar event in the past to an on-going remembrance and liturgical celebration of the event and the provision for its continuance in succeeding generations is most clearly expressed by the keeping of the Passover. A year after the first Passover in Egypt, the feast of Passover is celebrated in Num 9:5. Some clarification of who is eligible to eat the Passover is given in 9:6-14. Num 28:16-25 records the requirements of offerings for all subsequent observances of Passover. The itinerary in Numbers 33 again recalls the first Passover to the new generation who had not experienced the exodus out of Egypt.

The itinerary of the movement of both generations in Numbers also contributes to their characterization as two distinct groups of God's people. Their movement and fate represent an exemplar history which is reactualized for every new generation.[10] The first generation begins in the midst of the wilderness (Num 1:1--"in the wilderness of Sinai"). The second generation begins its journey, poised in expectation on the edge of the promised land (Num 26:3--"in the plains of Moab by the Jordan at Jericho"). One is a place of hardship and despair, the other a place of promise and expectation. The first generation had been at the edge of the promised land once before when Moses had sent the spies to reconnoiter Canaan. But the people rebelled and so were condemned to return to wander in the wilderness for forty years (Numbers 13-14). They wandered from place to place, condemned to die in the wilderness. They were granted the privilege of again coming to the brink of the promised land (22:1), but again they rebelled and so suffered their final death (Numbers 25).

In contrast, the new generation begins its life on the edge of the promised land (26:3) and remains there until the end of the book of Numbers (36:13). The new generation is reminded of the wanderings of its predecessors (33:1-47) and of the place where the new generation now stands (33:48-49) as well as the goal of the promised land to which they are going (33:50).

In some ways, this promised land of Canaan is an idealized land. It is an "exceedingly good land" (14:7) with figs, pomegranates and grapes, a land "flowing with milk and honey" (13:23-27). Its inhabitants are larger than life, "men of great stature" (13:32). The dimensions of the land are immense and are never attained in Israel's actual history (34:1-12).[11] This is the land about which the LORD had spoken to generations past, to Abraham, Isaac and Jacob (11:12; 14:16, 23; 32:11). Now the new generation is on the

brink of entering this marvelous land and enjoying the fulfillment
of the promise. And yet the book of Numbers ends with the new
generation still at the doorstep of Canaan. Its future lies open
before it. Thus, the new generation which ends the book of Numbers
stands as a paradigm for each succeeding generation who likewise
stands on the edge of the promised land, awaiting the fulfillment
of the promises of God.

Another frequent feature in Numbers is the recurring phrase,
"a perpetual statute throughout your generations." The phrase is
often appended to a legal ordinance. The phrase underscores the
concern of the movement of one generation to the next and the maintenance of the integrity of God's law into the future. The statement occurs at several points throughout the book (10:8; 15:15;
18:23; 35:29). Several other phrases relate similar ideas of remembrance and continuance to future generations (15:21, 23, 38; 18:8,
11, 19; 19:10, 21). Another feature of the legal material in
Numbers is its flexibility and openness to the new circumstances or
questions of new generations. Num 9:6-14 relates the legal case
involving the issue of eligibility to celebrate the Passover. The
adjustment and clarification of old laws and the adjudication of
conflicting regulations are also involved in Numbers 27 and 36. A
norm which prohibits the inheritance of property by women and a
norm which mandates the preservation of a lineage's property within
the lineage are in conflict and are resolved in these narratives.
The dispute involving Gad and Reuben in Numbers 32 and the compromise which is reached is part of the same flexibility within the
law which adjusts to the new circumstances of succeeding generations.

THE QUESTION OF INTENTIONAL EDITORIAL SHAPING

We have seen that numerous formal and thematic indicators
within Numbers suggest that the census lists in Numbers 1 and 26
constitute the major structural divisions of the book. In its
present form, the major unifying theme of Numbers is the death of
the old generation and the birth of the new generation which stands
on the edge of the promised land. One may well ask, however,
whether this central structure and theme which we have discerned
is the result of intentional editorial work by one or more redactors
or simply a result of our own reading or "misreading" of Numbers in
a way it was never intended to be interpreted.

We would argue that the abundance of clear formal indicators
and of explicit thematic formulations of the structure and theme of
Numbers which we have presented above already implies a significant
degree of probability that our interpretation corresponds to a

conscious editorial shaping of the book at some point in the later
stages of its composition. We have indicated above our agreement
with the great majority of scholars in assigning this later stage
of redaction to one or more levels in the Priestly tradition who
were responsible for the definitive structure and arrangement of
Genesis through Numbers in its present form. The issue with which
we will wrestle in this section is this: can we discern any connection or relation between the editorial structure of the book of
Numbers and the editorial structure of the other books of Genesis,
Exodus and Leviticus? Do the census lists in Numbers 1 and 26 and
the theme of the death of the old and the birth of the new generation find any correlates in the later editorial structure and themes
of the first three books of the Pentateuch?

It is not our intention at this point to present an exhaustive
survey of the discussion among scholars concerning the redactional
structure used by the Priestly writer or editor and his purpose.[12]
We do, however, wish to focus on two elements which most scholars
suggest form the basis for the redactional structure of the Priestly
tradition. These two elements are 1) the so-called toledot or genealogical formulae, and 2) the itinerary notes of Israel's movement
from place to place, particularly the wilderness itineraries of
Exodus-Numbers.

The Toledot Formulae and the Pentateuch

The toledot formula consists of the phrase, אלה תולדות ("these
are the generations of ..."), followed by the name of a patriarch
or ancestor. The formula is then followed by a series of genealogies or narratives which involve the offspring of the named ancestor.
The following is a list of the toledot formulae as they appear in
the biblical text:

        Gen 2:4a---"These are the generations of the heavens and the
                    the earth."
        Gen 5:1----"This is the book of the generations of Adam."
        Gen 6:9----"These are the generations of Noah."
        Gen 10:1---"These are the generations of the sons of Noah,
                    Shem, Ham and Japheth."
        Gen 11:10--"These are the generations of Shem."
        Gen 11:27--"These are the generations of Terah."
        Gen 25:12--"These are the generations of Ishmael."
        Gen 25:19--"These are the generations of Isaac."
        Gen 36:1---"These are the generations of Esau, that is, Edom."
        Gen 36:9---"These are the generations of Esau, the father
                    of the Edomites."
        Gen 37:2---"These are the generations of Jacob."
        Num 3:1----"These are the generations of Aaron and Moses."

The precise meaning or semantic range of the word, תולדות, (toledot)
is a matter of debate since it seems at times to refer to different
things. The phrase, "these are the toledot of N.N.," is sometimes

immediately followed by a vertical or linear genealogy which runs
a depth of several generations, usually mentioning only one ancestor
in each generation (e.g., Gen 5:1ff., from Adam to Noah; Gen
11:10ff., from Shem to Terah).[13] Sometimes the formula is immediately followed by a horizontal or segmented genealogy which usually
has a depth of only two or three generations with several members
of each generation mentioned (e.g., the offspring of the three sons
of Noah; Gen 25:12ff., the offspring of Ishmael; Gen 36:1ff., the
offspring of Esau). At other times, the toledot formula is immediately followed by narratives (e.g., Gen 2:4a; 6:9; 11:27; 25:19;
37:2).

Walther Eichrodt argued some years ago that this multiplicity
of uses for the phrase, "these are the generations of N.N.," implied
that the formulae as a series could not all belong to the same
author or editor.[14] Thus, he denied that the formulae belong to
Pg (the Grundschrift of the Priestly tradition). Eichrodt's conclusion, however, has not been sustained, and it is generally agreed
that most of the toledot formulae do indeed belong to one or more
early stages of the Priestly tradition.[15] The apparent variety of
referents for the term, toledot, may be subsumed under a broader
definition, i.e., "the stories of the offspring of N.N."[16] or
"those who were born of N.N. and what happened to them."[17] It has
been argued by some that the toledot formulae derive from a more
original "Toledot Book" or a "Book of Generations," chiefly on the
basis of Gen 5:1 which reads, "This is the book of the generations
of Adam."[18] This claim has been recently disputed by Peter Weimar
among others.[19]

The original number of the toledot formulae is also debated.
There are now twelve toledot formulae; eleven are in Genesis and
one is in Num 3:1. It is often assumed that one of two formulae in
Gen 36:1 or Gen 36:9 is secondary since they are repetitious, both
referring to the toledot of Esau. In order then to restore a round
number of twelve or ten, one of two things is conjectured. Either
one of the original toledot formulae is assumed to have fallen out
and so an additional formula is manufactured; or it is suggested
that another secondary formula has been added at a later stage and
so it is eliminated (usually Num 3:1).[20] Norbert Lohfink has argued,
for example, that the ideal depth for genealogies in the ancient
world was a depth of ten generations. Thus, Pg organized the entire
work into ten "toledot" or generations, each preceded by a toledot
formula. The number ten is achieved by assigning Gen 36:9 and
Num 3:1 to Ps, the later supplementary layer of the Priestly tradition.[21] Others would assign Gen 2:4a rather than Num 3:1 to a

secondary redactional level.[22]

This debate raises an important issue for our study: the
relation of the toledot formula, "These are the generations of Aaron
and Moses," in Num 3:1 and the other toledot formulae in the book
of Genesis. The central question which has occupied scholars is
whether Num 3:1 was actually part of the original Priestly layer
(Pg) or the work of a later editor (Ps or some other redactor). The
positions of Eissfeldt and Lohfink illustrate the two sides of the
question. Both assume that the original toledot series contained
ten members. Both eliminate the formula in Gen 36:9 as a secondary
and unnecessary repetition which then leaves eleven formulae
remaining. They assume that one more formula must then be eliminated in order to achieve the round number of ten toledot formulae.

On the one hand, Eissfeldt argues that Gen 2:4a is a later
addition. The original toledot series began with Gen 5:1, "This is
the book of the generations of Adam." He defends the originality
of Num 3:1, "These are the generations of Aaron" (the phrase, "and
Moses," is secondary), by observing that the primary movement in
the toledot series is a narrowing from a broader context to a smaller
and more specific circle of people. The inclusion of Num 3:1 as part
of the original series is consistent with this narrowing process,
as it moves from the representative of all humanity in Adam to the
sons of Jacob who represent Israel and finally to the priests who
are represented by Aaron. Thus, Num 3:1 stems from the same writer
as the other toledot formulae.[23] The fact that the narrowing function of Num 3:1 is consistent with the literary function of the
previous toledot formulae in Genesis, however, does not prove that
they are from the same hand. It is still at least conceivable that
a later editor, recognizing the process of narrowing in the earlier
tradition, may have added the formula in Num 3:1 and thereby extended the series one more step beyond its original termination with
the sons of Jacob (Gen 37:2). Eissfeldt's argument is not conclusive.[24]

On the other hand, Lohfink has argued that Gen 2:4a is not a
later addition but part of the original series. In order to maintain the original number of ten toledot formulae, he eliminates
Gen 36:9 and Num 3:1 as secondary additions. The final toledot
formula is thus in Gen 37:2, "these are the generations of Jacob,"
which stands as a superscription to the entire text from the departure to Egypt up to the entrance into Canaan in the book of Joshua.[25]
One may question Lohfink's assumption that the Priestly tradition
extends as far as the book of Joshua, given Noth's work on the
Priestly Tetrateuch of Genesis-Numbers and its relationship to the

Deuteronomistic History of Deuteronomy-Kings. One may also question
Lohfink's suggestion that Gen 2:4a is not a later addition, given
its apparently secondary redactional role of linking two originally
separate creation accounts. One may also question the presupposi-
tion of both Lohfink and Eissfeldt that the original toledot series
or collection contained ten and only ten members.[26]

This last assumption has been contested by Peter Weimar's
analysis of the varying syntactical forms of the toledot formulae
and the narrative contexts in which they occur.[27] Weimar acknowledges that only some of the eleven toledot superscriptions in
Genesis derived from a Vorlage used by the earliest Priestly writer.
The other formulae were written by the Priestly writer at the time
of composition. The variations in syntactical form and narrative
contexts among the formulae in Genesis suggest a variation in
origin.[28] Weimar maintains that the eleven toledot formulae in
Genesis provide the basic framework for the first part of the earliest layer of the Priestly tradition (Pg) which extends from Gen 1:1
through Exod 1:7. After Exod 1:7, Pg uses the itinerary notes as
the major structuring devices for its narrative. The toledot formulae are used most often in the creation narrative and the Jacob
cycle because they are both focused on the theme of "blessing" and
the multiplication of descendants which comes to a climax with the
formation of the people of Israel in Exod 1:7. Throughout Genesis,
the toledot formulae narrow the horizon of people until the spotlight
finally falls on the newly constituted people of Israel.[29]

Weimar is only interested in the function of the toledot
formulae in the earliest layer of the Priestly tradition (Pg). He
argues that Num 3:1 is a later and secondary extension of the original toledot series. The original conclusion or goal of the series
was the people of Israel, not the priestly clan of Aaron or Moses.
Thus, he completely ignores the interpretation and function of Num
3:1 in its present context. We would argue that Weimar's assessment
of the secondary nature of the toledot formula involving Aaron and
Moses in Num 3:1 may well be correct. The formula itself and its
relationship to its immediate literary context provide evidence of
editorial reworking.[30] However, even given the secondary nature of
the toledot formula in Num 3:1, the role which the later redactor
has assigned to it in the present shape of the narrative calls out
for study. This is precisely the deficiency in previous studies of
the toledot formula in Num 3:1. The debate has focused almost
exclusively on whether or not the formula belongs to the original
toledot series of Pg or to a later redactor. Eissfeldt and others
argued that it was part of the original collection. Lohfink and

Weimar among others argued it was secondary. We would tend to
agree with the latter position, but then the question arises as to
the effect of attaching Num 3:1 to the toledot series. How are we
to understand the toledot of Genesis in relation to the book of
Numbers?

The answer to that question begins with an attempt to discern
more precisely the indices of redactional development within the
third chapter of Numbers as a whole. Our starting point is the
basic outline of Diether Kellermann's redactional study of the
chapter as well as the ways we would alter or extend his analysis.[31]
Kellermann argues that the earliest layer of the Priestly tradition
(Pg) is not found at all in Numbers 3 but only in the surrounding
chapters of Numbers 1, 2 and 4. Kellermann detects several layers
of editing even in these three chapters, but the major content of
each is established in the early layer of the Priestly stratum:
the census of the twelve tribes (Numbers 1), the arrangement of
the Israelite camp in the wilderness (Numbers 2), and the census of
the Levites from thirty to fifty years of age (Numbers 4).[32]

We should at this point consider a question which Kellermann
does not ask. What is the Priestly writer's motivation for including a special Levitical census (Numbers 4) alongside a census of all
twelve tribes of Israel (Numbers 1)? The answer is perhaps best
illustrated by what intervenes between the two chapters in Pg, the
early Priestly version of the arrangement of the Israelite wilderness camp in Numbers 2. There the whole people of Israel are
included in the march and ongoing life of the community under God's
guidance. This corresponds to the inclusive character of the census
list in Numbers 1 which involves all twelve of the tribes of Israel.
On the other hand, the Israelite camp in Numbers 2 is arranged in
such a way that the priests and Levites occupy the inner circle of
the holy camp along with the tent of meeting, the vehicle of God's
presence in the midst of his people. The priests and Levites are
the focal point of the camp's structure. This arrangement corresponds to the exclusive character of the census list in Numbers 4
which involves only the special tribe of Levi. Thus, the simultane-
ous juxtaposition of the twelve-tribe census in Numbers 1 and the
Levitical census in Numbers 4 by the early level of the Priestly
tradition seems intended to portray two concurrent emphases in the
portrait of Israel in the wilderness: an emphasis on the inclusion
of all the tribes of Israel and an emphasis on the exclusive and
special character of the priests and Levites. The literary and
theological implications of these concurrent themes will be explored
in more detail later. We now turn to consider the redactional

history of Numbers 3.

Kellermann detects numerous stages in the literary growth of Numbers 3.[33] We will not enter into all the details of his redactional analysis of the whole chapter. Instead, we will group the editorial layers into three broad stages. The earliest section which itself is not unified is Num 3:11-51. It recounts the commissioning and the census of all the Levites over a month old who now constitute the vicarious redemption for all the first-born of Israel (Num 3:11-13). The content and structure of this section betrays a dependence on the earlier Priestly layer in Numbers 2 and 4.[34] The Levitical census in Numbers 4 which is redactionally earlier recounted the numbering of the Levites from thirty to fifty years old without reference to their role as a substitute for Israel's first-born. We would suggest that the inclusion of Num 3:11-51 intends to stress the role of the Levites as serving on behalf of and for the sake of the larger community of Israel. They are the substitute for the first-born of Israel who are dedicated to the LORD.

A second editorial stage is the later addition of Num 3:5-10 and 3:2-4.[35] Num 3:5-10 defines the role of the Levites not only in relation to all Israel but also in relation to Aaron the priest and his sons. The LORD commands Moses:

> "Bring the tribe of Levi near, and set them before Aaron the priest, that they may minister to him. They shall perform duties for him and for the whole congregation before the tent of meeting, as they minister at the tabernacle" (Num 3:6-7).

We see here another variation on the themes of inclusiveness and exclusiveness with the Levites now as a middle term of the equation. They not only serve the larger community of Israel but also the more exclusive group of Aaron and his sons.[36] The focus has now narrowed to the Aaronic priesthood as the special vehicle of the presence and blessing of God to his people:

> "And you shall appoint Aaron and his sons, and they shall attend to their priesthood; but if any one else comes near, he shall be put to death" (Num 3:10).

The identity of the "sons of Aaron" is made explicit by the addition of Num 3:2-4:

> These are the names of the sons of Aaron: Nadab the first-born, and Abihu, Eleazar, and Ithamar; these are the names of the sons of Aaron, the anointed priests whom he ordained to minister in the priest's office. But Nadab and Abihu died before the LORD when they offered unholy fire before the LORD in the wilderness of Sinai; and they had no children. So Eleazar and Ithamar served as priests in the lifetime of Aaron their father.

Once again the field of vision is narrowed to an even smaller circle
within the sons of Aaron: only Eleazar and Ithamar will serve as
priests.[37] This section appears to be based on an earlier Aaronic
genealogy, perhaps one like Exod 6:23 in the context of a wider
Levitical genealogy. It also presupposes the narrative of the
death of Nadab and Abihu in Leviticus 10.

The third and final stage in the growth of Numbers 3, according
to Kellermann, is the addition of a superscription in the form of
a toledot formula in 3:1, "These are the generations of Aaron and
Moses when the LORD spoke with Moses on Mount Sinai."[38] We will
deal with four issues involved in this occurrence of the toledot
formula: the significance of the chronological note, the inclusion
of Moses, the origin of the formula, and the redactional motivation
for the formula in 3:1. First of all, the accompanying chronological note, "when the LORD spoke with Moses on Mount Sinai," is
similar to other chronological statements which accompany the
toledot formulae in Genesis (e.g., Gen 2:4; 5:1). The problem is
that the note refers to the time when the LORD spoke to Moses on
Mount Sinai which at this point in the narrative is already past
(Lev 27:34). Beginning with Num 1:1, the setting has changed. The
LORD now speaks to Moses in "the wilderness of Sinai." The problem
may best be resolved by reference to the verses which follow. The
toledot formula of Aaron and Moses is immediately followed by a list
of all four of Aaron's sons, including Nadab and Abihu whose death
is recorded in Leviticus 10. Before Leviticus 10, the toledot of
Aaron included all four sons. After Leviticus 10, the toledot or
offspring of Aaron are limited to Eleazar and Ithamar. Thus, all
four sons constitute the toledot of Aaron only "when the LORD spoke
to Moses on Mount Sinai" as the chronological note in 3:1 makes
clear. This is at least one rationale for a redactor's inclusion
of the note in the form in which it appears in the present text.

The second issue in connection with Num 3:1 is suggested by
the preceding discussion of the sons of Aaron. The toledot formula
here includes "the generations of Aaron and Moses." A difficulty
arises in that no offspring of Moses are listed immediately after
the formula or, for that matter, in the entire Pentateuch. Only
the sons of Aaron are mentioned. Why is Moses then included in the
formula at all? Another difficulty is the order of the two names
in the formula. When Aaron and Moses are named together elsewhere,
it is almost always in the sequence, Moses and Aaron, not Aaron and
Moses. On the basis of these two difficulties, many scholars believe that the reference to Moses is not an original part of the
formula and should be removed as extraneous.[39]

One item which is typically passed over by the proponents of
such a view is the designation of Moses and Aaron as brothers in
Priestly forms of the Levitical genealogy (Exod 6:20, 26; Num
26:59). The Priestly tradition thus portrays them as members of
the same family and generation. Therefore, the offspring of the
clans of Aaron are in a sense related to the clan of Moses. Moreover, the sequence of the names, Aaron and Moses, may not be caused
only by the secondary attachment of Moses' name at the end of the
formula. The names of Moses and Aaron are mentioned together in
the Pentateuch approximately 75 times. In only three of these
instances is the sequence, Aaron and Moses, used:

> Amram took to wife Jochebed his father's sister and she bore
> him Aaron and Moses. . . These are the Aaron and Moses to
> whom the LORD saud: "Bring out the people of Israel from
> the land of Egypt by their hosts" (Exod 6:20, 26).

> These are the generations of Aaron and Moses at the time
> when the LORD spoke with Moses on Mount Sinai (Num 3:1).

> The name of Amram's wife was Jochebed the daughter of Levi,
> who was born to Levi in Egypt; and she bore to Amram Aaron
> and Moses and Miriam their sister (Num 26:59).

The first instance is a genealogy of the tribe of Levi which links
Aaron and Moses to the twelve-tribe genealogy of Jacob. The second
is the toledot formula in Num 3:1. The third instance is a genealogy within the census list in Numbers 26 which presents the second
numbering of the twelve tribes and the Levites in the book of
Numbers. The genealogical contexts of these passages suggest that
the reason for the sequence of Aaron and Moses in Num 3:1 is that
Aaron is the first-born and Moses is the younger brother. In genealogical contexts, therefore, Aaron is listed first and Moses
last.[40] At other times, since Moses remains the primary mediator
between God and the people throughout the Pentateuch, his name is
typically listed before Aaron.

All of this does not make it certain that the phrase, "and
Moses," was an original part of the toledot formula when it was
inserted in Num 3:1, but it does at least suggest that the possibility remains open. We would concede that the alternative explanation
that the phrase was added secondarily by a later redactor also
remains a possibility. In either case, one must still ask the
question concerning the effect of having Aaron and Moses together
in a toledot formula. If Num 3:1 originally referred only to the
toledot of Aaron, the exclusivistic or narrowing tendency of the
earlier redactional layers of Numbers 3 which centered on Aaron
and his sons would have been emphasized. The inclusion of the name
of Moses, however, widens the purview of the toledot formula in

Num 3:1.

One needs to remember the function of the toledot superscriptions in the other parts of the Pentateuch. They not only introduce genealogies which immediately follow them. They introduce the entire section which follows, beginning with the toledot introduction and extending to the end of the section which is marked by another toledot formula, the end of the work, or some other structural device.[41] In other words, the toledot of Aaron and Moses refers not only to the genealogy of Aaron's sons but to all the events which happen to Israel under the leadership of Aaron and Moses. In the present shape of the text, this section would extend through Numbers to the end of Deuteronomy which concludes the Pentateuch and narrates the death of Moses, the last member of his generation. Moreover, Gen 2:4a, "the toledot of the heavens and the earth," makes it clear that the meaning of "toledot" is not restricted in the present form of the text to actual physical offspring. It has been generalized to designate the carriers of the promise and blessing of God into succeeding generations. Thus, the inclusion of Moses in the toledot formula in Num 3:1 is meaningful and appropriate, even if perhaps secondary and redactional.

The third issue is the origin of the toledot formula in Num 3:1. Was the formula a new creation by a later redactor based on the form of earlier toledot formulae in Genesis? Or has the formula been transferred by a redactor from elsewhere, namely Exod 6:14-25 which lists the offspring of Levi, including Aaron and Moses? The toledot formulae in Genesis function as superscriptions, often before genealogies. Since the first occurrence of a genealogy involving Moses and Aaron does not appear in Num 3:1 but in Exod 6:14-25, it has been argued that the toledot formula has been moved from the beginning of Exodus to Numbers 3 where another genealogy and census of the Levites is introduced.[42] The evidence for deciding between the two options is scanty, and any conclusion would tend to be speculative.[43]

In any case, the redactor who placed the toledot formula in Num 3:1 did so in a way which consciously imitated or reflected the form and structure of the preceding toledot formulae in Genesis. The obvious use of the key phrase, "these are the toledot of N.N.," the chronological note which comes after the formula (cf. Gen 2:4; 5:1), and the naming formula which also follows the toledot statement in Num 3:1, "these are the names of the sons of Aaron," (cf. Gen 25:13; 36:10) are all characteristic of several of the toledot formulae in Genesis.[44] Whatever the origin of the phrase, "these are the toledot of Aaron and Moses," a redactor has carefully

molded it into its present shape and context. The formula is
preceded by the census list of all the twelve tribes of Israel and
the account of the organization of the Israelite camp which includes
all Israel and yet also focuses on the priests and the Levites.
The toledot formula is followed by a list of the sons of Aaron and
a census of all the Levites (Numbers 3) as well as the Levites from
thirty to fifty years of age (Numbers 4). It is also followed by
the continuing events of the wilderness march of the Israelites
under the leadership of Moses and Aaron.

This brings us to the fourth and final issue related to the
toledot formula in Num 3:1. What was the intention or goal of the
editor or writer in placing the toledot formula of Aaron and Moses
into the text at this point? Because, as we noted above, the
redactor has carefully shaped the formula in Num 3:1 in accordance
with the preceding toledot phrases in Genesis, a connection is
clearly intended between the toledot of Aaron and Moses in Num 3:1
and the toledot series in Genesis which ends with the toledot of
Jacob in Gen 37:2. Num 3:1 has been added as the last toledot
formula in the chain which now extends beyond Genesis into Numbers.
Furthermore, the formula in Num 3:1 continues the narrowing of the
focus which we have seen to be part of the toledot chain in Genesis.
The focus is now narrowed from the sons of Jacob who come to represent the twelve tribes of Israel to two members of one of those
tribes, Aaron and Moses of the tribe of Levi. The suggestion that
these emphases were part of a later redactor's intentional motives
seems very probable.

Perhaps a less certain but still probable claim can be made
that the same redactor also intended to maintain the counter current
of an inclusive perspective. This was achieved by the addition of
the name of Moses so that the spotlight was not only on Aaron and
his sons which had been a tendency in some of the preceding redactions of Numbers 3. The fact that the toledot formula in Num 3:1
was placed immediately after the census list of all twelve of the
tribes of Israel and the camp which included all the Israelite
tribes also lends credence to the redactor's concern to stress the
inclusion of all Israel in the continuing life and story of God's
people as well as the exclusive uniqueness of the Aaronic priests
and Levites (Numbers 3-4).

Thus, the latest redactor of Numbers 3 has in some ways taken
the concerns of both inclusion and exclusion which were implied in
the shape and content of the earliest Priestly layer in Numbers 1,
2 and 4 and made them more explicit. The writer who added the
toledot formula in Num 3:1 also made more explicit the connection

with the genealogies and toledot formulae in Genesis. This connection was already implied in the early layer of P through the affinity
and dependence of the census lists in Numbers 1 (the twelve tribes
of Israel) and Numbers 4 (the Levites) on the tribal genealogies
in Genesis and Exodus. Therefore, the redactional insertion of the
toledot formula in Num 3:1 is essentially consistent with and
further highlights the themes of the earliest stage in the Priestly
tradition in Numbers 1-4.

Up to this point, we have concentrated our attention on the
redactional layers and intentions which accompanied the eventual
insertion of the toledot formula in Num 3:1. We now turn to a
separate but related question. What is the overall literary effect
of extending the toledot series beyond Genesis into Numbers? How
is one now to read the structure of Genesis through Numbers and also
Deuteronomy in light of Num 3:1? The question is related to the
discussion of the redacitonal processes at work since much, if not
most, of the larger literary effect is a product of the intentions
of the several redactions or writers who reworked this material.
But the possibility remains that the final effect on the reading of
the literature may transcend any one redactor's intentionality.
The whole may in fact transcend, as it were, the sum of the redactional parts. It would be difficult to prove that all of the
following observations on the effect of Num 3:1 on the interpretation of the book of Numbers stem from the conscious purpose of one
or more redactors. Nevertheless, the present shape of the literature suggests the following interpretations of the function of the
toledot formula in Num 3:1 in relation to the wider Pentateuchal
context.

It has long been recognized that the toledot superscriptions
mark significant turning points in the Priestly writer's depiction
of the primeval and patriarchal histories in Genesis.[45] By the
addition of the toledot formula, "these are the generations of Aaron
and Moses," in Num 3:1, a later redactor has extended the same
function into the beginning of Numbers. For the first time after
the formative events of the Exodus deliverance and the revelation
on Mount Sinai, the people of Israel are organized into a holy
people on the march under the leadership of Aaron and Moses with
the priests and Levites at the center of the camp. A whole new
chapter has opened in the life of the people of Israel, and this
new beginning is marked by the toledot formula. It is interesting
to note the analogous use of the formula at the beginning of Genesis.
The first chapter of Genesis portrays God's organization of the
chaos of the heavens and the earth and the assignment of each part

to its correct place. The section is followed by the toledot formula, "these are the generations of the heavens and the earth," which links the preceding section to the material which follows. Likewise, the book of Numbers portrays God's organization of the people of Israel. He orders a census to be taken and assigns each tribe to its correct place in the holy camp which will march through the wilderness (Numbers 1-2). Then the section is followed by the toledot formula, "these are the generations of Aaron and Moses," which introduces the material which follows.

The toledot superscriptions do not only introduce significant turning points in the narrative portrayal of the creation of the world and its inhabitants and emergence of the people of Israel. They also function to narrow the horizon and perspective of the narrative to an ever smaller circle of people. The focus is increasingly narrowed as the toledot formulae move from the heavens and the earth to Adam and Noah and to Abraham, Isaac and Jacob. With the addition of the toledot formula in Num 3:1, the circle is narrowed once again to Aaron and Moses.[46] In this way, the line of promise is traced like a thread from one generation to another through the narrative. However, another countermovement is also detectable. Josef Scharbert has correctly seen not only the narrowing function of the toledot superscriptions in the book of Genesis but also their function of keeping the wider sphere of the cosmos and the peoples other than Israel clearly in view.[47] Israel exists within a wider world and in the context of many other peoples. The people of God do not exist in isolation but within the framework and for the sake of the larger human community (Gen 12:1-3).

This is best illustrated by the frequent connection between the toledot formulae and the genealogies with which they are often associated. The genealogies, as we have seen, have basically two forms. One form is a linear or vertical genealogy. It functions in the present literary context to trace the line of promise from generation to generation (e.g., Gen 5:1; 11:10). This form is consistent with the narrowing of the promise or blessing to a smaller and smaller circle of people. The second form is a segmented or horizontal genealogy which functions in the present context to continue to keep the peoples who are excluded from the central focus of the narrative in view (e.g., Gen 10:1ff.; 25:12ff.; 36:1ff.).[48] The primary interest of the story remains on the narrower line of promise, but the segmented genealogies remind the reader of the wider context of peoples in which the chosen line lives and with whom a solidarity is established.

Scharbert correctly sees the movement of exclusion and the
countermovement of inclusion in regard to Israel and its relation
to the wider sphere of humanity in general as it is worked out in
Genesis. His analysis of the redactional intention of Genesis,
however, can be extended even further into the book of Numbers. It
is our contention that the toledot formula in Num 3:1 along with the
census lists in Numbers 1 and 26 portray an analogous movement of
narrowing or exclusion and a countermovement of widening or inclusion. By itself, the toledot formula in Num 3:1 does in some way
further restrict the focus of the story from the toledot of Jacob
(Gen 37:2) to a smaller and more concentrated sphere, the toledot
of Aaron and Moses. The line of promise is seemingly narrowed once
again. The narrative of the rejection and punishment of Korah,
Dathan and Abiram who claimed the same authority given to Moses and
Aaron is an example of the same exclusivistic motif (Numbers 16-17).
The separate census of the Levites which included Moses and Aaron
(Numbers 3-4 and 26:57-62) is another indication of the special
status given to this smaller group among the tribes of Israel.
Even more important is the organization of the camp in Numbers 2.
Moses and Aaron stand with the priests and Levites at the center of
the camp, near the tent of meeting. The other twelve tribes of
Israel are arranged in stations outside the inner circle of priests
and Levites.

But there is also a countermovement of inclusion in Numbers.
The toledot formula in Num 3:1 is preceded by the census list of
all the tribes of Israel. In Chapter Four above, we saw that the
list of tribes in this census list was probably dependent upon the
preceding genealogical lists in Genesis. An intentional redactional
link between the tribal lists in Genesis and the lists in Numbers
is evident. The census lists of the twelve tribes function in a
way similar to the segmented genealogies in the book of Genesis.
The census lists keep the wider context of the whole people of
Israel in view. The census lists also continue the toledot of
Jacob which is introduced in Gen 37:2. The smaller group of the
priests and Levites, the toledot of Aaron and Moses, does not exist
in isolation. They live within the context of and for the sake of
the larger community of God's people.[49]

This inclusive motif is reinforced by the two census lists of
the twelve tribes in Numbers 1 and 26 as well as the numerous other
lists of the twelve tribes which occur in the book. All twelve
tribes are included in supervising the census (Num 1:5-15), in the
arrangement of the camp (Num 2:3-31), in presenting offerings at
the dedication of the altar (Num 7:12-83), in the inauguration of

the march (Num 10:14-28), in spying out the land of Canaan (Num
13:4-15), and in supervising the future division of the land of
Canaan (Num 34:16-29). Thus, the dual perspective of a narrowing
focus within the broader context of humanity which is evident in
Genesis has been given an additional dimension by a later redactor
of the book of Numbers. The more concentrated focus on the representatives of the priestly and Mosaic offices in Aaron and Moses
is counterbalanced by attention to the inclusion of all Israel in
the important events in the life of the community. Thus, the
toledot of Jacob, the descendants of the twelve sons of Jacob,
continue on in the book of Numbers. They are represented by the
census lists of the twelve tribes of Israel in Numbers 1 and 26.
The toledot of Aaron and Moses also continue on as represented by
the special Levitical censuses in Numbers 3-4 and 26.

What then is the final goal of the toledot series in the
present form of the Pentateuch? As we have seen, scholars have
tended not to ask this question. They have been more concerned
with the original conclusion or goal of the toledot in an earlier
layer of the Priestly tradition. Thus, Eissfeldt and Scharbert
saw Aaron and the priestly clan as the original end point of the
toledot series.[50] Lohfink understood the original end of the series
as the toledot of Jacob which extends from Gen 37:2 up to the
entrance into Canaan in the Priestly portions of the book of
Joshua.[51] Weimar believed that the original end of the toledot
superscriptions was Gen 37:2 which introduced the section up to
Exod 1:7 where the people of Israel had finally become a people.[52]
The patriarchal promises of blessing and countless progeny had now
been fulfilled with the seventy members of the family of Jacob who
went down to Egypt. This was the goal for the early layer of the
Priestly tradition (Pg), the formation of the people of Israel.
Weimar held that the secondary addition of the toledot formula in
Num 3:1 (Ps) destroyed this original structure and goal. Num 3:1
replaced the goal of the formation of the people of Israel (Pg) with
the goal of the appearance of the priests (Ps).

Our analysis would contradict Weimar's position that the goal
of the formation of the people had been entirely concluded and
fulfilled for the early layer of P with the seventy-member family
of Jacob in Exod 1:7. We would argue that those seventy persons
represented only a partial fulfillment of the prior promises of
blessing and descendants. The census lists in Numbers 1 and 26 are
also typically assigned to the early layer of the Priestly tradition.
They report an increase of the people of Israel to about 600,000
persons, excluding women and children. This represents a further

step along the way in the fulfillment of the earlier patriarchal
promises. But the Priestly tradition, particularly in its present
form but perhaps also at an earlier stage, viewed the patriarchal
promises of innumerable descendants (Gen 15:5; 16:10) as only
partially fulfilled. The people could still be counted as they
stood on the edge of the promised land (Numbers 26). By the end
of Numbers and Deuteronomy, the goal and promises of the past await
complete fulfillment.

The logic of the toledot formulae throughout Genesis and in
the book of Numbers further corroborates this formward-looking
stance toward the goal or fulfillment of the past promises which
have been given to the people of God. The formula, "These are the
toledot of N.N.," refers to the offspring of the person named and
what happened to them. The formula looks forward to the next
generation and is often preceded by an account of the death of the
previous ancestor (e.g., Gen 9:29 and 10:1; 25:7 and 25:12, 19).
The name of the ancestor which is included in the toledot formula,
as Skinner has argued, is the genitive of the progenitor, not of
the progeny. The formula always refers ahead to the future events
of the new generation rather than backward as subscription.[53] Thus,
the goal of the toledot series in its present form which ends with
"the toledot of Aaron and Moses" looks ahead to the future destiny
of the leaders and the whole people of Israel. They await the
ultimate fulfillment of the past promises of innumerable descendants
and the promised land which has not yet been achieved.

The generation which begins the book of Numbers clearly does
not experience the fulfillment of the promises. That possibility
and hope is left to a new generation of the toledot of Jacob (the
twelve tribes of Israel) and the toledot of Aaron and Moses (the
priests, Levites and the holders of the Mosaic office). This new
generation begins with the second census list in Numbers 26. There
a census of the twelve tribes of Israel is once again taken which
expresses the continuation of the toledot of Jacob. A census of
the Levites is also taken in chapter 26 which constitutes the
continuation of the toledot of Aaron and Moses. Thus, the final
goal of the toledot series within the Pentateuch is the new generation which ends the book of Numbers (Numbers 26-36) and extends to
the end of Deuteronomy, the final book of the Pentateuch.

As we noted in Chapter Four, the expanded segmented genealogy
of sub-clans in Numbers 26 functions in the present text to herald
the advent of this new generation. Just as the simple Priestly
twelve-tribe genealogy in Gen 35:22-26 is followed by an expanded
segmented Priestly genealogy in Gen 46:8-27, so the census of the

twelve tribes in Numbers 1 is followed by the census of the twelve
tribes in Numbers 26 which likewise lists another generation of
sub-clans. Both of these transitions, the one in Genesis and the
one in Numbers, signal important turning points. In Genesis, it
marks the formation of the people of Israel from the sons of Jacob.
In Numbers, it marks the formation of a new generation who had not
experienced the exodus or the revelation at Sinai. They now stand
on the edge of the promised land with the warnings and promises of
the past to guide them into the future. These two transitions in
Genesis and Numbers have striking formal and functional similarities
in the present text.[54] They provide further evidence of a conscious
editorial connection between the structure of Genesis and the structure based on the census lists which we have described for the book
of Numbers.

The toledot formulae, then, provide an overarching redactional
structure for the Pentateuch which recounts the death of one generation and the birth of a new generation. The promises of the past
are time and again threatened. Each generation encounters its own
difficulties and obstacles. And yet the promises of land and
descendants continue in an unbroken line and are in fact partially
fulfilled for each generation. The promise of countless descendants
is partially fulfilled as each new generation is born, a transition
which is marked by the toledot formulae and the genealogical and
tribal lists. The promise of the land is likewise proleptically
fulfilled as all the patriarchs in Genesis sojourn for at least a
time in the land of Canaan. At their death, they are all eventually
buried in the promised land as well (Abraham--Gen 25:7-10; Isaac--
Gen 35:27-29; Jacob--Gen 50:12-13; Joseph--Gen 50:24-26 and Exod
13:19; cf. Josh 34:32). These features are typically assigned to
the Priestly writer. They are in accord with the definitive editorial theme and structure which we have detected in the book of
Numbers which may also be assigned to the Priestly tradition.

Hence, the extension of the toledot formulae in Genesis to
Numbers, the relationship of the census lists in Numbers with the
genealogical lists in Genesis and the first part of Exodus, and the
consistency of the major theme of the promises being passed on after
the death of one generation and the birth of a new generation all
suggest an intentional and thoroughgoing editorial shaping of the
material in Genesis through Numbers. This redactional shaping
occurred most probably in one or more stages at a point relatively
late in the history of the literature. The result of this definitive redaction on the present structure of the Pentateuch may be
outlined briefly as follows.

I.   Genesis   Prologue--The First Generations of God's
                  People to Whom the Promises Are Made and
                  Given in Each Succeeding Generation Up to the
                  Toledot of Jacob

II. Exodus   The First Generation of God's People Who
                  Experience the Exodus out of Egypt and God's
                  Revelation at Mount Sinai--The Toledot of
                  Jacob

III. Leviticus   Further Instructions to the Generation of the
                  Exodus and Sinai--The Toledot of Jacob
                  Continued

IV. Numbers   The Death of the Old Generation and the Birth
                  of the New
                  A. The Continuation of the Toledot of
                     Jacob and the Introduction of the
                     Toledot of Aaron and Moses (Numbers
                     1-25)
                  B. The Continuation of the Toledot of
                     Jacob and the Toledot of Aaron and
                     Moses into a New Generation (Numbers
                     26-36)

V.   Deuteronomy Epilogue--Moses' Last Words as a Final
                  Exhortation to the New Generation

The structure which is suggested by the use of the toledot formulae
in conjunction with the genealogies and the census lists in the
present shape of the Pentateuch suggests an overarching redactional
structure for Genesis-Deuteronomy which is consistent with the
definitive structure of the book of Numbers in its present form.[55]
Thus, we would conclude that the structure and theme of Numbers
which we have discerned is the result of an intentional editorial
shaping of previous traditions by one or more writers or redactors.[56]

The Wilderness Itineraries and the Pentateuch
     One final issue remains in our consideration of the structure
of Numbers and its relationship with the redacitonal structure of
previous material in Genesis, Exodus and Leviticus. That issue
concerns the role of the so-called wilderness itineraries which
trace the movement of the Israelites from place to place from Egypt
to the promised land in Exodus, Leviticus and Numbers. The wilderness itineraries have been the object of study from a number of
perspectives. There exists a long tradition of attempting to
determine their actual historical locations, particularly in the
Sinai peninsula.[57] The apparent relationship of the itinerary
notices scattered throughout the text to the itinerary in Numbers
33 has also been a prominent issue.[58] The methods of source and
form criticism have also been recently reapplied to the geographical
notices in the Pentateuch.[59]
     The issue on which we wish to concentrate is the role of the
itinerary notices in structuring the material which runs through

Exodus, Leviticus and Numbers. The issue is significant since our
survey of the outlines used by commentaries on Numbers in Chapter
One revealed that the majority of commentators used the itinerary
notices in Numbers as the primary structure for the book. In relation to the structure of the entire Pentateuch, it is often suggested
that the Priestly writer used one major structural device in Genesis
and another in Exodus-Numbers. The formulation by Frank Cross is
typical. In the book of Genesis, he argues that the Priestly redactor used the toledot formulae and genealogies for the major framework for structuring the narrative. However,

> a new framing device was taken up in Exodus-Leviticus-Numbers
> by the Priestly tradent. He apportioned his epic and Priestly
> tradition in blocks, according to the stations of Israel in
> the journey from Egypt to the Plains of Moab.[60]

This frequent portrayal of a dichotomy in the Priestly redactor's strategy for structuring his material in Genesis through
Numbers must be rejected for several reasons. First of all, the
attribution of the itinerary notices to a single unified redaction
by one Priestly tradent has been questioned by recent research.
Walsh has endeavored to show that at least two independent versions
of the itinerary now appear in Exodus-Numbers which correspond to
at least two different sources.[61] Moreover, G. I. Davies has
argued that very few of the itinerary notices in Exodus-Numbers
actually stem from the Priestly tradition.[62] The majority of the
most significant itinerary notes are the product of a later
Deuteronomistic editor who added the itinerary notes in order to
reconcile the account in Exodus-Numbers with the geographical
material in parts of the Deuteronomistic History. The arguments
are suggestive and at least call into question the notion of a
unified redactional structure in Exodus-Numbers based on the
itineraries.

Secondly, the bifurcation of the structure of an allegedly
early Priestly layer into toledot for Genesis and itineraries for
Exodus-Numbers entirely ignores the present shape of the redactional
structure of Genesis-Numbers. The present extension of the Genesis
toledot formulae into Num 3:1 along with the clear connection of
the genealogies and lists of the sons of Jacob in Genesis with the
census lists in Numbers 1 and 26 suggest an overarching and unified
redactional framework for the whole of Genesis-Numbers. The primary
framework is based on the series of succeeding generations, not on
the itinerary notices of Israel's movement from place to place.
This framework may or may not have been the basic structure of the
earliest layer of the Priestly tradition. In any case, the

overarching framework which now exists is consistent and thoroughgoing as it relates the succession of the experience and eventual
death of the old generations and the subsequent birth of each new
generation.

Thirdly, what role then do the itinerary notices play in the
narrative? We would argue that they do indeed play a role in
structuring the material in Exodus-Numbers, opening and closing
scenes.[63] However, the itinerary notes operate at a secondary
level within the overall structure. The primary framework of
Genesis-Numbers, and by extension Deuteronomy, remains the succession of one generation to another. Obviously, because the section
introduced by the formula, "these are the toledot of Jacob," in
Gen 37:2 and the lists of the offspring of Jacob is so long and
extensive, a secondarly level of organization was needed within
this broader section. The itinerary notices helped in fulfilling
this need.

Fourthly, a fact which is often ignored is that notices of
geographical location or movement from place to place may also be
found in abundance in the book of Genesis. Not surprisingly, they
perform precisely the same function, organizing the larger sections
introduced by the toledot formulae and genealogies into smaller
subsections or scenes.[64] Each of the geographical notices in some
way closes or opens a narrative scene and thus plays a role in the
substructure within the larger toledot framework.[65] The same is true
of the other major toledot sections within Genesis. Within all the
eleven toledot sections of Genesis, one may count at least 68 geographical notices which serve to divide and give structure to the
events recounted within each toledot section. The analogous character of the function of the itinerary notes in Exodus-Numbers and
the function of the geographical notes in Genesis should be apparent.
They both provide a secondary level of structuring the larger
toledot blocks.[66]

In short, the later Priestly writers or redactors of Genesis
through Numbers have followed a consistent strategy in providing
a structure for the material contained within those books. The
toledot formulae and the genealogies and tribal lists, including
the census lists in Numbers 1 and 26, make up the major overarching
framework for Genesis through Numbers in its present form. The
editorial division of the Pentateuch into five books, at whatever
later stage it occurred, did not destroy but rather complimented
this definitive generational framework. As our outline of the
Pentateuch above suggests, the book of Genesis acts as a prologue
as it recounts the several toledot up to the most important one,

the toledot of Jacob. The introduction to the book of Exodus
summarizes the toledot of Jacob in a tribal list which includes the
seventy members of Jacob's clan who represent a new generation:

> Then Joseph died, and all his brothers, and all that
> generation. But the descendants of Israel were fruitful
> and increased greatly; they multiplied and grew exceedingly
> strong; so that the land was filled with them (Exod 1:6-7).

The books of Exodus and Leviticus follow and recount the formative
events in which this new generation was involved: the exodus out
of Egypt and the revelation at Mount Sinai.

The book of Numbers then begins in the wilderness of Sinai
with the census and organization of this same generation into a
holy people on the march in the wilderness. For the first time,
this generation is called to put into full practice its vocation
as the holy people of God on the move. Although signs of hope
appear intermittently, this generation ultimately fails in its
calling and dies in the wilderness. A new generation is again
born and marked by the new census in Numbers 26, a generation which
remains at the edge of the promised land of Canaan.

Insofar as the new census includes both the twelve tribes of
Israel who represent the twelve sons of Jacob (26:1-51) as well as
the special census for the Levites (26:57-62), the toledot of Jacob
and the toledot of Aaron and Moses continue on in tandem into a new
generation. Thus, no new toledot formula is required since the
focus of the story has not narrowed any further to a smaller group
of people. The focus remains fixed on all the descendants within
the toledot of Jacob (the twelve tribes of Israel) and the toledot
of Aaron and Moses (the priests and Levites and the Mosaic successor). Thus, the book of Numbers as a unit within the Pentateuch
represents a crucial transition. The book moves from the old
generation who had themselves experienced the exodus and the events
of Mount Sinai and yet who ultimately failed in their calling to the
new generation who are likewise called to be God's holy people.
They are called to remember the warnings and promises of the past
and the future hope of the promised land.

As an epilogue, the book of Deuteronomy closes the Pentateuch.
The book is Moses' last will and testament to the new generation
who now stand on the precipice between the wilderness and the
promised land. Deuteronomy and thus the Pentateuch appropriately
end with the death of the last member of the old generation, Moses,
who is allowed to see but not enter the promised land. The addition
of the book of Deuteronomy, at whatever stage it occurred, did not
seriously disrupt the overall framework since it simply continues

to assume the same generation and location (the plains of Moab)
with which the book of Numbers ends. The division of the Pentateuch
into five books, then, retains and compliments the generational
structure which we have described.

We should again remind ourselves that this definitive structure
may not have been the final stage of the editing of these books.
Deuteronomistic or even later unknown editors may have added certain
itinerary notices which further subdivided and structured the
material in Exodus-Numbers within the larger toledot framework.[67]
The division of the Pentateuch into five separate books may well
have also occurred at a later date. Certainly a multitude of other
subsideary structural devices may be discerned within the Pentateuch,
but the generational framework remains the clearest, the most consistent and the primary structure of the whole.[68] Our analysis
further upholds the contention that the framework is the result of
an intentional editorial shaping of the material.

In light of our earlier observations on the formal and thematic
indicators of the framework of the book of Numbers and its correla-
tion with the overarching redactional structure of the Pentateuch,
it seems highly probable that the census lists in Numbers 1 and 26
form the foundation for the later definitive structure of the book.
It is time to examine that structure in more detail as we return
again to study the book of Numbers itself.

A STRUCTURAL OUTLINE OF THE BOOK OF NUMBERS

Having given evidence that the two census lists mark the major
divisions in the book of Numbers, we will now present a more
comprehensive outline of the book. The outline will show how this
understanding of the structure of Numbers shapes the message which
is conveyed to the reader.

The Book of Numbers:
The Death of the Old and the Birth of the New

I. The End of the Old: The First Generation of God's People out
   of Egypt on the March in the Wilderness--Num 1:1-25:18

   A. The Preparation and Inauguration of the March of the Holy
      People of Israel--1:1-10:36
      1. Preparation and ritual organization of the march--1:1-10:10
         a. Census of the twelve tribes (the toledot of Jacob) and
            the tribe of Levi (the toledot of Aaron and Moses) and
            the arrangement of the holy camp--1:1-4:49
         b. Laws for preserving the holiness of the camp involving
            lepers, women suspected of adultery, and Nazirites--
            5:1-6:21
         c. Offerings from the tribal leaders after the census to
            prevent a plague and preserve the holiness of the
            camp (cf. Exod 30:11-16)--7:1-89

d. Setting up the lamps in accordance with the command of the LORD--8:1-4
e. The consecration of the Levites as a substitute for the first-born of the people who were consecrated to the LORD when he slew the first-born of Egypt--8:5-26
f. The observance of the second Passover and a legal case involving one who is ritually unclean and the observance of Passover--(:1-14
g. God's guidance of his people in the cloud covering the tent of meeting and the people's obedient following of the cloud--9:15-23
h. The blowing of the trumpet as a signal of the gathering and the departing of the holy camp of God's people-- 10:1-10
2. The inauguration of the march--10:11-10:36
    a. The holy camp sets out for the first time from the wilderness of Sinai to the wilderness of Paran-- 10:11-13
    b. The march of the twelve tribes and the Levites in prescribed order--10:14-28
    c. The request for Hobab, the desert guide, to stay with the camp--10:29-32
    d. A three day journey from the mount of the LORD with the ark of the covenant leading and the people obediently following--10:33-36

B. The Cycle of Rebellion, Death and Deliverance of the Holy People of Israel with Elements of Hope but Ultimate Failure and Death--11:1-25:18
    1. Repeated incidents of rebellion and atonement, each involving the death and/or the threat of death of a portion of the first generation--11:1-20:29
        a. The first rebellion by the people against God--11:1-3
        b. A second rebellion as the people crave meat--11:4-35
        c. A third rebellion by Miriam and Aaron against Moses-- 12:1-16
        d. A fourth rebellion by the people against Moses and Aaron on account of the negative report of those who spied out Canaan (the first generation is condemned to wander forty years in the wilderness and to die there--13:1-14:45
        e. A sign of hope--cultic regulations for when the people properly enter the promised land--15:1-36
        f. A fifth rebellion of the laity and Levites against Moses and Aaron and the LORD in two stages--16:1-19:22 (16:1-17:5 and 17:6-19:22)
        g. The end of the first generation draws closer: the ultimate rebellion by Moses and Aaron against the LORD--20:1-21
        h. The death of Aaron and the succession of the priesthood to Eleazar: a proleptic signal of the end of the first generation and the beginning of a new generation-- 20:22-29
    2. The end of the first generation: signs of hope coupled with ultimate failure--21:1-25:18
        a. The LORD delivers the king of Arad into the hands of the Israelites--21:1-3
        b. Another rebellion of the people against the LORD and and Moses--21:4-9
        c. Israel on the march again with victories over Sihon and Og--21:10-35

d. A crescendo of hope: Balak and Balaam and the blessing of Israel (including Balaam's final eschatological oracle--"in the latter days"--which points to blessings for Israel in a more distant future in 24:14-25, esp. v. 17)--22:1-24:25

e. The death of the remainder of the first generation: the final rebellion by the people against the LORD in apostasy--25:1-18

II. The Birth of the New: The Second Generation of God's People out of Egypt As They Prepare to Enter the Promised Land-- Num 26:1-36:13

A. The Preparation and Organization of the New Holy People of God As They Prepare to Enter the Promised Land--26:1-36:13

1. The second census of the twelve tribes (the toledot of Jacob) and the Levites (the toledot of Aaron and Moses): a new generation--26:1-65

2. The daughters of Zelophehad: the preservation of the lineage line from the previous generation in an orderly manner through the women's inheritance of property-- 27:1-11

3. The commissioning of Joshua by Moses to lead the new generation into the promised land since Moses can only see and not enter the land--27:12-23

4. Further cultic and legal regulations for the new generation--28:1-30:16

5. Moses' last act of military leadership: revenge against the Midianites in holy war for tempting the first generation into apostasy--31:1-54

6. The request by Reuben and Gad for the allotment of land in Transjordan: a potential crisis averted and a reminder of the past with words of warning and encouragement--32:1-33:56

a. The bargain struck between Moses and the tribes of Reuben and Gad: Transjordan in exchange for their assistance in conquering Canaan--32:1-42

b. A recapitulation of the journey by the first generation from Egypt to the edge of the promised land and words of warning and promise--33:1-56

7. Law as promise: divine commands concerning the antici- pated residence of the people in the promised land-- 34:1-36:13

a. Boundaries and divisions of the land--34:1-26

b. Establishment of Leviitical cities and cities of refuge as instruments by which to maintain the land's holiness--35:1-34

c. The daughters of Zelophehad revisited: the maintenance of tribal property in the same lineage group as one generation gives way to the next--36:1-13

B. Will This Second Generation Be Faithful and Enter the Promised Land (Promise) or Rebel and Fail as the First Generation (Warning)?

This structural outline of the book of Numbers attempts to illustrate the way in which the census lists in Numbers 1 and 26 function as the major divisions of the book. It also illustrates the way in which the remaining material would be understood within the narrative setting of the movement from one generation of God's people on the march to another. The criteria for structuring the

book of Numbers as we have done will not be discussed for every
point of division, but it is important to demonstrate the ways in
which some of the major divisions are marked. We will begin with
the division of Numbers into its two halves on the basis of the
census lists.

The Division of Numbers into Two Parts--1:1-25:18 and 26:1-36:13

The primary criteria and evidence for using the census lists
as markers of the major structure of the book has already been
discussed in some detail above. The placement of the first census
list at the very beginning of the book, the chronological and
geographical indicators, the theme of the death of one generation
and the beginning of a new generation as it is developed and
continued from the spy story throughout the book, the concern for
succession of offices, the motif of the death of leadership in
Miriam, Aaron and Moses, the emphasis on the enduring quality of
the laws of God as perpetual statutes from one generation to
another, and the climactic eschatological promise oracle of Balaam
which is addressed to the first generation of God's people but
points to a later generation all support the understanding of the
two-generation scheme and the census lists as the overarching
and unifying structure. This basic structure embraces and gives
comprehensible order to the disparate material which comprises the
book of Numbers. We now turn to consider the major divisions
within each half of the book.

The First Generation in Numbers 1:1-25:18: Structure and Themes

The basic structure of this first half is as follows:

I. The End of the Old: The First Generation of God's People out
of Egypt on the March in the Wilderness--1:1-25:18

   A. The Preparation and Inauguration of the March of the Holy
People of Israel--1:1-10:36
      1. Preparation and ritual organization of the march--1:1-10:10
      2. The inauguration of the march--10:11-10:36

   B. The Cycle of Rebellion, Death and Deliverance of the Holy
People of Israel with Elements of Hope but Ultimate Failure
and Death--11:1-25:18
      1. Repeated incidents of rebellion and atonement, each
involving the death and/or threat of death of a portion
of the first generation--11:1-20:29
      2. The end of the first generation: signs of hope coupled
with ultimate failure--21:1-25:28

The major break in this first half of the book occurs between 10:36
and 11:1. There is no chronological indicator here and a geographical note occurs only at 11:3 in the form of an etiological formula.
Hence, most commentators do not make a major break here. Yet if

one reads through this first half of Numbers without considering
the geographical and chronological markers as the only means of
structuring and with the structure of the first generation in mind,
one cannot help but notice the extremely abrupt and wrenching break
in the narrative at 11:1. All of the material through 10:36
describes the ordering of God's people according to the commands of
the LORD and their faithful obedience to those commands. Everything
is set in a positive tone. The narrative in 10:35-36 relates the
customary and repeated leadership of the ark as the people obediently traveled under Moses' leadership. The stress is completely
on the faithfulness of the people as they prepare for and inaugurate
the march.

But at 11:1 we encounter the first complaint and rebellion by
the people in the book of Numbers, a rebellion for which the reader
is totally unprepared. The shattering abruptness in the break of
the narrative flow between 10:36 and 11:1 matches the shattering
abruptness of the break in the relationship between God and his
holy people. While 1:1-10:36 is a completely positive picture of
the relationship of God and his people, 11:1-25:18 is overwhelmingly
dominated by a series of rebellions and plagues and death with
periodic glimmers of hope but ultimate failure.

Commentators often suggest that the division between 10:10 and
10:11 marks one of the two major disjunctures in the whole book
because of the time indicator and the geographical note in 10:11-12
which signals the inauguration of the march through the wilderness.
Scholars are also aware that the transition from purely Priestly
material to a mixture of J, E and P material occurs at this point.
Furthermore, the transition from Noth's tradition-historical theme
of the "revelation at Sinai" to the theme of the "guidance in the
wilderness" occurs here. While these may be helpful in determining
divisions, neither they nor the geographical or chronological
indicators can be definitive in understanding the structure of the
book as the book itself defines it for its readers. We would agree
that there is a break at this point, albeit more minor as our
outline proposes. We would understand a more major division at
11:1 and a still more major division at 26:1. Establishing a
primary division between 10:10 and 10:11 ignores the more important
two-generation structure of the book in favor of a premature
imposition of other criteria which contravene the present redactional
markers of the division of the book.

The second part of 1:1-25:18 extends from 11:1 to 25:18 and
can best be divided into two sections: 11:1-20:29 and 21:1-25:18.
The break between 20:29 and 21:1 is marked by a geographical

indicator, but a specific chronological note is lacking. Nevertheless, a major break is evident here in that a positive tone is
struck for the first time in this predominantly negative section
with the story of Israel's victory over the Canaanite king of Arad
which begins at 21:1. Up to this point Israel has continually
rebelled, and the LORD has punished the people with plagues and
military defeats.

This section begins with the positive conquest story (21:1-3)
followed by another rebellion (21:4-9) and then another positive
conquest story with victories over Sihon and Og (21:10-35) and the
lengthy narrative of Balak and Balaam with its climactic promise
oracles (22:1-24:25). A final rebellion story follows and recounts
the death of the remaining members of the first generation (25:1-18).
This section is marked by a mingling of profound promise with
ultimate failure which is not true of the overwhelmingly negative
picture of Israel in 11:1-20:29. Once again, factors other than
chronological and geographical notations must be factored into the
equation when determining the structure of Numbers.

The Second Generation in Numbers 26:1-36:13: Structure and Themes
       The structure of this second half of the book of Numbers may
be presented as follows:

II. The Birth of the New: The Second Generation of God's People out
    of Egypt As They Prepare to Enter the Promised Land--26:1-36:13

    A. The Preparation and Organization of the New Holy People of
       God As They Are About to Enter the Promised Land--26:1-36:13

    B. Will This Second Generation Be Faithful and Enter the
       Promised Land (Promise) or Rebel and Fail As the First
       Generation (Warning)?

       The outline is intended to highlight the way in which 26:1-
36:13 roughly parallels the tone, themes and function of 1:1-10:36
which describes the preparation and ordering of the life and march
of the first generation of God's people. Both sections are positive
in character. They portray the people as faithfully preparing for
a march into new territory. Both sections contain a large proportion of legal material.

       The fate of the first generation, as it attempted to put this
law and its life as a holy people of God into operation, led to
ultimate death and failure (11:1-25:18). But the fate of the
second generation is left open. There are signs of hope as disputes
are resolved in a positive way rather than leading to rebellion
(27:1-11; 32:1-42; 36:1-13). Laws are given to the second generation which can only apply to residence in the promised land and
thus give a promising note to the fate of this second generation.

The Midianites are avenged in an obedient execution of holy war
by Israel for their temptation of Israel to apostasy at the very
end of the life of the first generation (Numbers 25). Moses
himself, the leader of the first generation, is the one who leads
this war of vengeance on Midian as his last major act of leadership.
The fate of the first generation is remembered as both warning and
promise (33:1-56). The second generation is a new beginning, and
its destiny still lies before it as it stands on the doorstep of
the promised land. Thus, the second half of the story of the
second generation remains undecided and untold. Its fate is a
question mark. It is with this undecided future that the book of
Numbers comes to an end.

CONCLUSION TO PART TWO

The major arguments in favor of analyzing the book of Numbers as a separate literary unit and of describing its unifying redactional framework in the manner in which we have done have now been presented. The literary boundaries of the present shape of the book of Numbers were shown to be the result of a conscious editorial shaping within the wider five-fold division of the Pentateuch (Chapter Three). Within these literary boundaries, we argued that the census lists in Numbers 1 and 26 play a pivotal role in providing the primary and overarching structure for the book of Numbers in its present form. Recent trends in the study of the census lists show much interest in seeking the historical referents or more original forms of the twelve-tribe lists and the lists of census numbers which is certainly a legitimate and helpful enterprise. However, a full interpretation of the census lists necessitates an examination of their role within the present shape and context of the book of Numbers (Chapter Four).

We have attempted to describe and substantiate the important role of the census lists in Numbers 1 and 26 as the unifying literary and theological framework of the book. The book's structure may best be summarized under the theme of "the death of the old and the birth of the new." The old generation who experienced the exodus and the revelation at Mount Sinai is condemned to die in the wilderness (Numbers 1-25). A new generation arises, signaled by the new census in Numbers 26. This generation stands on the edge of the promised land and recalls the warnings and promises of the past as it looks forward to its own destiny (Numbers 26-36). This unifying generational framework and theme is indicated by a number of formal and thematic indicators throughout the book. It is also consistent with the definitive redactional structure of Genesis through Numbers and, indeed, of the the entire Pentateuch (Chapter Five). We now will seek to explicate the implications of this unifying structure for the interpretation of selected portions of the book, of the book of Numbers as a whole, and of the function of Numbers within the broader context of the Pentateuch.

PART III

THE INTERPRETATION OF NUMBERS: IMPLICATIONS

CHAPTER SIX

THE SPY STORY IN NUMBERS 13-14

The central problem in modern interpretations of the book of
Numbers has been the widespread disagreement on the structure of
the book and the subsequent absence of a cogent and convincing
proposal for the book's unifying literary framework. As a result,
individual narratives and laws in Numbers are often interpreted
without reference to their role within the larger context or structure of the book as a whole. This in turn has led to presentations
of the theology of Numbers which are typically impressionistic and
which ignore the important contours of the book's definitive editorial framework. Furthermore, the important role of Numbers within
the wider context of the Pentateuch has not been adequately described
or appreciated.

The preceding chapters have offered and defended an alternative
proposal for the structure of Numbers based on the census lists in
Numbers 1 and 26 which divide the book into two different generations of God's people on the march in the wilderness toward the
promised land. In this third part of our study, we will attempt to
illustrate the theological implications of this overarching literary
framework. Chapters Six, Seven and Eight will consist of interpretations of three selected portions of Numbers: the important narrative of the spy story in Numbers 13-14 (Chapter Six) along with the
Balaam cycle in Numbers 22-24 (Chapter Seven) and selected legal
material in Numbers (Chapter Eight). A brief overview of critical
issues will introduce our analysis of each passage. The emphasis
of our study will be on the role which the passage plays within the
larger structure of Numbers and its theological implications.
Chapter Nine will summarize the theological interpretation of the
book of Numbers as a whole in light of its structure. We will also
consider the function of Numbers within the larger structure of the
present form of the Pentateuch.

In the present form of the book of Numbers, the narrative of
the Israelite spy mission into Canaan which is recorded in Numbers
13-14 is of great significance. The narrative is the first clear
and explicit exposition of the book's unifying theme and structure.
The story begins with the Israelites in the wilderness of Paran on

the edge of the promised land of Canaan. God commands Moses to
send twelve men, one from each tribe, to spy out the land. After
forty days, the spies return with a favorable report of the great
fruitfulness of the land. But they also report that the inhabitants
of the land are strong, their cities large and fortified. Caleb
and later Joshua, two of the spies, give a minority report. They
argue that the Israelites are indeed able to overcome the inhabitants and conquer the land.

The people respond in disbelief. In despair, the Israelites
wish for their own death in the wilderness and then desire to choose
their own leader and return to Egypt. God appears and tells Moses
that he will disinherit the people and make of Moses an even greater
nation than the Israelites. Moses refuses to accept the offer.
Instead, he appeals to God's reputation among the nations and asks
God to forgive his people. God does pardon the people but only
insofar as he will allow only the second generation of Israelites
to enter the promised land. The present generation will suffer the
fate they wished upon themselves: all those who were counted in
the census in Numbers 1 will die in the wilderness. A plague
strikes down the ten unfaithful spies; only Joshua and Caleb remain
alive. The next day the condemned people decide to go up to conquer
the land against Moses' warning that the LORD is not among them.
The episode in Numbers 13-14 ends with the rebellious people soundly
defeated by the inhabitants of the land, unable to obtain the
promise by their own efforts. We will begin our study of these
two important chapters with a summary of the critical issues associated with them.

OVERVIEW OF CRITICAL ISSUES

Because of the apparent doublets and tensions within the
narrative, a major critical approach to Numbers 13-14 has involved
the division of the two chapters into literary sources. The chapters appear to consist of an earlier J or JE account and a later
P account with a few secondary supplements or glosses. Apart from
minor disagreements on individual verses, a fair degree of consensus
exists on which verses belong to the respective layers. Martin
Noth's proposed source division is typical. The J tradition consists of 13:17b-20, 22-24, 27-31; 14:1b, 4 39-45. Noth suggests
that 14:11b-23a is a secondary expansion of this earlier J source.
The P tradition contains 13:1-17a, 21, 25-26, 32-33; 14:1a, 2-3,
5-10, 26-38.[1] Sean McEvenue has done a careful study of the sources
in Numbers 14.[2] McEvenue concludes that there is a basic JE
source,[3] a supplement concerning Moses' intercession for the people

in 14:11-24 which has been added to JE before the P source,[4] a
later supplemental layer to JE before P in Num 14:3, 30-33 and
39-45, the basic P source,[5] and a later post-Pentateuchal gloss in
14:34 which presupposes the completed story in Numbers 13-14 as
well as the later reverberation of the spy story in Num 32:6-15.[6]
The important difference between McEvenue and most others is his
characterization of 14:3, 30-33 and 39-45 as a supplemental layer
which is neither JE nor P and his suggestion that 14:34 is a very
late post-exilic gloss.

It is clear in McEvenue's The Narrative Style of the Priestly
Writer that he is concerned to isolate only the sections which most
certainly belong to the earliest Priestly stratum in order to
illustrate the stylistic and narrative art of the Priestly writer.
Thus, he is more concerned than most in distinguishing passages
which probably or possibly are not early P sections from those
which do belong to the early part of the P layer. In this way, he
combines the method of source criticism with a literary method of
discerning the rhetorical style and techniques used by the early
Priestly writer. McEvenue understands the P version as part of a
documentary source which is separate from but dependent on the J
source. P is not merely a redactor of J. Thus, he attempts to
isolate the early P stratum from the previous J layer and from any
later glosses. He then proceeds from a literary perspective to
explicate the style of P in relation to J. In this narrative, the
Priestly writer "tends to replace action with theology, suspense
with symmetry, interiorly motivated conflict with objective
tableau."[7]

The Priestly writer has also added what McEvenue terms a
"fairy tale dimension" which involves motifs and techniques familiar
to the reader from children's literature. Some of these motifs
include fixed roles with a world order clearly separating good and
evil (the good Caleb and Joshua vs. the bad spies and people), the
personification of the cloud as God's presence and the earth as one
which eats its inhabitants (Num 13:32), and the people's ironic
self-condemnation to death which casts a spell on their fate (14:1-
2).[8]

McEvenue is careful to say that the Priestly writer is not
rewriting the spy story into a fairy tale but only using techniques
which moderns are accustomed to see in children's literature of this
type.[9] Many of McEvenue's literary observations lead to a greater
appreciation of the literary skill of the early Priestly writer.
One potential problem is that his use of alleged parallels in
motifs often appears impressionistic and selective with few

controls. It is a problem of which McEvenue himself seems aware.[10]
The most recent commentator to deny the existence of literary
sources in the spy story is Gordon Wenham.[11] Source critics often
point to the numerous doublets in Numbers 13-14 as evidence of two
sources (e.g., 13:21-P and 13:22-J; 14:26f.-P and 14:11ff.-J).
Wenham acknowledges the doublets but suggests that "repetition is
a characteristic feature of biblical narrative" so that doublets do
not necessarily imply separate sources. Surely such a position is
theoretically possible, but it seems far more probable that the
doublets suggest the existence of at least two separate layers
which have been joined. Wenham admits the presence of other tensions in the text, but he attempts to explain them away. For
example, the territory covered by the spies, according to the verses
usually assigned to J (13:22) centered in sourthern Palestine around
Hebron. The verses assigned to P (13:21), on the other hand,
suggest that they covered the whole land from north to south.
Wenham counters that the supposedly J verses in 13:29 implies that
they went further than Hebron since it mentions the Canaanites
living by the Mediterranean Sea on the west and the Jordan River on
the east. Apart from the fact that some scholars suggest that
13:29 is a later gloss,[12] a significant tension remains between the
P version which emphasizes the whole land from north to south and
the J version which emphasizes the south with some allusions to
people on the eastern and western ends of southern Palestine.

      Wenham also attempts to explain why Caleb alone appears as a
faithful spy who opposes the negative report of the majority of the
spies in an early scene in the narrative while later both Caleb and
Joshua appear as the faithful spies. Source criticis take this as
evidence of two different sources. J includes only Caleb; the later
P section includes both Caleb and Joshua. Wenham psychologizes the
story in order to explain this apparent tension. Joshua was Moses'
assistant and would have been expected to disagree with the negative
report of the other spies. Thus, it was more effective for Caleb
to speak up first and then have his testimony supported by Joshua.[13]
This reading brings more into the text than is there. Nor does it
explain why Caleb and not Joshua is singled out later in Num 14:24.
Whatever the final literary effect, it seems more reasonable to
explain the original cause for the tension as the result of two
different layers embedded within the text.[14]

      A new avenue into the spy story of Numbers 13-14 was opened
by the form-critical work of Hugo Gressmann.[15] Gressmann sought to
describe the original form, function and sociological setting of
the saga which he detected underneath the layers of the present

text. The original form of the story was an ethnographic and
etiological saga which described the entrance of the Calebites into
southern Palestine and explained why they had settled in and around
Hebron. The Calebites were formerly a non-Israelite people who only
later were assimilated into the community of Israel.[16] The early
form of the saga celebrated the courage and bravery of Caleb, the
ancestor of the clan, who alone of all the spies who searched out
the land of southern Palestine was willing to go and conquer the
land. God then chose him as the only one who would inherit the
choice area around Hebron. Gressmann then hypothesized that the
original conclusion which has been lost in the present text told
how the other people turned again into the wilderness while Caleb
and his clan set off and conquered Hebron. Thus, the spy story was
originally "an introduction to the story of the conquest of
Hebron."[17] This saga was carried by the southern tribes. Later
the story was "mutilated" by a northern Israelite redactor "who
upheld the fiction of the unified conquest by all Israel from the
east via the Jordan."[18] The later Priestly version of the story
lacks the vividness of the old saga and has pushed the religious
element to the fore at the expense of the historical interest of
the saga.[19]

A more recent example of a form-critical study of the spy
story is one by Siegfried Wagner.[20] Wagner collects and compares
all of the spy stories or traces thereof in the Old Testament. He
cites the story in Numbers 13-14 and its repetition in Deuteronomy
1 and the allusion to it in Josh 14:7-8. A second spy story is in
Joshua 2, a third in Judges 18, and a trace of another spy story in
Josh 7:2-4a. Wagner argues that there are six elements in the
traditional literary form of the spy story: 1) choosing or naming
the spies, 2) sending the spies out with instructions, 3) an account
of the fulfillment of the instructions, 4) an announcement of the
return of the spies and their report, 5) a statement in the perfect
tense that God has given the land into their hands, and 6) the
beginning of the invasion or conquest.[21]

There are several problems in Wagner's procedure. First of
all, Sean McEvenue correctly observes that the number of examples
in the Old Testament on which to base his claim are meager. He has
only four different stories, one of which is repeated three times.
Moreover, only some of the six elements of the form occur in all
four stories, and even those are not always in the same order.[22]
Another consideration is that most of the six formal elements,
especially elements 1-4, would naturally be associated with any
spy mission anywhere. They do not represent a special literary or

oral convention with a particular sociological setting which is the
proper goal of form criticism.   This is simply the way humans must
carry out or speak about spy missions in any circumstances.   Much
of Wagner's analysis also relies on the conclusions of Gerhard von
Rad who spoke of the so-called "historical credo" and its setting
in the ancient Israelite cult in the Feast of Weeks located at
Jericho or Gilgal.[23]   Much of this involves assumptions based on
von Rad's hypothetical and now much disputed reconstruction which
was simply taken for granted by Wagner.   Nothing inherent in the
material or in Wagner's analysis would place the spy story in such
a setting.

　　　　A further inadequacy of the form-critical method of Wagner
and even Gressmann was a blurring of the distinction between the
oral and literary levels.   They focused on the original form and
function without a full appreciation of the complex and long processes of reshaping and amalgamating in connection with other
traditions which occurred on both the oral and literary levels.
Martin Noth's tradition-critical method attempted to trace the
development of the tradition of Caleb in Hebron which is reflected
in Numbers 13 and 14.[24]   According to Noth, the story was orginally
part of the Pentateuchal theme of the conquest of Canaan.   Because
the tradition of an all-Israelite conquest from the east across
the Jordan became normative, however, the Caleb story was trans-
formed from a story of Caleb's successful conquest of Hebron to an
abortive attempt by Israel to occupy the promised land.   Israel and
even Caleb were condemned to wander forty more years in the wilderness.   Thus, the story was shifted from the conquest theme to the
Pentateuchal theme of guidance in the wilderness in order to explain
the delay in the conquest.   As a result, the story was incorporated
at a relatively late point in the oral stage into the murmuring
motif within the larger theme of the guidance in the wilderness.

　　　　The origin of this murmuring motif was not the spy story itself
but the story of the quails in Num 11:4ff. which involved the
reshaping of a folk etiology of a wilderness site known by the
name of "Graves of Craving."   The quail story itself was originally
a positive story about God's providing food for a hungry people.
Its association with the ominous name, "Graves of Craving," led it
to become a negative story of the people's unjustified murmuring
and subsequent punishment.   This, according to Noth, began the
murmuring motif which then attracted other stories of similar
content.[25]   Although this is one possible explanation for the
emergence of the murmuring motif within Israelite tradition, it is
no more than a possibility.   The lack of solid evidence suggests

that Noth's conjecture is little more than speculation. Our view
of other difficulties with Noth's concept of Pentateuchal themes
which act as free-floating magnets for other traditions has been
given in Chapter One. The strength of Noth's work, however, is
that it does open up the question of the continual use and reshaping
of traditional material throughout Israel's history. In other
words, one cannot restrict the creative shaping of a given tradition
only to one point in the literary stage (the tendency of source
criticism) or primarily the original oral stage (the tendency of
form criticism).

After Noth, tradition-historical studies on the spy story have
tended to focus on the narrower question of the origin of the
murmuring motif in relation to Numbers 13-14. George Coats in his
work on the murmuring motif in the Old Testament argues that the
motif originated in a Judaean polemic against northern Israel
(Ephraim) from early in the period of the divided monarchy.[26] The
crucial link in Coats' argument is his interpretation of the spy
story.[27] He attempts to uncover the earliest strand of the story
from the J source. Coats argues that this earliest version of the
story involved a rejection of the people of Israel who here stand
for the northern tribes. The only exception is Caleb, the faithful
spy from Judah (Num 13:6), who will enter the land and whose
descendants will possess it (Num 14:24). The land here is not only
Hebron but the whole land of Canaan, according to Coats. The rejection of the rest of the people is absolute. In Coats' words,
"neither this generation nor their offspring shall have another
chance to become the heirs to the election faith."[28]

Simon de Vries has presented a case against both Noth and Coats
on the question of the origin of the murmuring story.[29] He concludes
that

> the murmuring tradition did not arise, as Noth claims, in the
> quail story; nor as Coats believes, in a Judean polemic
> against the north; but simply out of the theological reflex
> that faced the necessity of calibrating the southern conquest
> tradition (the original Caleb-Hebron story) with the already
> dominant tradition of the central amphictyony (of a unified
> conquest from the east).[30]

The arguments which de Vries presents against Noth and Coats are
cogent and convincing. The "Graves of Craving" etiology in the
quail story which Noth sees as the origin of the murmuring tradition
is a later and secondary addition to the narrative. Therefore, it
cannot serve as the origin of the murmuring motif which is firmly
embedded in earlier layers of the story.[31] Against Coats, de Vries
correctly argues that the evidence that the spy story could have

been used as covert propoganda by Judaeans against northern Israel
at some point in its history "is no proof that it was created for
that purpose."[32]

The murmuring motif is firmly anchored in the J source which,
according to de Vries, is typically dated to the Solomonic period.
This, however, seems to contradict Coats' placement of the motif's
origin at a point which is later: the period of the divided monarchy.[33] Another point made by de Vries concerns Coats' reading
of Num 14:22-24 (J):

> None of the men who have seen my glory and my signs which I
> did in Egypt and in the wilderness and yet have put me to the
> proof these ten times and have not hearkened to my voice shall
> see the land which I swore to give to their fathers; and none
> of those who despised me shall see it. But my servant Caleb
> I will bring into the land into which he went, and his
> descendants shall possess it.

Coats suggests that the land which is mentioned includes not only
Hebron but all of Canaan. He also maintains that these verses imply
that only Caleb and his descendants will ever inherit the land. As
for the rest of the people in the J account, neither that generation
nor their offspring will inherit the land. One difficulty in such
a reading is that an Israelite during the monarchy would presumably
know that this was never the case. Caleb was not the only one who
conquered or occupied the land of Canaan. Another difficulty is
that the J account itself seems to leave the question of who will
not inherit the land open or at least ambivalent. In point of fact,
the J passage makes a distinction between Caleb himself who will
see the land and his descendants who will possess it. This difference in the fate of the two generations is then explicitly extended
by P to all the Israelites: one generation will die in the wilderness, and only the second generation will see the land. But this
may already be implicit in the J version.[34]

Coats also makes much of the link of Caleb, the faithful spy,
and the tradition that he is of the tribe of Judah. Yet we would
note that nowhere among the verses assigned to J is a specific
connection made between Caleb and Judah. Only P makes the association explicit in the list of spies in Num 13:6. It might be said
in reply that J assumed Caleb was a Judaean or that the J verse
which made the association has been deleted. Then, however, Coats'
thesis must rely on a hypothetical reconstruction which weakens
his position. The identification of Caleb the Kenizzite with the
tribe of Judah seems to be due at least in some part to the
ethnographic reality that Calebites or Kenizzites dwelling near
Hebron were indeed part of Judah in the period of the Israelite

monarchy. Thus, it is difficult to determine how much intentionality to read into Caleb's connection with Judah as an anti-north
polemic. The ethnographic reality may have also played an important
role.

One final observation needs to be made. Whatever the intention
of the original J or pre-J account, the Priestly tradition has
shaped the present form of the text in such a way as to clearly
include Joshua, an Ephraimite from the north, alongside Caleb, a
Judaean from the south, as faithful spies. A later tradent has
theologically shaped the material in such a way that it resists a
political reading as southern propoganda against the north. The
present story is inclusive. It traces the promise of God which
continues through faithful representatives of the people of God
from both northern and southern Israel.

The critique of Noth and Coats by de Vries is, by and large,
a convincing one. Not so convincing is his alternative explanation
of the origin of the murmuring tradition as a theological reflex
to harmonize the tradition of a southern conquest by Caleb at
Hebron and the normative tradition of an all-Israelite conquest
from the east across the Jordan. De Vries argued that the harmoni-
zation was achieved by refashioning the Caleb conquest narrative
into an abortive conquest story. A delay was introduced to allow
one generation to die for its rebellion and another generation to
enter the land. These considerations, we admit, may have helped
to shape the tradition at some point along its development. But
there is no way to prove that this attempt to harmonize two traditions was the original starting point for the murmuring tradition.
It remains one more possible option among others. Another option
which remains only possible as well is that the murmuring tradition
has some historical rooting in the wandering of all or some part of
the Israelite people in the actual wilderness period before the
occupation of the land. None of these proposed alternatives for
the origin of the tradition, however, has sufficient proof to claim
to be more than one possibility among others.

Volkmar Fritz has written a tradition-historical study of the
Yahwist's wilderness tradition.[35] In the course of his study,
Fritz attempts to reconstruct the pre-Yahwistic version of the spy
story. When he compares his reconstruction with the present J
account, he arrives at the conclusion that the Yahwist has reworked
a literary Vorlage, not a set of oral traditions as some previous
tradition historians had assumed. His evidence involves detecting
the specifically Yahwistic redactional intrusions into the previous
source material and showing that the type of intrusions involved

require a literary Vorlage and could not be achieved on an oral
level. The major shortcoming of the work is the difficulty of
establishing sound criteria for determining the kinds of redactional
procedures which are possible and those which are not possible on
an oral level and which can only be performed literarily. Thus,
his claims that a certain editorial addition or deletion requires
a literary and not an oral context are many times less than obvious.
The myriad of minute glosses and divisions between various layers
sometimes blunts the impact of his analysis. His study is at best
a refinement of earlier work without much which is significantly new.

One other line of critical inquiry into the spy story is a
strictly historical one which depends to some degree on the other
critical methodologies in assessing the biblical evidence. Historians of Israel's early history must also rely on evidence from extra-
biblical texts and other archaeological artifacts. The primary
historical interest surrounding the spy narrative is its relation
to the history of the Israelite conquest or occupation of Canaan.
Many have suggested that the Calebite tradition in the spy story
represents a vestige of an actual conquest from the south of
Palestine by one group of Israelites. This, of course, is in
contrast to the normative biblical tradition in Joshua and Judges
of one conquest from the east across the Jordan.[36] The historical
crux in Num 13:22 which notes that Hebron was built seven years
before the Egyptian city of Zoan has also occasioned interest among
scholars.[37]

THE SPY STORY AND THE EDITORIAL FRAMEWORK OF NUMBERS

Previous critical studies of the narrative of the Israelite
spies have focused on the questions of the origin of the traditions
and on distinguishing the various layers of the text. Even Sean
McEvenue's literary study of the story sought only to isolate the
earliest level of the Priestly tradition and describe its characteristics. These are legitimate enterprises and need to be pursued
as far as the evidence allows. One facet of the narrative which
has not been adequately explored, however, is the relationship of
the spy story to the larger editorial structure of Numbers. The
relationship is an important one since the spy story, more than
any other part of Numbers, has been clearly linked by later editors
to the census lists in Numbers 1 and 26 which form the basis for
the structure of the entire book. As such, the story has been
elevated to a key position and plays a significant role in the
present shape of the book.

The spy story is explicitly connected to the preceding census
list in Numbers 1 in God's judgment speech in 14:28-30 which follows
the people's refusal to enter the land:

> (28) "As I live," says the LORD, "what you have said in my
> hearing I will do to you. (29) Your dead bodies shall fall
> in the wilderness; and of all your number, numbered from
> twenty years old and upward, who have murmured against me,
> (30) not one shall come into the land where I swore that I
> would make you dwell, except Caleb the son of Jephuneh and
> Joshua the son of Nun."

The phrase, "from twenty years old and upward," is the recurrent
age formula which is used in the census in Numbers 1. The formula
occurs in the LORD's instructions to Moses in Num 1:3, 18 and in the
census totals of each of the twelve tribes (Num 1:20, 22, 24, 26,
28, 30, 32, 34, 36, 38, 40, 42) as well as in the final census total
for all Israel (Num 1:45). These people, all those numbered "from
twenty years old and upward" in Numbers 1, are those who are condemned to death in the wilderness in Numbers 13-14. It is almost
universally held that the verses which contain the age formula in
Numbers 1 and the verse in Numbers 14 (v. 29) belong to the same
early Priestly tradition.[38] An intentional editorial link between
Numbers 1 and Numbers 13-14, therefore, appears very probable.

Other less explicit connections between the spy story and the
census list are also present. The census in Numbers 1 is designed
to count the number of males from twenty years old and upward "who
are able to go forth to war" (Num 1:3). The census is immediately
followed in Numbers 2 with a description of the camp of the twelve
tribes. This elaborate military organization intimates that an
upcoming military venture is in the offing.[39] The setting for the
intial census, however, is in the wilderness of Sinai where Israel
encounters no military enemies. It is not until the people finally
reach the wilderness of Paran at the edge of Canaan that the first
military expedition, the spy mission into Canaan, is about to take
place (Num 12:16; 13:1). Thus, the first military operation for
which the reader is prepared by the military census in Numbers 1
is the spy story in Numbers 13-14. In this way, the census list
and the spy story are implicitly connected.

The spy story is also directly linked to the second census
list in Numbers 26 which marks the new generation of Israelites.
The link is achieved by the relatively late editorial addition of
Num 26:63-65 which concludes the census:[40]

> (63) These were those numbered by Moses and Eleazar the
> priest, who numbered the people of Israel in the plains of
> Moab by the Jordan at Jericho. (64) But among these there
> was not a man of those numbered by Moses and Aaron the priest,

who had numbered the people of Israel in the wilderness of
Sinai. (65) For the LORD had said of them, "They shall die
in the wilderness." There was not left a man of them except
Caleb the son of Jephuneh and Joshua the son of Nun.

Verse 65 clearly recalls the spy story. Verse 64 intends to distin-
guish this new census of a second generation from the census in
Numbers 1. The death sentence imposed on the generation of people
who were counted in the wilderness of Sinai in the first census
and who rebelled and refused to enter the land in Numbers 13-14 has
been fulfilled. The plague which killed twenty-four thousand
people in Num 25:9 presumably took the last remaining members of
the old generation. The new generation in Numbers 26 stands on the
threshold of Canaan just as the old generation in chapters 13-14
had stood before the promised land in the wilderness of Paran.
The old generation had failed in their mission, condemned to die
in the wilderness. The fate of the second generation is undecided.

     This important connection between the spy story and the second
census of the new generation is missed by Sean McEvenue. He applies
the concept of "fulfillment in nuce" in relation to the punishment
of death on the entire generation of Israelites in Numbers 13-14.[41]
McEvenue states that the Priestly account of the spy story leaves
the promised death of the whole generation unfulfilled except for
the symbolic death of the ten unfaithful spies in 14:36-38. The
question of the final fate of this sinful generation remains open.
This, according to McEvenue, reflects a question which the Priestly
writer is addressing to the exile: will the sinful generation
survive? This question, McEvenue says, is unanswered.[42]

     McEvenue has failed to see the important role of the second
census list in Numbers 26 which marks the end of the first sinful
generation and the beginning of a new generation. This is not
"fulfillment in nuce" but complete fulfillment of the promised
punishment. The question of the book of Numbers is not whether
the sinful generation which experienced the Exodus and Sinai will
survive. The question of Numbers is this: what will be the fate
of the new generation who did not see the Exodus and Sinai and who
did not participate in the rebellion of the golden calf or the
spy story? Will they also fail or will they be the recipents of
the promise and enter the promised land?

     The census in Numbers 26 does not function only as a negative
indication that the punishment of the old generation has been completed. The census is also a tangible sign that the promise of
innumerable descendants and the land of Canaan has been extended
to a new generation which includes all Israel. This is important
in light of the spy story in Numbers 13-14. In Num 14:11-12 God

tells Moses he will disinherit the people and offers to make of
Moses alone a nation even greater and mightier than they. Here
God is suggesting a further narrowing of the line of promise to the
toledot of Moses alone. But Moses refuses. Appealing to the
reputation of God among the nations, he asks God to forgive. God
does pardon the people and yet the rebellion must be punished.
Thus, the old generation will die in the wilderness; only the new
generation of Israelites will have the opportunity to see the
promised land.[43] The census list in Numbers 26 is a confirmation
of God's words. A whole new generation has indeed arisen. This
new generation is not limited only to the toledot of Moses but
includes a census of all twelve tribes (the toledot of Jacob) and
a census of the Levites (the toledot of Aaron and Moses). Thus,
the spy story and the second census list together affirm the inclusiveness of God's continuing promise. The two accounts also affirm
that Moses' leadership is performed for the sake of the larger
community, not for the sake of self glorification. And the appeal
of Moses to God in Num 14:13-19 also affirms that the continuing
existence of God's people is for the sake of God's glory among the
nations.

We have seen that the spy story is closely tied to the census
lists in Numbers 1 and 26. The spy story contributes an essential
component to the overarching editorial unity and structure of the
book. Other reverberations of the spy story in the second half of
Numbers further promote a sense of a unifying redactional reading
of the book. The most obvious is the reapplication of the spy
story to the new generation in Num 32:6-15. There verses are
typically understood as later editorial supplements, perhaps included
at the same time as Num 26:63-65.[44] The verses recount the request
by the sons of Reuben and the sons of Gad to settle in the Transjordan rather than cross the river into Canaan. Moses interprets
the request as a rebellious move which would discourage the other
Israelites from entering the land. Moses says to them,

> "Shall your brethren go to the war while you sit here? Why
> will you discourage the heart of the people of Israel from
> going over into the land which the LORD has given them?
> Thus did your fathers, when I sent them from Kadesh-barnea
> to see the land. For when they went up to the Valley of
> Eshcol, and saw the land, they discouraged the heart of the
> people of Israel from going into the land which the LORD had
> given them" (Num 32:6-9).

Thus, Moses draws a clear parallel between the rebellious actions
of the spies in Numbers 13-14 and the request by the sons of Gad
and Reuben. Moses then reminds them of the consequences of the
actions of the former generation:

"And the LORD's anger was kindled on that day, and he swore, saying, 'Surely none of the men who came up out of Egypt, from twenty years old and upward, shall see the land which I swore to give to Abraham, to Isaac, and to Jacob, because they have not wholly followed me; none except Caleb the son of Jephuneh the Kenizzite and Joshua the son of Nun, for they have wholly followed the LORD. And the LORD's anger was kindled against Israel, and he made them wander in the wilderness forty years, until all the generation that had done evil in the sight of the LORD was consumed" (Num 32:10-13).

The lesson of the past is then applied as a paradigm which interprets the potential rebellion of the new generation.

"And behold, you have risen in your father's stead, a brood of sinful men, to increase still more the fierce anger of the LORD against Israel! For if you turn away from following him, he will again abandon them in the wilderness; and you will destroy all this people" (Num 32:14-15).

These important verses suggest that the fate of the second generation is still an open question. If they rebel, God may again consign the people to the wilderness and destroy them. The people of God continue to live under the threat. But the last word in this episode is one of promise. The sons of Gad and Reuben pledge to join the other Israelites in conquering the land of Canaan. Only then will they return to settle in Transjordan. Moses accepts the compromise offer, the crisis is averted, and the promise is made by Moses to the sons of Gad and Reuben: "This land shall be your possession before the LORD" (Num 32:22; cf. 32:33).

The central themes of the spy story are here taken up and recapitulated for the new generation. All those who were "twenty years old and upward" and were counted in the first census were condemned to wander for forty years and to die there because of their lack of faith. Only Caleb and Joshua would see the land which God "swore to give to Abraham, to Isaac, and to Jacob." And now the new generation stands again on the edge of the promised land. The whole Pentateuchal tradition of the promise to the ancestors and to Israel as well as the warnings of the past generation are focused on this new generation. The final fate of the new generation remains unknown, but a note of hope and promise brings the episode to a close.

Another reverberation of the spy story in the latter chapters of Numbers which is not as explicit but still important is Numbers 34. The chapter outlines the procedures for the future division of the land. The chapter begins with a detailed description of the boundaries of the promised land. The LORD gives precise instructions on where the boundary lines are to be drawn. The instructions, of course, are not immediately relevant but are to be executed at

a future time "when you (i.e., the people) enter the land of
Canaan. This is the land that shall fall to you for an inheritance,
the land of Canaan in its full extent" (Num 34:3). The description
of the extent of the land corresponds closely to the description
of the territory covered by the spies in Numbers 13-14. The
southern boundary is in the wilderness of Zin (Num 34:3; cf. "the
wilderness of Zin," 13:21) while the northern boundary extends "to
the entrance of Hamath" (Num 34:8; cf. "the entrance of Hamath,"
13:21). The land will also reach from the eastern border at the
Jordan River (Num 34:12; cf. "the Jordan," 13:29) to the Great Sea
on the western boundary (Num 34:6; cf. "the sea," 13:29). These
rather precise correspondences between the spy story and the later
description of the boundaries of the promised land suggest that
the promise of the land originally given to the old generation has
now been extended in all its fullness to the new generation.[45]

Another link between the spy story and Numbers 34 is the list
of twelve tribal leaders who are commissioned to supervise the
future division of the land among the tribes (Num 34:16-29). Three
such lists of the leaders of the twelve tribes are found in Numbers:
the list of twelve census supervisors in Numbers 1, the list of
twelve spies in Numbers 13, and the list of those who will divide
the promised land in Numbers 34. Each of these lists mark significant turning points in the book: the organization and inauguration
of the march of the holy people of God in the wilderness toward the
promised land (Numbers 1), the decisive rebellion of the wilderness
generation who were numbered in the first census which led to their
death in the desert (Numbers 13), and the future allocation of the
promised land to the members of the Israelite tribes who were
counted in the second census (Numbers 34). These lists help to
bind the beginning, middle and end of the book together, signaling
key turning points in the narrative. It should also be noted that
none of the persons mentioned in the list in Numbers 34 are mentioned
anywhere else in Numbers with the exception of Caleb and Joshua and
the successor to Aaron, Eleazar. This emphasizes the newness of
the generation who will inherit the land as well as the faithfulness
of God's promise to Joshua and Caleb, the only two faithful spies
in the story in Numbers 13-14. Of the old generation, they alone
will see the land of Canaan.

It should be clear from our analysis that the spy story in
Numbers 13-14 has been assigned a crucial role within the unifying
literary and theological structure of Numbers. The story is closely
and directly related to the two census lists in Numbers 1 and 26
and is recalled in important ways in the second half of the book

in Numbers 32 and 34. Although many of these connections are the
result of later editorial supplements, the relationships have
achieved a unifying framework which brings a degree of coherence
to the whole. They provide evidence of an intentional redactional
reworking in several stages, each of which aided in making explicit
a cohesion which was only implied in the earlier Priestly framework
of the census lists in Numbers.

THEOLOGICAL IMPLICATIONS

A degree of cohesion is not the only result of the shaping of
the spy story in its present form within the wider framework of
Numbers. A more important result is the interpretation of the
theological significance of the story in its present context. The
following discussion will be organized under the rubrics of the
nature of the rebellion, the nature of the punishment, the extension
of the promise, the remaining threat, and the second generation as
paradigm.

First of all, the nature of the rebellion of the Israelites
in Numbers 13-14 is in some ways similar to previous rebellions in
the wilderness. The characteristic word for the people's "murmuring"
(lun) in the wilderness is used (e.g., Num 14:2, 27). The people's
wish that they had died in Egypt (Num 14:2) is also typical of the
other wilderness rebellions (e.g., Exod 14:11; 16:3). The unusual
appeal of Moses to the reputation of God among the nations as a
reason to forgive the people and God's offer to disinherit the
people and to make of Moses a great nation are signs of the gravity
of the Israelites' rebellion (Num 14:13-19). But even these have
parallels in the earlier story of the golden calf in Exod 32:10-14
(cf. also Exod 34:6-9).

And yet the rebellion in Numbers 13-14 is unique, forming a
climax to all the previous rebellions and murmurings of the people
in the wilderness. The immediately preceding context tells of the
abrupt and unexpected rebellion of the people (Numbers 11) and of
the leaders, Miriam and Aaron (Numbers 12). The rebellion of Aaron
and Miriam is the first outright challenge against Moses and the
LORD by the leaders of the people. Numbers 13-14 follows with the
culminating rebellion of both the leaders who are represented by
the spies (Num 13:2) and all the people (Num 14:1-2). The uniqueness and severity of the rebellion is also indicated by the people's
desire to choose their own leader and return to Egypt (Num 14:4).
George Coats correctly observes that

> here, for the first time, the murmuring is followed by a
> move to return to Egypt. The murmuring tradition therefore

involves not simply an expression of a wish that the Exodus
had not occurred or a challenge of Moses' authority in
executing the Exodus, but now an overt move to reverse the
Exodus. Yahweh is the God "who brought Israel out of Egypt."
The murmuring results in a rejection of this deity and a move [46]
to elect a new leader to take the people back to Egypt.

The only episode which approaches the severity of the people's sin
in the spy story is the making and worshiping of the golden calf in
Exodus 32. Yet the people worshiped the golden calf as the god
who led them out of Egypt and as an image of the LORD:

> And he (Aaron) received the gold at their hand and fashioned
> it with a graving tool, and made a molten calf; and they said,
> "These are your gods, O Israel, who brought you out of the
> land of Egypt!" When Aaron saw this, he built an altar before
> it; and Aaron made proclamation and said, "Tomorrow shall be
> a feast to the LORD."

The golden calf episode does not involve so much a rejection of
God and his power and faithfulness as an attempt by the people to
shape God into their own image.[47] Much more is at stake in the
spy story where the people repudiate the power and faithfulness of
God to fulfill his covenantal promises. In seeking another leader
to return to Egypt, they have renounced God and his covenant with
his people.

The fall of the people in the spy story is so low because the
sense of expectation and hope which the entire Pentateuchal narrative attaches to this one moment is so high. All the patriarchal
promises in Genesis and the reiteration of the same promises to
the Israelites since Exodus 1 have looked forward to this time when
the people are at last on the verge of entering the promised land.
Coupled with this high sense of anticipation, the census in Numbers
1 which counted an enormous army of over 600,000 men and the elaborate organization of the tribes into a carefully ordered military
camp with God in its midst should have provided the foundation for
the utmost confidence and faith.

The tone of events in Numbers 1-10 is entirely positive. Only
the abrupt rebellions in Numbers 11 and 12 interrupt the atmosphere
of positive expectation. One is led to wonder if these rebellions
are portents of greater acts of rebellion or only temporary setbacks.
The reader remains hopeful as the people reach the border of the
long awaited land of Canaan. Certainly now the people will faithfully follow their God. The initial reconnaissance of the land
reveals a beautiful and fruitful land "flowing with milk and honey."
The picture is bright indeed.

But then comes the strong and fateful adversative, "yet" (epes
ki) in the spies' report:

> "Yet the people who dwell in the land are strong, and the
> cities are fortified and very large; and besides, we saw
> the descendants of Anak there" (Num 13:28).

Caleb, the faithful spy, does not deny the facts of their description but argues that they will be able to conquer the inhabitants.
He exhorts the people: "Let us go up at once and occupy it, for
we are well able to overcome it" (Num 13:30). The spies respond
with an even more pessimistic description of the land and its
inhabitants.

> "The land, through which we have gone, to spy it out, is a
> land that devours its inhabitants; and all the people that we
> saw in it are men of great stature. And there we saw the
> Nephilim (the sons of Anak, who come from the Nephilim);
> and we seemed to ourselves like grasshoppers, and so we
> seemed to them."

The report of the spies leads the people into a fatal rebellion and
mutiny. They state their desire to choose their own leader and
return to Egypt. Aaron and Moses fall to the ground, knowing that
such words will provoke the wrath of God. Joshua and Caleb tear
their garments and thereby further illustrate the severity of the
people's sin. The two faithful spies, Joshua and Caleb, then get
to the heart of the issue. It is God, not themselves, whom they
must trust to bring them into the exceedingly good land.

> "If the LORD delights in us, he will bring us into this land
> and give it to us, a land which flows with milk and honey.
> Only, do not rebel against the LORD; and do not fear the
> people of the land, for they are bread for us; their protec-
> tion is removed from them, and the LORD is with us; do not
> fear them" (Num 14:8-9).

The people's rejoinder is an attempt to stone Joshua and Caleb at
which point God intervenes with his judgment of death on this sinful generation. The next day the people decide to go up and fight
the Canaanites. But Moses warns them that God is not with them and
that they will therefore be defeated. They proceed anyway and are
soundly defeated (Num 14:39-45).

The crucial issue in the nature of the rebellion is not a difference of opinion concerning the human military potential of the
Israelites in relation to the Canaanites. Nor is it a question of
human courage or lack thereof, as Gressmann's form-critical reconstruction of the spy story which celebrated the courage of Caleb
suggests. The crucial question in the present form of the story is
this: who will conquer the promised land? In what do the people
trust in obtaining the inheritance of the land? Do they trust in
God's power and faithfulness to fulfill his own promises, or do the
people trust in their estimates of their own human potential?
Caleb and Joshua are obedient followers who have faith in God.

The faithless spies and people do not trust in God but only in
themselves and in their own misguided perceptions which place
limits on God's ability and desire to accomplish what he has
promised.

This rebellious lack of faith extends to all the people. All
the tribes are represented by the twelve spies who reconnoiter the
land. Joshua and Caleb are the only spies who witness to the good-
ness of the land and God's ability to bring his people into it.
Contrary to Coats' description of the original murmuring tradition
as a Judaean polemic against northern Israel, the present shape of
the spy narrative is neither anti-north or anti-south. Joshua is
from the north (Ephraim) and Caleb is from the south (Judah), and
both are cast in a positive light. The dividing line in the story
is not a political boundary but a theological boundary: those who
trust in God versus those who reject God and his promises and trust
in themselves.

Except for the two faithful spies, all the people fall into
this latter category. This is underscored by the three-fold repetition of the word "all" in the people's initial response to the
negative report of the spies:

> Then all the congregation raised a loud cry; and the people
> wept that night. And all the people of Israel murmured
> against Moses and Aaron; all the congregation said to them,
> "Would that we had died in the land of Egypt! Or would that
> we had died in this wilderness" (Num 14:1-2).

The nature of the rebellion, then, included the unique and climactic
intensity of the rebellion, its repudiation of God's ability and
faithfulness in fulfilling his covenantal promise, and its inclusion
of all Israel in the rebellion.

The nature of the punishment in the spy story corresponds in
its severity and inclusiveness to the grave nature of the rebellion.
The issue is one of life and death. Those who trust in God live;
those who do not die. Yet the judgment and punishment which God
places upon the people is not an arbitrary one. In a series of
correspondences and ironic parallels, God gives the people exactly
what they desired. The people had wished for their own death:
"Would that we had died in the land of Egypt! Or would that we
had died in this wilderness" (Num 14:2). The LORD grants their
wish: "'As I live,' says the LORD, ' what you have said in my
hearing I will do to you; your dead bodies shall fall in this
wilderness'" (Num 14:28-29; cf. also 14:32, 33, 35).

The people want to return to Egypt (Num 14:4), and God obliges
by sending them back into the wilderness toward the Red Sea in a
reversal of the Exodus (Num 14:25). The people ask in despair,

"Why does the LORD bring us into this land, to fall by the sword"
(Num 14:3)? Later, the people are unwilling to accept the sentence
of death which God has imposed upon them, and they decide to invade
Canaan on their own. Moses then turns their own previous fears of
falling by the sword back upon them:

> "Do not go up lest you be struck down before your enemies,
> for the LORD is not among you. For there the Amalekites and
> the Canaanites are before you, and you shall fall by the
> sword; because you have turned back from following the LORD,
> the LORD will not be with you" (Num 14:42-43).

The people use their concern for the women and children as
excuses for not risking the invasion of Canaan: "Our wives and
little ones will become a prey; would it not be better for us to
go back to Egypt" (Num 14:3)? But ironically, it is precisely
because of the people's refusal to trust God and carry out the
invasion that their little ones will have to suffer: "And your
children shall be shepherds in the wilderness forty years, and shall
suffer for your faithlessness, until the last of your dead bodies
lies in the wilderness" (Num 14:33). Moreover, in the end God will
take good care of the little ones, despite their parents' rebellion.
"But your little ones who you said would become a prey, I will
bring in, and they shall know the land which you have despised"
(Num 14:31). The people's sin, then, brings to them not only the
punishment that they deserve but also what they had wished upon
themselves.

The ten spies experienced the judgment of death immediately
(Num 14:36-38). It is only by interpreting the spy story within
the larger framework of Numbers that the execution of the judgment
upon the rest of the sinful generation can be fully understood.
The judgment upon the people does not remain unfulfilled in Numbers,
as McEvenue argued.[48] Instead, the gradual death and disappearance
of the wilderness generation is implied for the remaining chapters
of the first half of the book. These chapters include further
rebellions (Numbers 16-17, Numbers 20--the judgment on Moses and
Aaron). The final rebellion occurs in Numbers 25 and causes the
outbreak of a plague which kills 24,000 Israelites, presumably the
last remnants of the sinful generation. This is confirmed in the
second census in Numbers 26 which includes none of those counted in
the first census for they have all died in the wilderness (Num 26:
63-65). Just as the rebellion in the spy story included all the
people, so too the punishment has been meted out to all the people.

No hope of repentance is held out to this wicked generation.
God does forgive Israel but that only means that the people will
not be totally annihilated. A future generation will have the

opportunity to see the promised land. There appears, however, to be no avenue of recourse or appeal for the rebels. But if any question of a reprieve remains, the further rebellions after the spy story (Numbers 16-17; 20; 21:4ff.; 25) dispel any hope for this sinful generation. The intensity of their lack of faith is only confirmed all the more by these later chapters.

The third rubric for the theological implications of the narrative of the Israelite spies is the extension of the promise to the second generation. Scholars have often seen the spy story as a predominantly negative story of punishment and faithlessness which gives the entire book of Numbers an essentially negative perspective and theme.[49] Such a view, however, is altered when one reads the story within the context of the larger structure of the book. The tragedy of the sin and death of the wilderness generation is deep and intense. Never before had a whole generation of God's people been condemned to die in the wasteland of the desert. But out of the darkest night of the whole Torah comes the dawn of a new generation. The old generation will die, but their children whom the rebels used as an excuse for not entering the land (Num 14:3) will become the new carriers of the promise (Num 14:31). The census list of the new generation in Numbers 26 is a concrete sign that the promise to all Israel continues into the future. The instructions for the future division of the land and its boundaries in Numbers 34 also testify in a specific way to the continuance of hope and expectation to the new generation. The spy story in Numbers 13-14 is the first military venture after the mustering of the troops in Numbers 1. It ends in dismal failure and death. The later military engagements in Numbers 21 and 28, however, describe an obedient Israel as victorious over its enemies outside the promised land. Hope has again entered the picture. Perhaps this new generation will fare better when they again invade the land of Canaan. Indeed, the whole tone of the second half of the book in Numbers 26-36 is positive and hopeful. It may be seen as a return to the basically positive outlook of Numbers 1-10 which preceded the series of rebellions in Numbers 11-14.

The extension of the promise to the second generation was was not automatic. God initially wanted to eradicate the people entirely and make Moses alone a great nation (Num 14:11-12). Moses resists the temptation of pride and denies himself for the sake of the people. Moses intercedes for the people, renouncing his own glory and appealing instead to the glory of God among the nations. God then repents and forgives the people.

The difficulty is that God pronounces forgiveness and in the
same breath condemns the whole generation to death in the wilderness (Num 14:20-23). Coats argues that "the only consequence of
the forgiveness announced in v. 20" is that "the rebels will not
be destroyed immediately but may wander through the wilderness until
the natural end of their lives."[50] Katherine Sakenfeld's study of
divine forgiveness in the spy story correctly perceives that the
consequence of the forgiveness is much more than Coats suggests.[51]
Divine forgiveness means the repeal of the intention to annihilate
the entire people and the assurance of the extension of the promise
to a second generation. Our discussion of the specific signs of
the extension of the promise (the second census in Numbers 26, the
future division of the land in Numbers 34, the positive tone of
Numbers 26-36) would appear to support and enrich such a reading.

The fourth theological theme connected with the spy story and
the larger framework of Numbers is the remaining threat which hangs
over the second generation. Although the promise of the land and
the continuing existence of the people is extended to the children
of the wilderness generation, this does not entail an easy assurance
of the fulfillment of the promise. The new generation may itself
experience the same fate of death in the wilderness if they rebel
and despise the promises of God. This theme is most clearly
espoused in the story of the sons of Gad and Reuben who desire the
Transjordan as their territory in Numbers 32. Moses fears that this
will only discourage the rest of the Israelites and cause them not
to enter the land again. He then recounts the spy story and the
judgment of death which was the consequence of the previous generation's rebellion. He concludes,

> "And behold, you have risen in your father's stead, a brood
> of sinful men, to increase still more the fierce anger of the
> LORD against Israel! For if you turn away from following him,
> he will again abandon them in the wilderness; and you will
> destroy all this people" (Num 32:14-15).

The past is reinterpreted for the present. The tragic fate of the
past generation may also be the fate of the new generation. In
principle, the threat remains. There is no certain guarantee that
this generation, unlike their predecessors, will enter the land.

The last word in the story in Numbers 32, however, is not a
threat but a promise. The sons of Gad and Reuben agree to accompany
and aid the other Israelites in their taking of the land of Canaan.
Only afterward will they return to their inheritance in the Transjordan (Num 32:20-24, 29-30). The crisis is averted, and the
chapter ends with Moses giving them the land in the Transjordan.
Indeed, the last word of the entire book of Numbers as depicted in

the second half of the book (Numbers 26-36) is basically positive
and hopeful. After all the deaths of the first generation, not
one death of a member of the second generation is recorded.
Military engagements are successful (Numbers 28), potential crises
are resolved (Numbers 32), and laws which look forward to the future
life in the land of Canaan are promulgated (Numbers 34).[52] The
threat remains, but the promise of the future is the dominant note
which is sounded at the end of the book.

One final rubric in the theology of Numbers 13-14 within the
structure of Numbers is the portrait of the second generation in
Numbers as a paradigm for all succeeding generations.[53] The book
of Numbers as well as Deuteronomy and the entire Pentateuch ends
with the present generation of Israelites facing an open and unresolved future on the edge of the promised land. In its present
form, the Pentateuch is cut off as a unit from the books which
follow (Joshua, Judges, Samuel, Kings) and elevated as the primary
and constitutive definition of the life of Israel before God. The
closing chapter of Deuteronomy concludes the Pentateuch with a
reminder of the uniqueness of Moses, Israel's leader since the
Exodus and the mediator of God's revelation of the Torah (Deut 34:
9-12; cf. Josh 1:7-8). The Torah is thus the unique and definitive
statement of what constitutes the people of God.

The unresolved character of the future of the new generation
at the end of Numbers and the Pentateuch as a whole invites every
succeeding generation to identify itself as the new generation of
God's people. This is part of the theological implication of the
spy story in Numbers 13-14 since the account of Numbers 32 which
we discussed above is the paradigm for the reapplication of traditions of the past (the spy story) in light of present circumstances
and future hopes. For the first time, the members of this new
generation are not witnesses to the formative events of the Exodus
and Sinai. They must rely on the testimony of the past to shape
and guide their understanding of the present and future life as a
holy people before God. This second generation stands, as each
succeeding generation does, on the edge of the promised land with
promises awaiting final fulfillment.

Israel, throughout her history, remained in a sense on the
boundary of the promised land. The fullness of the promises of
the past were never achieved completely or for long. The conquest
is incomplete. The period of the judges is interrupted by cycles
of rebellion. The monarchy is marred by the frequent disobedience
of the kings, even of David, which leads to the fateful division of
Israel into north and south. The devestation of the exile

definitively shapes Israel and its understanding of its traditions.
And the return to the promised land after the exile is something
less than the complete fulfillment of the prophetic promises of the
past. Furthermore, the traditions which continued to appropriate
the Hebrew Scriptures as their normative religious literature,
whether Jewish or Christian, have always identified themselves as
a people who likewise stand on the threshold of the promised land,
awaiting the final fulfillment of the promises of the past, however
defined.

We have endeavored to show that the theological interpretation
of the spy story in Numbers 13-14 is enriched by attention to its
function within the context of the larger framework of Numbers. We
have seen that the relationship of the spy story to this larger
framework is explicit and direct. The connections of the spy
narrative to the census in Numbers 1, the second census in Numbers
26, the reapplication of the spy story in Numbers 32, and the future
division of the promised land in Numbers 34 are carefully indicated
in the text. These connections clearly illustrate how the generational framework of Numbers establishes the final and definitive
interpretive context for the book and for the Pentateuch as a whole.
We now turn to an analysis of material in Numbers which is not as
explicitly related to the larger structure of Numbers as the spy
story: the Balaam cycle in Numbers 22-24 (Chapter Seven) and
selected legal material in Numbers 15, 27 and 36 (Chapter Eight).
Although these sections are not as clearly tied to the framework
of Numbers we will attempt to show that an appreciation of the
place and role which the present editorial structure of Numbers
assigns to them can significantly enhance their theological interpretation.

THE BALAAM CYCLE IN NUMBERS 22-24

The story of Balaam relates how Balak, king of Moab, commissions a professional seer named Balaam to curse the Israelites who are encamped in the plains of Moab. God initially prohibits Balaam to go to Balak. Without explanation, God rescinds his prohibition. Balaam saddles his ass and sets out to meet Balak. Again without explanation, an angel of God stands in the way of Balaam and his ass, but only the ass sees the angel standing before them. After beating his ass three times, Balaam's eyes are opened and he too sees the angel who now tells him to continue on his journey. Finally, Balaam comes to Balak and in three different settings which are each prepared with elaborate cultic preparations, Balaam blesses the Israelites with glorious images of their multitude and strength. These magnificent blessings are the very antithesis of what Balak desired, but he is powerless to change the seer's words. What God has spoken through Balaam will be done. Balak's own words to Balaam confirm the efficacy of his blessings: "For I know that he whom you bless is blessed, and he whom you curse is cursed" (Num 22:6). Four poetic oracles of blessing are embedded in the narrative, each spoken by Balaam. The final oracle forms the climax to the series of blessings:

> "I see him, but not now;
> I behold him, but not nigh:
> A star shall come forth out of Jacob,
> and a sceptre shall rise out of Israel;
> it shall crush the forehead of Moab,
> and break down all the sons of Sheth.
> Edom shall be dispossessed,
> Seir also, his enemies, shall be dispossessed,
> while Israel does valiantly.
> By Jacob shall dominion be exercised,
> and the survivors of cities be destroyed"
> (Num 24:17-19).

OVERVIEW OF CRITICAL ISSUES

A wide range of methods have been used to interpret these chapters. The presence of doublets, alterations in the designation of God and other tensions in the text have led source critics to detect two basic sources in the Balaam cycle, a Yahwistic and an Elohistic layer. The Priestly source is evident only in Num 22:1. One example of a proposed source-critical division of the Balaam cycle would be the following:[1]

Num 22:2-21-----E, with some traces of J---the introductory
                                            narrative
Num 22:22-40----J, with some traces of E---Balaam and the ass
Num 22:41-23:27-E for the most part-------two oracles embedded
                                            in the narrative
Num 23:28-24:19-J for the most part-------two oracles embedded
                                            in the narrative
(Num 24:20-25----later additions)

The disagreement on the source division of some of these sections,
however, is considerable, particularly with regard to the sections
containing the oracles.[2]

    One factor which has hampered a clear source-critical deline-
ation of literary layers is the long and complex oral history which
is evident in the material. While the tendency of some earlier
source critics was to date the poetic oracles of Balaam as later
compositions,[3] form critics isolated and reconstructed much earlier
oral forms of a saga about Balaam as well as earlier forms of his
oracles. Gressmann reconstructed an earlier form of the narrative
in which Balaam was an Arabic seer who was forced to bless rather
than curse Israel. Gressmann argued that the conclusion of this
earlier form of the story related a subsequent military victory by
Israel over Moab.[4] In the ending of the present story, this has
been deleted. Balak and Balaam simply go on their separate ways
(Num 24:25).

    The reconstruction of the role of Balaam as seer or diviner
has been considerably sharpened since Gressmann with the aid of
comparative ancient Near Eastern texts. Babylonian and other Near
Eastern sources have provided insights into the function of inter-
mediaries like Balaam.[5] The most striking parallel to the biblical
figure of Balaam is an Aramaic text from Deir ʻAllā in modern Jordan
which dates from about 700 B.C. The contents of the text are
ascribed to "Balaam son of Beor." He is called "a seer of the gods"
who apparently acted as a professional curser. Scholars are generally agreed that some connection exists between the biblical Balaam
and the Balaam of the Deir ʻAllā texts.[6] Other form-critical
studies of the Balaam cycle have focused on the form of the "seer
speech," traditonal formulae which may be detected in the Balaam
oracles, and a form-critical study of the prose portions of the
Balaam story.[7] Tradition-historical studies of the Balaam cycle
have sought to illumine the numerous stages of reshaping which the
cycle has undergone from earlier to later stages.[8]

    Another major avenue was opened by W. F. Albright's text-criti-
cal and philological analysis of the Balaam oracles as examples of
early Hebrew poetry.[9] Albright sought to date his reconstruction

of the Balaam oracles to the twelfth or thirteenth century B.C. on
the basis of parallels to the grammar, lexicography and epigraphy
of other Northwest Semitic texts from approximately the same period.
The oracles were written down in about the tenth century B.C.[10]
Albright was responding most directly to Sigmund Mowinckel's
attempt to date the two earliest Balaam oracles to the time of
David or Solomon (tenth century B.C.) and the later two oracles to
the time of Josiah (seventh century B.C.).[11] Albright's discussion
provides a good deal of convincing evidence for dating the origin
of the oracles at a time earlier than Mowinckel's proposed dates.
On the other hand, one must also admit the possibility that the
circumstances of the reigns of David, Solomon or Josiah may have
occasioned editorial reinterpretations and reworking of these
oracles, traces of which Mowinckel has perhaps correctly detected.
In any case, it appears very likely that these ancient oracles have
experienced a long history of transmission and editing up to their
present literary context in the book of Numbers.

Although studies of the Balaam story have concentrated on
determining the origin of its parts or describing its various layers,
some have endeavored to analyze the narrative in its present literary form. Thus, L. M. Pakozdy examined the theological intention
of the final redactor in his various uses of the divine name, particularly in the interplay of Yahweh and Elohim.[12] Ruth Mackensen
argued that the purpose of the present literary shape of the Balaam
narrative was to counteract a rising Hebrew exclusiveness as well
as the claim of the classical pre-exilic prophets to have the sole
right to interpret the will of God.[13]

A brief but insightful study of the present literary form of
the Balaam pericope has also been presented by Robert Alter.[14]
Alter uses the Balaam story as an example of the repetition of
key-words and actions as a literary technique of biblical narration.
He acknowledges that the story is made up of more than one layer,
but he seeks to discern the literary artistry of the later editors
of the story. Alter detects a key-word (Leitwort) in the use of
the verb, "to see," throughout the story. The structure of the
story involves the symmetry of the three episodes with Balaam and
his ass (cf. the emphasis on three in Num 22:28) which is matched
by the three different settings for Balaam's proclamation of the
oracles which Balak mechanically prepares for him each time (Num
23:1-4; 23:14-15; 23:27-30). The mechanistic character of the
repetition of Balak's cultic preparations represents a world view
which is at odds with the God of Israel   who is beyond mechanical manipulation and human control.[15] Alter's proposal is

particularly suggestive, but it should be noted that all these
attempts to study the present shape of the Balaam narrative do not
extend their analysis far enough. They fail to consider the important question of the role of the story within the larger literary
framework of the book of Numbers.

One final area of study which has surrounded the Balaam cycle
is the theological interpretation of the story. The most significant aspect of such interpretations has been the messianic interpretation of Num 24:17:

> "I see him, but not now;
> I behold him, but not nigh:
> A star shall come forth out of Jacob,
> and a scepter shall rise out of Israel."

The identification of the star and sceptre with a messianic figure
became part of the Jewish and Christian traditions early in their
respective developments.[16] Other theological interpretations have
dealt with the figure of Balaam or with the theology of the story
of Balaam's ass in Numbers 22.[17] Once again, the missing element
in these various theological interpretations of the Balaam story,
whether messianic or not, is that they do not analyze the theological
function which the story's larger literary context assigns to it.
It is to this concern that we now turn.

THE FUNCTION OF THE BALAAM CYCLE WITHIN THE STRUCTURE OF NUMBERS

As the above summary of scholarship shows, most previous
attempts to interpret the Balaam cycle tend to ignore its role
within the larger structure of the book. The chapters in Numbers
22-24 are typically isolated as an independent unit from their
surrounding literary context. As one scholar puts it,

> it becomes increasingly evident that the narrative of Numbers
> xxii:2-xxiv breaks into the text of the book and must be
> handled as a separate literary creation. It has nothing to
> do with the material that precedes and follows. Hence, little
> can be judged from the context as to its purpose or its place
> in the history of Israel.[18]

Such a disregard of the wider literary context, however, leads to
an impoverished reading of the Balaam story. The story's full
literary and theological significance is properly perceived only
when one has a clear conception of the larger structure of Numbers
as a whole and the story's strategic position within that structure.

One study which purports to analyze the role of the Balaam
narrative within the wider context of Numbers and the Pentateuch
was done by M. Margaliot.[19] Margaliot argues that Num 22:2-24:25
was written as a whole by one author and thus was not compiled from
various sources. Moreover, the entire unit dates from the time of

Moses.[20] Such a position, however, ignores the evidence of a long
history of editing and reshaping which may be detected through
numerous tensions and seams within the story. The sense of unity
and symmetry which does exist in the present form of the Balaam
story is best explained as the work of one or more later redactors
or writers and need not be attributed to one original author at the
time of Moses. The relation of the chapters preceding and following
Numbers 22-24 is also best understood as the result of later editing
and not as original.

     A more serious fault in Margaliot's interpretation is the
description of the intended purpose of the Balaam narrative in the
Pentateuch. The purpose of the story of Balaam, according to
Margaliot, is to increase the stature of Moses as the true prophet
of God by depicting Balaam as a false prophet and as an "anti-Moses"
figure. Margaliot emphasizes the negative picture of Balaam and his
encouragement of the Israelite apostasy (cf. Num 31:8, 16) as a foil
to the positive portrait of Moses.[21] Such an interpretation of the
primary intention of the Balaam story in its present context encounters several difficulties. First of all, the evaluation of Balaam
in Numbers is ambivalent and not as one-sided as Margaliot implies.
Balaam's oracles of blessing are certainly cast in a positive light
and Balaam himself is portrayed as basically an obedient and loyal
intermediary of God in chapters 22-24. The negative picture which
later emerges in Num 31:8, 16 is almost parenthetical in nature with
little elaboration of the reasons for Balaam's actions. Although
the addition of Num 31:8, 16 does put Balaam in a more negative
light, the overall literary characterization of Balaam as at least
a temporary messenger of God is not obliterated. Thus, the primary
intent of the present form of the Balaam narrative seems to lie
elsewhere. Balaam himself is not presented as a purely negative
foil.[22]

     Another difficulty in Margaliot's analysis is that the texts
never make an explicit comparison between Moses and Balaam. Nowhere
is such a comparison even subtly intimated. As a matter of fact,
the shape of the present literary context of the Balaam story
suggests that such a comparison is not intended at all. For example,
Num 20:12 which is in close proximity to Numbers 22-24 relates the
LORD's condemnation of Moses and Aaron:

> And the LORD said to Moses and Aaron, "Because you did not
> believe in me, to sanctify me in the eyes of the people of
> Israel, therefore you shall not bring this assembly into the
> land which I have given them."

Such a passage so near the Balaam story seems to mitigate against
an emphasis on the role of Moses as a more suitable prophet of God

than Balaam as the central concern of Numbers 22-24. Furthermore,
the incident which immediately follows the Balaam narrative in
Numbers 25 exalts the faith and actions of Phinehas the priest, not
Moses. Moses simply stands with the rest of the congregation of
Israel while Phinehas zealously kills the apostate Israelite and
the Midianite woman. The action of Phinehas stops the plague and
evokes the praise of God and a promise of a perpetual priesthood
(Num 25:8-13). Again, the literary context of the Balaam story does
not suggest a primary intention to exalt Moses over Balaam.

Finally, the Balaam oracles themselves, especially in chapter
24, seem to point to a time or generation or person in the future
rather than the present:

> "I see him, but not now;
> I behold him, but not nigh:
> a star shall come forth out of Jacob,
> and a scepter shall rise out of Israel" (Num 24:17).

The primary concern of the Balaam oracles is not to exalt the present generation of Israelites or their present leader, Moses. The
Balaam oracles ask the reader to look toward the far off horizon in
the future. Thus, we would reject Margaliot's claim that the Balaam
narrative in its present literary context is designed primarily to
magnify Moses as the true prophet of God and to denigrate Balaam as
a false prophet. Margaliot has failed to discern the proper literary effect of the material which immediately precedes and follows
the Balaam story as well as the function of the story in the larger
structure of the book of Numbers.

What then is the function of the Balaam cycle in its present
literary setting? In terms of its immediate context, the section
preceding the Balaam narrative in chapter 21 strikes a positive
note for the first time since the definitive rebellion of the
Israelites in the spy story in Numbers 13-14. Israel defeats the
Canaanite king of Arad which is Israel's first military victory in
the book of Numbers (21:1-3). Another rebellion of the people
follows which is in turn followed by a positive story of the conquest of Sihon and Og (21:10-35). Thus, the promises of God are
shown to continue as God remains with his people. For the first
time since the spy story, the victories over Israel's enemies in
chapter 21 again place the people of God on the edge of the
promised land ("in the plains of Moab"--Num 22:1). God has not
abandoned his people, and his promises to the people are reaffirmed.
This hopeful setting provides the stage for the climactic promise
oracles which Balaam utters in the name of God. Numbers 21 leads
the reader to see the primary intent of Balaam's oracles of blessing
to be a dramatic reaffirmation of the faithfulness of God to his

promises to his people.

The section which follows the Balaam story in Numbers 25 also affects the way the Balaam story is to be read. The link between the Balaam story and the apostasy of the Israelites at Shittim involving the god Ba'al of Pe'or has been clearly and intentionally made by later redactors in Numbers 31:8, 16. These verses occur in the context of the Israelite victory over Midian in revenge for the Midianites' role in the apostasy of chapter 25. Among those killed is Balaam. Moses, however, chastises the Israelites for not also killing the Midianite women:

> Moses said to them, "Have you let all the women live? Behold, these caused the people of Israel, by the counsel of Balaam, to act treacherously against the LORD in the matter of Pe'or, and so the plague came among the congregation of the LORD" (Num 31:15-16).

Balaam is seen as the one who encouraged the Midianite women in the actions which led to the Israelite apostasy in Numbers 25. By means of this explicit link between the two episodes, a sharp contrast is drawn between the tenacious faithfulness of God as portrayed in Balaam's oracles in Numbers 22-24 and the extreme lack of faithfulness on the part of the people. The Balaam cycle emphasizes the unswerving dedication and ability of God to bless his people in face of all opposition from Israel's enemies. Even the apparent and unexplained inconsistency of God's commands to Balaam to go and then not to go to meet Balak (Num 22:12, 20, 22, 35) shows the absolute and mysterious power of God to control even those who would desire to curse his people. God leads Balaam the professional curser to bless his people with acolades and promises which are unsurpassed in the entire Pentateuch.

In face of the demonstration of the extreme fidelity of God to preserving the welfare of his people in Numbers 22-24, the incident in Numbers 25 stresses the fickle and shallow faith of God's people. The people have every reason to be hopeful and faithful. The Balaam oracles describe the glorious future which is theirs as they stand on the threshold of the promised land. The setting is a replay of the spy story in Numbers 13-14 where the people likewise had every reason to have hope and trust in God. And yet the Israelites quickly and easily turned from their God in apostasy. The Balaam narrative describes how even an ass can recognize an angel of God and how even a pagan seer can see God and do his will. The same cannot be said of this generation of God's own people. Balaam sees glorious visions of a great future. The Israelites see only their own people playing the harlot with the daughters of Moab and Midian in apostasy (Num 25:1-3, 6-7).[23] In short, the immediate

literary context of the Balaam story in Numbers 22-24 serves to
heighten the contrast between the faithfulness of God in continuing
his promises to the people (the military conquests in Numbers 21
which bring the people again to the threshold of the promised land)
and the faithfulness of the people (the apostasy at Shittim in
Numbers 25).

The Balaam cycle also plays an important role within the larger
framework of the whole book of Numbers. The pericope in Numbers
22-24 is positioned at the very end of the first generation which
is counted in the census in Numbers 1 and immediately before the
second generation which is counted in the census in Numbers 26.
The Balaam oracles sound a crescendo of hope and promise at the
conclusion of the first generation. As we have seen, however, the
first generation returns immediately to the way of rebellion and
disobedience. The apostasy in Numbers 25 stands in the present
structure of Numbers as the final rebellion of the old generation.
The plague which ensues apparently kills the last members of the
generation which was counted in Numbers 1. The new census in Numbers
26 begins "after the plague" (26:1), that is, after the last of the
rebellious generation had died (cf. 26:63-65).

The old generation had not learned from its forty years of
wandering in the wilderness. Its actions at the end of its life
in the wilderness were the same as its actions at the beginning.
The apostasy at Shittim in Numbers 25 and the spy story in Numbers
13-14 are mirror images of each other. In both cases, the people
stand on the brink of entering the land of Canaan, a setting filled
with hope. The immediate response in the two stories, however, is
open rebellion against God. A plague kills the people involved
(Num 14:37; Num 25:9). One or two faithful people separate themselves from the majority and act faithfully on behalf of God (Caleb
and Joshua--Num 14:6-10; Phinehas--Num 25:6-7). A special promise
is then given to the faithful few (the land--Num 14:24, 30; a perpetual priesthood--Num 25:10-13). In the midst of the dismal end
of the old generation, however, a new generation of hope arises and
is affirmed by the oracles of Balaam. The oracles herald the coming
of a star out of Jacob and a scepter out of Israel. They point
beyond themselves to a time to come, a time of prosperity, strength,
victory and hope. Balaam stands at the end of one generation and
points ahead to the coming of a new generation of God's people.

The person of Balaam, however, is enigmatic. He acts obediently
as an intermediary of God in Numbers 22-24. In Numbers 31:8, 16,
on the other hand, Balaam is killed for causing the apostasy at
Shittim in Numbers 25. The history of interpretation of the figure

of Balaam is a fascinating chronicle of later reflections on Balaam as saint or sinner, as the prophet par excellence or the personification of evil. One side of his character is typically emphasized to the exclusion of the other.

The present literary portrait of Balaam in Numbers, however, holds the two together in a way which is theologically significant. Balaam is a legitimate instrument of God by which God affirms and continues his promises to the people. He is a true servant of God. But Balaam's subsequent actions which incite rebellion and apostasy oppose God's will and purpose which leads to Balaam's death. Balaam is a paradigm for the ways of God in the world, whether Israel or any other people. Obedience to the will of God leads to life; disobedience leads to death.

The death of Balaam in Numbers 31 occurs in the midst of the victory over the Midianites by the new generation. Balaam's death is a reminder that while the promises made through Balaam remain valid (the victory over the Midianites), Balaam himself must die on account of his rebellion. Similarly, the promises made through the wilderness generation who experienced the Exodus and Sinai remain valid, but the generation itself must die in the wilderness because of their disobedience. The fate of Balaam in Numbers 31 is also a reminder to the second generation that it likewise lives under both the threat and promise of God. No less than Balaam or the wilderness generation, the new generation will live if they act faithfully, but they will come under judgment if they act rebelliously.

THEOLOGICAL IMPLICATIONS

Above all, the Balaam oracles in Numbers 22-24 affirm that God's promises to his people continue in the form of a climactic collection of blessings for Israel's future. The oracles of Balaam again take up the Pentateuchal promises of a multitude of descendants (Num 23:10) and of the conquest of the land (Num 24:6-8, 17-19). The oracles set the stage for the coming of a new generation filled with hope. The Balaam cycle in its present context proclaims the inability of anyone or anything to sway God from his desire to bless his people. Ironically, Balak the king of Moab, the one who desired to have Israel cursed, ends up being the one cursed (Num 24:17). God controls Balaam, telling him when to go to Balak and when not to go, telling what to speak and what not to speak. The apparent inconsistencies in God's commands to Balaam may be the result of the combination of two or more layers of tradition. But the overall literary effect is to heighten the sense of God's unquestionable mastery of the pagan seer. God's

capacity to execute his promises extends beyond the boundaries of
Israel.

There is also a negative side to the Balaam narrative. The
bright future proclaimed by Balaam heightens the tragic failure of
the old generation as it rebels once more for the last time (Numbers
25). The plague which punishes the rebels marks the final death of
a whole generation. God had done everything to prevent Israel's
enemies from cursing his people, but in the end the people brought
the curse upon themselves. The possibility of such failure continued
on into the new generation. The death of the once obedient messenger of God, Balaam, in Numbers 31 reminds the new generation that
God is a jealous God who will not allow disobedience to go unpunished.

The Balaam oracles impel the reader to look to a far off future
for the coming of one who will conquer Israel's enemies and reign
over them. This eschatological note is struck most forcefully in
Num 24:17:

> "I see him, but not now;
> I behold him but not nigh:
> a star shall come out of Jacob,
> and a scepter shall rise out of Israel."

This verse has been variously interpreted as a vaticinium ex eventu
(a prophecy after the fact) which was designed to legitimate retro-
actively the reign of David or Solomon or perhaps Josiah. Others
have understood the verse as an eschatological or messianic oracle
which pointed to the Messiah, whether Jesus of the New Testament or
another messianic figure within Judaism.[24]

Such interpretations, however, too often ignore the more
immediate context of the Balaam oracles within the structure of
Numbers. Hence, Martin Noth understands Balaam's oracles of
blessing to be "without any immediate historical consequences."[25]
Such a view fails to see the significance of the Balaam oracles in
the present form of the text as words of glorious promise spoken in
the midst of the death of one generation and addressed to another
future generation. Thus, the immediate consequences of the promise
oracles in Numbers are the emergence of a second generation of hope,
the new leaders who emerge in both the priestly office (Phinehas)
and the Mosaic office (Joshua), and the hope of a successful and
obedient entrance into the promised land which is anticipated but
not yet consummated at the end of the book.

This forward-looking perspective of the present literary form
of Numbers functions to invite the reader into the story. The
people of this new generation who themselves have not experienced
the Exodus or Sinai and who still look for the future fulfillment

of the promises made by God to his people may easily be identified
with the reader's own generation. In one way or another, the experience of standing between glorious promise and final fulfillment has
characterized every generation of God's people, Christian or Jewish.
Because the story is open-ended and because a member of the community
of faith in any period may identify his or her own time with the
new generation which arises in the second half of Numbers, the story
is designed to make a claim upon the reader. The reader is asked
to include himself or herself as a participant in the promise and
challenge of this new generation of God's people.

One other theological implication of the Balaam narrative is
its illustration of God's wider involvement in the world. M.
Margaliot argued that the story of Balaam showed that the office of
a prophet of God was not in principle limited to Israel but that it
became limited to Israel

> because of the moral calibre of those men on whom the LORD
> bestowed his spirit: these non-Israelite prophets, unworthy
> of their task, were disloyal to their God and betrayed their
> mission.[26]

This assessment depends, of course, on the judgment of death on
Balaam for his role in luring the Israelites into apostasy (Num 31:8,
16). Nevertheless, the oracles which Balaam speaks are treated
favorably, and nothing in the text suggests that these words of
blessing were not valid expressions of a legitimate intermediary of
God. The subsequent punishment of death which the non-Israelite
Balaam experienced for his later rebellious behavior is not different
in kind from the punishment of death which the wilderness generation
of the Israelites experienced for their continual rebellions. Even
the prophet Moses himself must experience a judgment of death and a
prohibition against entering the land for his lack of faith (Num
20:12).

Clearly, a contrast is not intended between the moral calibre
of Israelites and the moral calibre of non-Israelites. What is
shown here is the extension of God's sovereignty and activity among
peoples other than Israel. The Balaam story again recalls the
inclusive motif associated with the genealogical lists in Genesis
which are concerned not only with the narrowing of the line of
promise to Israel but also with the inclusion of other peoples of
the world in the purview of the on-going biblical narrative. The
Balaam cycle illustrates the fact that God may use even a pagan
seer to accomplish his purposes. But in any case, both Israel and
the nations live under the threat of death if they act in disobedience to the will of God.

Thus, we have seen that the role of the Balaam story within
its immediate literary context and within the larger structure of
Numbers has important consequences for the interpretation of the
story. This is true, despite the fact that the Balaam cycle is
not as directly and explicitly related to the framework of Numbers
as was the spy story in Numbers 13-14. Nevertheless, the uniqueness
and striking quality of the story, the narratives which precede and
follow it, and the strategic position which the story occupies
within the structure of Numbers all have dramatically shaped its
intended function and significance within the book of Numbers.

CHAPTER EIGHT

SELECTED LEGAL MATERIAL IN NUMBERS

Much of Numbers consists of material which is legal in nature,
particularly in the first ten and the last ten chapters of the book.
Any study of Numbers must give at least some attention to the
significance of this legal material. Commentators have often
observed that the ordinances and prescriptions which are scattered
throughout Numbers have no real function in the text or connection
to the surrounding narrative.[1] What then was the motivation for
later editors to have included these legal sections? Some suggest
that later redactors simply wanted their favorite laws to be
included among the authentic Sinai or Mosaic laws and so secondarily
inserted them in Numbers at the end of the Sinai section.[2] Others
simply see no motivation other than to preserve ancient traditon.
We hope to show, however, that at least some of the laws in Numbers
do have a more meaningful role to play in the book's overall structure and theme and that a literary connection with theological
consequences is often apparent between law and narrative.

OVERVIEW OF CRITICAL ISSUES

The concept of law in the Pentateuch raises a host of problems
and issues which we cannot begin to treat fully. The amount of
research on the Decalogue, the question of law and covenant, the
isolation of the Covenant Code of Exodus, the Holiness Code of
Leviticus and the Deuteronomic Code in Deuteronomy, the use of
ancient Near Eastern law as parallel and contrast to biblical law,
and the recent employment of sociological or anthropological methods
in studying ancient Israelite law is enormous.[3] The laws in Numbers,
however, have not been studied as carefully as other legal sections
in the Pentateuch. In part, this is due to the fact that the laws
in Numbers are not part of a larger unified law code or collection
in their present form. Rather, they appear intermittently among
the narrative sections of Numbers. Moreover, the history of the
development of many of the laws, apart from possible ancient Near
Eastern parallels, is every difficult to reconstruct so that little
can be known of their dates and origins. Concerning the date of

the inclusion of the laws in their present literary contexts, Martin
Noth is probably correct in his estimate that most of the laws have
been inserted at a relatively late stage in the growth of the
Pentateuchal literature. They are for the most part later than
any of the literary sources (including P), and they may even have
been inserted at a time later than the joining of the Tetrateuch
of Genesis-Numbers with the book of Deuteronomy.[4] This later date
for their inclusion does not, however, preclude the possibility
that the laws have origins which are much earlier in time.

We will examine two sections of legal material in Numbers in
our effort to determine what literary or theological role may have
been attributed to them by virtue of their present position and
context within the structure of Numbers. One section is Numbers 15
which is a compilation of laws concerning sacrifices, the legal
case of a man gathering wood on the sabbath, and the ordinance to
wear tassels (ṣiṣith) as a remembrance of the commandments. The
other section involves the legal case of the daughters of Zelophehad
and the inheritance of their father's property in Numbers 27:1-11
and Numbers 36:1-12.

Critical studies on Numbers 15 have focused in part on the
origins and development of sacrifices in the Old Testament in light
of other biblical and extra-biblical parallels.[5] The extension of
the application of these sacrificial laws to the "foreigner" (ger)
as well as the native Israelite in Num 15:16, 29 is seen by some as
a late development of the Persian period.[6]

The legal case of the man gathering wood in Num 15:32-36 is
problematic in that it is not obvious why Moses must seek divine
direction in adjudicating the case. The judgment of death by
stoning is the prescribed penalty for violating the sabbath (Exod
31:14; 35:2). What then is the problem? One scholar has argued
that gathering wood was not in itself an open profanation of the
sabbath, but it suggested the intention to kindle a fire which would
be a clear violation of the law in Exod 35:2:

> "Six days shall work be done, but on the seventh day you shall
> have a holy sabbath of solemn rest to the LORD; whoever does
> any work on it shall be put to death; you shall kindle no
> fire in all your habitations on the sabbath day."

Thus, the real issue was whether the intent to commit a sin bears
the same guilt as actually committing it. God's judgment decided
this issue in the affirmative; intent is equivalent to doing the
act itself.[7]

Gnana Robinson's thorough summary of various attempts to
interpret this text concludes by rejecting Weingreen's arguments

and proposing that in the original version of the case, the
wood-gatherer was

> punished not for an intention to kindle a normal domestic
> fire on the sabbath, but for indulging in an act of kindling
> a "strange fire," a fire to strange gods

in an act of apostasy.[8] A later redactor did not understand the
ancient cultic prohibition against gathering wood in order to kindle
a "strange fire" to foreign gods. Thus, the redactor subsumed the
case of the wood-gatherer under the general prohibition of work on
the sabbath by adding the phrase, "on the sabbath day," to the end
of Num 15:32. An editor then placed the case in its present literary context as a practical example to illustrate the commandment
which immediately preceded in Num 15:28-31:[9]

> "And the priest shall make atonement before the LORD for the
> person who commits an error, when he sins unwittingly, to
> make atonement for him; and he shall be forgiven. . . But
> a person who does anything with a high hand . . . reviles
> the LORD, and that person shall be cut off from among his
> people. Because he has despised the word of the LORD and
> has broken his commandment, that person shall be utterly cut
> off, his iniquity shall be upon him."

The case of the wood-gatherer on the sabbath which follows these
verses now functions as an illustration of a person who acts "with
a high hand" (15:30), that is, one who sins openly and defiantly.
Robinson's reconstruction of the original intention of the legal
case is suggestive but relies to some extent on conjecture. More
probable is Robinson's view of the intended function of the case
of the wood-gatherer in its present form and context as an illustration of a high handed and deliberate violation of God's commandment (Num 15:30). We should recall that the preceding context in
chapter 15 has to do with sins of an unintentional nature. Therefore, the present form of Numbers 15 involves a collection of
material brought together under the theme of the significance of
intentionality in determining the degree of guilt and punishment.
Sins which are done unwittingly (Num 15:30) bear less guilt and so
can be atoned through sacrifice. On the other hand, an overt and
intentional violation of the commandments which is done "with a
high hand" (Num 15:30) implies a high degree of guilt and the
severest penalty.

The last section of the chapter, Num 15:37-41, instructs the
people to wear tassels on their garments as reminders of God's
commandments. This section was included in the Jewish liturgy of
the post-exilic period as part of the Shema prayer. One study has
suggested a connection between the Hebrew word for "tassels" and
Babylonian and Sumerian cognates with a similar meaning.[10]

Finally, attention has been drawn to the section in Num 15:22-
23:

> "But if you err, and do not observe all these commandments
> which the LORD has spoken to Moses, all that the LORD has
> commanded you by Moses from the day the LORD gave command-
> ment and onward throughout your generations . . ."

Most commentators have taken the chronological formula, "from the
day the LORD gave commandment and onward throughout your generations,"
as a reference to the time when the people will err or not observe
the commandments. Gershon Brin suggests an alternative interpretation of the chronological formula as defining the time, not when the
people err, but when the commandments were actually given.[11] The
verses would then imply that laws were given not only in Moses'
generation but "onward throughout your generations." Brin concludes
that since the author of these verses actually lived much later than
Moses, he is unknowingly providing "evidence of his knowledge that
his own writings include laws that are not Mosaic," even though they
are attributed to Moses.[12] Brin's reading, however, misconstrues
the syntactical function of the chronological formula. The formula
does not modify the object of the verb, as Brin suggests. Rather,
it defines the duration of the main verbal action of the clause, and
the placement of the chronological formula at the end of the clause
is the usual procedure in this case.[13]

Critical studies on the legal case of the daughters of
Zelophehad in Num 27:1-11 and Num 36:1-12 have principally involved
two areas of inquiry: 1) the reconstruction of legal procedures
and laws of inheritance in ancient Israelite society, and 2) the
reconstruction of the relationship of Manasseh and its sub-clans
(of which the daughters of Zelophehad are a part) to traditons
regarding settlement in both the territory east of the Jordan and
in the territory west of the Jordan. First of all, scholars have
used the case of the daughters of Zelophehad as an illustration of
the actual legislative procedure in ancient Israel by which a new
law may be promulgated in a case of unprecedented circumstances.
J. Weingreen has noted that the test case of the daughters of
Zelophehad is one of only three examples of such a procedure in
the Pentateuch.[14] He argues that these examples are indicative of
a much larger corpus of case law in ancient Israel which grew
progressively to meet the demands of a developing society. Weingreen
also uses the daughters' formal declaration that their father had
no part in the insurrection of Korah (Numbers 16) as evidence of a
law which is not mentioned in the Pentateuch: the property of a
person convicted of treason was forfeited to the governing authority
with the result that the heirs of such a person received no

inheritance. Zelophehad's daughters assured Moses that their father was not guilty of treason and that thus his property should be passed on to his heirs. A parallel to this implied law may be found in the story of King Ahab and Naboth's vineyard in 1 Kgs 21:1-16.[15]

A study of the institution of levirate marriage in ancient Israel, whereby a brother or close kin of a deceased person is obligated to marry the wife of the deceased, uses the case of Zelophehad's daughters to show that the levirate marriage not only ensured the continuity of the family line but also ensured that the ancestral land remained in the family. Num 27:4 indicates that the "name" of the deceased continued as long as his descendants remained associated with his land.[16] Two scholars have also attempted to uncover the Israelite practice of the inheritance of land by the daughters of a deceased man on the basis of ancient Near Eastern parallels from Nuzi.[17]

The second area of inquiry concerns traditions of the settlement of one part of the tribe of Manasseh in east Jordan (Num 32:39-42) and another part in west Jordan (Josh 17:3-6). The daughters of Zelophehad, members of the tribe of Manasseh, are allotted land in west Jordan (Josh 17:3-6). A host of historical, genealogical and geographical questions are raised by these various traditions. Andre Lemaire has sought to untangle some of the geographical and genealogical issues which involve the relation of Manasseh, Machir and Gilead (cf. Num 27:1).[18] Another study by N. H. Snaith argues against those whom we have mentioned above who believe that the case of Zelophehad's daughters represents actual legal procedure in ancient Israel.[19] Numbers 27 and 36, according to Snaith, have no historical value since they are purely literary creations which were written to account for the fact that the tribe of Manasseh came to hold land to the west of the Jordan (Josh 17:1-6).

Finally, David Jobling's structuralist analysis of the story of the daughters of Zelophehad notes the dualism of the tribe of Manasseh which is situated in both east Jordan and west Jordan.[20] Jobling argues that by setting their legal dispute in east Jordan (Numbers 27) and by relating it to Numbers 32 by their relation to Machir who settles in east Jordan, the narrative of Zelophehad's daughters implies that they are east Jordanian women. Jobling then maintains that the "deep structure" of the narrative "codes" west Jordan (Canaan proper) as "male" and thus as politically superior and primary. The narrative "codes" east Jordan (Transjordan) as "female" and thus as dependent, peripheral and inferior. "This," writes Jobling, "is the semantic force most deeply charging the manifest texts."[21]

Jobling's literary observations are at times suggestive, but
it is the jump to the "deep structures" which he detects which is
most troublesome. The plain sense of the text suggests that Zelophehad's   daughters are not primarily identified as east Jordanian
women. Their legal case takes place in east Jordan simply because
all the Israelite tribes are located in east Jordan in Numbers 27
and 36. They are together awaiting entrance into the promised land.
And indeed, the inheritance which the daughters receive in Josh 17:3-
6 is located in west Jordan, the land of Canaan. The biblical
narrative as a whole, then, seems to portray the daughters of
Zelophehad as primarily west Jordanian women who, in the book of
Numbers, stand in solidarity with the other tribes of Israel as
they look forward to the entry into Canaan. Thus, Jobling's
characterization of the structural correspondence between male/female
and west Jordan/east Jordan seems to misconstrue the present form
of the narrative. One last analysis of the significance of the
daughters of Zelophehad which should be mentioned is Katherine
Sakenfeld's analysis of the narrative as a case which raises interpretive issues from the perspective of a feminist hermeneutic.[22]

THE FUNCTION OF LAW IN NUMBERS 15 IN ITS NARRATIVE CONTEXT

As the summary of critical work on the laws in Numbers 15 and
in Numbers 27 and 36 demonstrates, very little work has been done
on the function of these legal sections within their narrative
framework. These laws have been embedded in the present narrative
by later redactors, whether by later editors of the Priestly tradition or post-Priestly redactors who worked after the joining of
Deuteronomy to the Tetrateuch, as Noth has suggested.[23] We intend
in this section to uncover the literary effect and theological
purpose which the work of these latest redactors accomplished. We
hope to illustrate the role of these legal sections within the definitive structure of the two census lists which divide Numbers into
two generations, a structure which had been established by earlier
redactors of the Priestly tradition. We will first examine the
function of Numbers 15 in its narrative context.

Numbers 15 is a conglomeration of legal material which has been
inserted between two narratives, the spy story in Numbers 13-14 and
the story of the rebellion of Korah, Dathan and Abiram in Numbers
16. Numbers 15 contains a series of laws concerning sacrifices and
offerings which are to be presented to the LORD when the people
inhabit the promised 'land (15:1-21). These are followed by laws
for atonement sacrifices for unintentional sins by the community
(15:22-26) and by an individual (15:27-32). The next section in

chapter 15 relates the legal case of a man gathering wood on the
sabbath (15:32-36). Because the degree of guilt and the required
punishment of the man is unclear, a divine judgment is sought. As
we saw above, the case in its present context provides an illustration of intentionally sinning with a "high hand" (Num 15:30) and
the severity of punishment which such an act entails. The last
section of chapter 15 is the LORD's command to the people to wear
tassels on the corners of their garments as a reminder to do the
commandments throughout their generations (15:37-40). The chapter
ends with God's reaffirmation that he remains the God of Israel,
the same God "who brought you out of the land of Egypt" (15:41).

Many scholars have failed to see any connection between the
laws in Numbers 15 and the surrounding narrative. For example,
Noth maintains that

> it is not quite clear why this rather unsystematically
> arranged collection of various cultic-ritual ordinances
> should have found a place at this particular point in the
> Pentateuchal narrative . . . Moreover, the individual parts
> of this collection have no connection with each other.[24]

In our opinion, Noth is wrong. The laws in Numbers 15 do have a
meaningful connection with the spy story which precedes it and the
story of Korah's rebellion which follows it. Furthermore, it seems
probable that this connection was the product of a redactional
intentionality which accompanied the inclusion of these laws at
this point in the narrative in Numbers.

We will first examine the relationship between the laws in
Numbers 15 and the preceding narrative context of the spy story in
Numbers 13-14. Gordon Wenham has drawn attention to the numerous
verbal allusions to the spy story which may be found in Numbers 15:
"the land" (15:2, 18; occurs over 30 times in Numbers 13-14),
"Egypt" (15:41; cf. Num 14:3-4, 19, 22), "congregation" (15:24-25;
occurs 10 times in Numbers 13-14), "be forgiven" (15:25-26, 28; cf.
Num 14:19-20), "look" (15:39; cf. Num 13:18, 33); "eyes" (15:39;
cf. Num 13:33), and "spy out/follow after" (Hebrew tur, 15:39;
occurs 7 times in Numbers 13-14).[25] The connection between Numbers
15 and the spy story, however, goes beyond merely verbal allusions
in that it also takes up and enhances the central themes of the spy
story. The rebellion and failure of the old generation who desired
to return to Egypt (Num 14:3-4) had put in question the whole venture
of God's bringing the people into the promised land. Indeed, God
had threatened to forsake the people entirely. Only after the
pleading of Moses did God decide that the old generation would die
but that a new generation would enter the land. The laws in Numbers
15 are to apply "when you come into the land you are to inhabit,

which I give you" (Num 15:2, 18). These laws presuppose the entry into the land by the new generation and therefore function in the narrative context as promises to the new generation that they will indeed live in the land of Canaan.

This function of Numbers 15 was understood by the medieval Jewish commentaries of Ibn Ezra and Nachmonides:

> The incident of the spies is immediately followed by the section containing laws which apply only to the Promised Land. This was intended to give confidence and assurance of the ultimate possession of the land to the next genera-tion, who might have been skeptical about the fulfillment of a forty-year-old promise.[26]

That this section of laws for life in Canaan is intended to function as promise for the new generation is underscored by the conclusion of Numbers 15:

> "I am the LORD your God, who brought you out of the land of Egypt, to be your God: I am the LORD your God" (Num 15:41).

This fundamental assertion of God's relationship to his people which is often repeated in the Pentateuch had experienced a profound challenge in the spy story, both in the people's desire to return to Egypt (Num 14:3-4) and by God's own initial plan to disinherit the people entirely (Num 14:11-12). The reaffirmation of God's covenan-tal relation to his people and his stance before them as their deliverer confirms the promise made to the new generation, despite the rebellion and death of the old generation in Numbers 13-14. Moreover, the juxtaposition of Numbers 15 and the conclusion to the spy story in which the people set out on their own to capture the land and are defeated (Num 14:39-45) serves to emphasize the fact that it is God and not the people who will bring Israel into the land. This is highlighted several times in Numbers 15: "The land to which I bring you" (15:2, 18); "I am the LORD your God who brought you out of Egypt" (15:41).

The importance of the theme of concern for the new generation which is central to the spy story is also demonstrated in other ways by the laws in Numbers 15. The phrase, "throughout your genera-tions," recurs five times in this one chapter alone (15:14, 15, 21, 23, 38). The redactors' intent to project their material beyond their own time to succeeding generations is clear and explicit. This is a message for all generations to come, not only for their own historical moment. The case of the wood-gatherer on the sabbath is an illustration of the application of a law to a new situation which requires a divine judgment. It functions as a paradigm and warrant for succeeding generations to interpret inherited tradition in light of new concerns. The law concerning the wearing of tassels

on the garments as a reminder of the commandments is specifically
directed to future generations to remind them of the covenant with
their God (Num 15:38). Thus, the themes of the continuing promise
to the new generation despite the death of the old, the emphasis
on God as subject of the people's deliverance, and the concern for
the new generation to come are themes which are uppermost in the
spy story and which are further enriched by the present shape of
the legal material in Numbers 15. Material which is cast in the
genre of legal discourse functions theologically here as promise
to the new generation which it addresses.

The laws in Numbers 15 also have a role to play in the interpretation of the narrative which follows, namely, the rebellion of
Korah, Dathan and Abiram in Numbers 16. The incident which occasions
the revolt by Korah and his company is not immediately evident
within the story itself. The charges against Moses concern his
right to be the sole authoritative mediator of God's words and laws
to the people (Num 16:3, 13, 28-29). The Targum Jonathan surmises
that it was Moses' regulation on wearing tassels on the people's
garments (Num 15:37-40) which was the specific cause of the revolt;
in this Moses had "gone too far" (Num 16:3).[27] In fact, the literary juxtaposition of Numbers 15 and the Korah rebellion implies
something close to the Targum's interpretation. Perhaps the ordinance of the tassels was not itself the specific cause, but the
LORD's speaking only to Moses which is noted throughout Numbers 15
(15:1, 17, 22, 23, 35, 36, 37) appears to provide the necessary
background for the otherwise unprovoked and unexplained rebellion
by Korah. In other words, while the spy story's relation to Numbers
15 suggested that these laws functioned as promise to a new generation, the story of the rebellion of Korah and his company suggests
that these same words were heard as a burden and a threat by others.
One kind of hearing brings life in the emergence of a new generation; the other hearing brings death to an old generation who will
not allow God to choose his own mediator or means of guiding the
people into the land and who instead seek to exalt themselves.

The content and structure of the laws in Numbers 15 also function to dramatize the grave nature of Korah's revolt which is a
deliberate and intentional rebellion against God's mediator. The
laws in Numbers 15 form a brief treatise on the role of intentionality in determining guilt. The chapter begins with laws on sacrifices
in the land and then moves to laws of sacrifices for unintentional
sins committed by the community and the individual. Unintentional
sins may be atoned through sacrifice which suggests that lesser
guilt is assigned to such sins as compared to sins which are

intentionally done. The case of the wood-gatherer on the sabbath
then follows and confirms the important role of intention: one
who sins intentionally and with a "high hand" in open and prideful
defiance must be "cut off from among his people" (Num 15:30, 32-36).
Finally, the law of the tassels as reminders of the commandments
encourage intentionality and devotion in obeying the commandments
and thus help to avoid unintentional transgressions of the law.
The present shape of the story of Korah's rebellion clearly emphasizes the blatant and intentional nature of the revolt. The guilt
of the rebels is thus not open to doubt and cannot be atoned; their
actions demand the judgment of death.

THE FUNCTION OF NUMBERS 27 AND 36 IN THEIR NARRATIVE CONTEXT

The legal case of the daughters of Zelophehad in chapters 27
and 36 is presented as an unprecedented set of circumstances surrounding the death of a man without male heirs. The daughters of the
deceased man request that they be designated the heirs. This
request raises a legal issue: can daughters inherit property when
there are no sons? The question is referred to God whose judgment
is that the daughters may indeed inherit the property in order to
ensure the continuance of the family line and the land associated
with it (Num 27:1-11). Another related issue arises in chapter 36:
may the daughters of Zelophehad marry outside their own tribe, or
must they remain within the confines of their own tribal group?
Again, a divine decision is sought and rendered. The daughters of
Zelophehad must marry within their own tribe in order to ensure
that the ancestral land remains within the tribe which originally
inherited the land.

Our review of critical studies on the daughters of Zelophehad
revealed a focus on historical reconstructions of legal procedure
or tribal and geographical relationships in ancient Israel. Unlike
Numbers 15, however, most scholars also acknowledge some literary
connection between the case of Zelophehad's daughters in Numbers 27
and the preceding narrative context of the census in Numbers 26.
G. B. Gray, for example, believes that Numbers 27 was placed after
the census in Numbers 26 because they are both related to the
question of the inheritance of the land. The case in Numbers 27
obviously concerns land inheritance. The census in chapter 26 is
taken to determine the size of each tribe and thus determine the
proportion of the land which the tribe will inherit (Num 26:52-56).[28]
But this is not the only literary link between the census list and
the case of Zelophehad's daughters. The genealogy of the tribe of
Manasseh in 26:29-33 which extends further than any other genealogy

in the census list gives specific mention to Zelophehad and his
five daughters. This genealogical link seems specifically designed
by a redactor to relate the two chapters. Furthermore, the case of
Zelophehad's daughters also depends on the report of the death of
all the members of the old generation in 26:64-65 which, by implication, includes the death of Zelophehad.[29] The accounts of the
daughters of Zelophehad in Numbers 27 and 36 play an additional
literary role in the larger structure of Numbers. They form an
inclusio for the events and organization of the new generation
whose emergence is marked by the second census list in chapter 26.
They frame the material associated with the new generation and
define the theological perspective which is assigned to the new
generation of God's people. It is this theological function within
the structure of Numbers which scholars have generally not considered
in their interpretation of Numbers 27 and 36.

The theological function of the account of the daughters of
Zelophehad within the larger context of Numbers falls into three
areas: a reaffirmation of the promise, the concern for inclusiveness, and the flexibility of the tradition and the need for reinterpretation. Our analysis of the laws in Numbers 15 attempted to
show how they functioned as a note of promise after the debacle of
the spy story. The overriding concern in Numbers 27 and 36 on
questions of the inheritance of the land of Canaan has a similar
function. The new generation has emerged and now stands on the
brink of entering the promised land. Its concern and perspective
are dominated by the prospect of God's fulfillment of long awaited
promises. It is this concern which is depicted in the two episodes
of the daughters of Zelophehad which act as keynotes for the new
generation. This interpretation is also supported by the designation of the purpose of the second census list as a guide for
allocating the land (Num 26:52-56) which invites the reader to view
this new generation with a more hopeful eye. The census of the
first generation in Numbers 1 made no explicit mention of the
promised land. In the second census in Numbers 26, entrance into
the land is almost taken as an assured and accomplished fact.
Moreover, the subject of most of the material between the two
accounts involving Zelophehad's daughters (Numbers 28-35) either
deals directly with the inheritance of the land (boundaries of the
land, supervision of its allocation) or presupposes a stable life
in the land (cultic and sacrificial regulations). Thus, the
purpose of the preceding census list, the concern of the material
in Numbers 28-35, and the issues involved in the case of Zelophehad's
daughters all suggest a reaffirmation of the promise of the land

to a new generation of hope who look for its fulfillment. Scholars
who interpret the case of Zelophehad's daughters either as actual
legal procedure in ancient Israel after its settlement in the land
(Weingreen) or as a literary device by which to identify the
daughters with east Jordan (Jobling) fail to discern the present
viewpoint of the material which is located outside the land of
Canaan but directed toward a future entrance into the promised land.

A second theological function of Numbers 27 and 36 is the
concern to maintain the inclusiveness of the promised inheritance
to all tribes. The reason given for allowing the daughters to
inherit their father's land in Numbers 27 is to ensure that each
tribe retain its full inheritance. No one tribe is to benefit from
circumstances which threaten to deprive another tribe of its land.
The same reason is given in Numbers 36. The daughters may marry
only within their own tribe to ensure that the tribe's land does
not transfer to another tribal group. As we have seen in previous
sections of our study, this concern to include all the tribes in the
promises of God to Israel is also evident in the construction of
the census lists and the other lists of the leaders of the twelve
tribes (supervisors of the census, spy story, supervisors of the
division of the land of Canaan).

The third theological function of the legal material in chapters
27 and 36 is the affirmation of the flexibility of the tradition
and the warrant for reinterpreting the past for the sake of the new.
The very nature of the legal question in Numbers 27 and 36 suggests
that no precedent exists in past traditions by which to adjudicate
the issue presented. Herein lies an implicit acknowledgment that
all the issues which may conceivably arise in the life of the new
generation may not find a direct answer in the traditions given at
Sinai. Past traditions require reinterpretations. This theme was
already noted in the case of the wood-gatherer in Numbers 15, but
here the theme is much stronger. Again, much of the material which
lies between chapters 27 and 36 may be subsumed under the theme of
the remembrance and reinterpretation of the past for the sake of
the new generation. Perhaps the most striking example is in Numbers
32 in which the spy story is recalled as a warning to the second
generation of what may again occur. Indeed, much of the legal
material throughout the book of Numbers consists of what may be
called "case law" which by its very nature suggests a realistic and
dynamic stance in the application of God's will for his people.[30]

At the beginning of the book of Numbers, an important shift
occurs from the immovable setting of Mount Sinai which is the locus
of God's definitive revelation of his will. The locus of God's

revelation in Numbers is now the portable tent of meeting. The
people are no longer stationary but on the move, and God and his
law moves with them. The tent of meeting thus functions in some
ways as a symbol of the flexibility and openness of God's revelation.
Thus, the book of Numbers as a whole and the case of the daughters
of Zelophehad in particular provide a literary and theological
warrant for future generations to continue to address their concerns
to the tradition which they have received. God's revelation to
his people does not consist of a sterile and entrenched legalism
but of a robust and living tradition which leans toward the future
in hope and anticipation. It is a tradition which respects the
past but lives in the present and looks toward the future.

CHAPTER NINE

THE BOOK OF NUMBERS, THE PENTATEUCH AND BEYOND

THE THEOLOGY OF THE BOOK OF NUMBERS AS A WHOLE

Chapter Two of our study demonstrated the lack of agreement on the structure of the book of Numbers. The foundation upon which commentators have built their proposals for the framework of Numbers were shown to be inadequate. Chronological indicators, geographical notations of Israel's movement from place to place, tradition-historical "themes," and the various documentary sources have all been used as the basis for proposed outlines of the book. We have seen, however, that these proposals fail to discern the definitive editorial structure of the book which is based on the two census lists of Numbers 1 and 26. The three preceding chapters of this study attempted to show the ways in which this definitive structure affected and enriched the theological interpretation of individual passages in Numbers.

The manner in which one understands the editorial structure of the book not only affects how one interprets specific passages but also how one interprets the theology of the entire book. Thus, the detection of the proper structure is crucial to the task of properly interpreting the purpose of the book. Our survey of commentaries in Chapter One revealed that descriptions of the theology of Numbers as a whole tended to be brief, general and impressionistic. This state of affairs reflects the disarray among commentators in formulating a definitive structure for the book. The most thorough presentations of the book's theology were given by J. de Vaulx and G. Bernini.[1] De Vaulx's description of the book's theology, however, depends in large part on his description of the book's structure which he based on the geographical notices of Israel's movement from one place to another. This geographical itinerary, according to de Vaulx, was also a spiritual itinerary of the gradual development and growth of Israel's faith:

> The time passed in the desert, therefore, has no other goal than to provoke the moral conversion and the spiritual progress necessary for the people to attain their destiny.[2]

Our analysis of the census lists in Numbers 1 and 26 as the primary structure of the book, however, does not portray a gradual

179

progress and improvement in Israel's spiritual life. Rather,
Numbers presents a radical and decisive distinction between the old
rebellious generation of death and the new generation of hope. God
condemns the old to death in the desert but gives birth to a new
generation whom he leads again to the doorstep of the promised land.
The focus is not on a gradual spiritual improvement on the part of
the people. Rather, the focus is on the activity of God who, though
intolerant of rebellion, remains faithful to his promise. The old
prideful generation which begins the book of Numbers never repents
but continues to rebel up to the very last moment of its life
(Numbers 25). God condemns this generation to death in the wilderness. The new generation of hope consists of the "little ones" who
are born in the desert with no claim to distinction other than that
God has chosen them to be heirs of his promise. God proclaims to
the old generation that

> your little one, who you said would become a prey, I will
> bring in, and they shall know the land which you have
> despised. But as for you, your dead bodies shall fall in
> this wilderness (Num 14:31-32).

But even this new generation of hope remains under the threat that
it too may fall into rebellion and experience the same fate as the
condemned generation of the past (Num 32:14-15). The book of
Numbers, then, is not so much an account of the progress of a people
on a gradual pilgrimage as the story of God's uncompromising justice
and mercy which condemns prideful rebellion but gives life and hope
to "little ones" who trust in God and his faithfulness to his
promises.

It is clear that the image which one has of the structure of
the book in large part determines the book's theological interpretation. De Vaulx's image of the primary structure of Numbers as a
series of geographical movements leads him to view the book as a
spiritual pilgrimage of gradual progress. Such a view, however,
fails to take into account the overriding structure based on the
census lists which divide the book into two generations: a generation of despair and death and a generation of hope and life. The
new generation at the end of Numbers has not progressed any further
than the old generation. It faces the same challenge of living as
God's holy people. It stands under the same promises and threats
as the generation past. The old generation had reached the edge
of the promised land and had gone no further (the spy story--Numbers
13-14). At the end of Numbers, the new generation has returned to
the edge of the promised land but it too has gone no further (Num
36:13). Its ultimate destiny remains in question.

Bernini has been the only modern commentator which we have
surveyed who made a major division with the second census list in
Numbers 26. He labeled the section in Numbers 26-36 as "the community of the new generation."[3] Bernini's view of the structure of
the book, however, was based on the notion of tradition-historical
"themes" or blocks of tradition. One block or theme concerned
traditions related to Sinai (Num 1:1-10:10), another concerned
traditions related to the march in the desert (Num 10:11-25:18),
and a third was related to ordinances in the plain of Moab (Num
25:19-36:13). This division of the book into three separate parts
did not allow Bernini to perceive that the two census lists in
Numbers 1 and 26 actually divided the book into two halves, the
death of the old generation and the birth of a new generation. The
result is that Bernini's theological exposition of the book tends
to be divided into three separate and unrelated parts which correspond to the three different blocks of tradition. In this way,
Bernini only provides interpretations of the three separate parts
of the book rather than a comprehensive interpretation of the whole
book of Numbers. Once again, the perceived structure of the book
significantly affects its theological interpretation.

Much has already been said in the preceding chapters concerning
our proposal for the structure of Numbers and its theological interpretation. Therefore, our view of the theology of Numbers as a
whole will come as no surprise and needs only to be summarized at
this point. The structure of Numbers is based on the two census
lists in Numbers 1 and 26 which divide the book into two generations,
a generation of rebellion and death and a generation of hope and
life. The first half of Numbers (chapters 1-25) begins with the
generation of God's people who had been eyewitnesses to God's
deliverance in the exodus out of Egypt and to God's revelation of
his will at Mount Sinai. In preparation for the march from Sinai
to the promised land, the Israelites are counted in a census and
organized into a holy camp of God's people (Num 1:1-10:10). The
tent of meeting stands in the middle of the camp as the locus of
God's presence in the midst of his people. The priests and Levites
surround the tent of meeting while the other twelve tribes of Israel
in turn surround the priests and Levites in concentric circles of
holiness and purity. Various ordinances are given by God to aid
the organization and ensure the holiness of the camp. The march is
finally inaugurated as the people begin to move toward the promised
land (Num 10:11-36). Everything up to this point in the narrative
is cast in a positive light. The laws which are given are gifts of
God by which the life of the people is organized and which enable

the march toward the promised land to proceed.
This positive picture is abruptly shattered by a series of
rebellions against God, first by the people and then even by the
leaders of the people (Numbers 11-12). A climactic rebellion occurs
as the people are on the verge of entering Canaan in the spy story
in Numbers 13-14.[4] The people fear death at the hands of the
Canaanites more than they trust God's promise to give them a full
and prosperous life in the promised land. Their fear of death
ironically leads to the fate which they bring upon themselves:
death in the wilderness. In spite of this ultimate rebellion, the
promise continues as God binds himself to a new generation. The
old generation will die, but the new generation will now carry the
promise forward into the future. The promise is confirmed by the
laws in the next chapter (Numbers 15) which will apply only when
the people enter the promised land. Further rebellions by the old
generation illustrate its total incapacity for repentance (Numbers
16-19). Even Moses and Aaron rebel and are condemned to die outside
the promised land (Numbers 20).

Signs of hope do continue to appear from time to time. God
gives victories to the Israelites as they encounter the foreign
kings of Arad, Sihon and Og (Num 21:1-3, 10-35). Still the people
rebel (Num 21:4-9). The oracles of Balaam follow with a climactic
note of blessing and hope which is directed to a distant time in
the future (Numbers 22-24). God will not allow a foreign king or
pagan seer to curse his people. But still the old generation rebels
and, in effect, curses itself and thereby brings final death upon
its members (Numbers 25). The sin of the old generation is so
entrenched that it cannot escape its destiny. The only remedy for
its incessant and undeterred rebellion against God is death in the
wilderness.

However, all is not lost. A new generation is born and again
counted and organized, just as the old generation had been counted
and organized (Numbers 26). This new generation has again been
brought to the threshold of Canaan as it stands on the plains of
Moab. The concerns of the daughters of Zelophehad for their inheritance in the promised land forms a positive and hopeful inclusio
for the matters pertaining to the second generation (Num 27:1-11
and 36:1-13). Joshua is commissioned by Moses to take his place as
leader of the people when they enter the land (Num 27:12-23).
Further ordinances for life in the promised land are given (Numbers
28-30). Moses leads a successful war of vengeance on the Midianites
for leading the last generation into apostasy (Numbers 31). This
was done in obedience to God's command given at the end of the last

generation (Num 25:16-18).

The new generation is then called to be aware of its own potential for rebellion and disobedience. God's promises are not to be taken lightly or for granted. The thoroughly hopeful tone of the new generation is threatened by the request by Reuben and Gad to settle in Transjordan rather than Canaan. Moses interprets the request as a potential rebellion and applies the lesson of the spy story as a word of warning. In the end, the potential crisis is averted and a compromise is reached (Numbers 32). The journey of the first generation from Egypt to the border of the promised land is recapitulated for the new generation, concluding with words of encouragement and warning in connection with the future settlement in Canaan (Numbers 33). The boundaries and division of the land of Canaan follow along with laws which establish Levitical cities and cities of refuge by which to maintain the holiness and purity of the land (Numbers 34-35). The book ends with a return to the case of the daughters of Zelophehad and the question of the future inheritance of the promised land (Numbers 36). The chapters associated with the second generation project a mood of hope and expectation. One senses that the fulfillment of the promises of the past are near at hand. But even this new generation must guard against the possibility that it, like the generation preceding, may fall into rebellion and also die in the wilderness (Num 32:15). Indeed, even when the people at last settle in the land, they are warned that the full promise may still elude them (Num 33:55-56). The new generation is reminded that it must remain constantly and diligently self-critical. The promise of the land, however, remains the last word (Numbers 34-36).

It is our contention that the new generation in the second half of Numbers functions as a paradigm for every succeeding generation of God's people. The basic theme of Numbers is the succession of generations and the means by which a new generation appropriates the tradition of the past for its own time. The old generation whose members were eyewitnesses to the formative events of the Exodus and Sinai are dead and gone. God calls a new generation of his people into being and actualizes for them the warnings and promises of the past.

The concern of the book of Numbers is not simply to narrate the history of the death of the generation of the Exodus and Sinai and the birth of the generation immediately following it. The concern of the book is to establish a model or paradigm which will invite every generation to put itself in the place of the new generation with which Numbers and the whole Pentateuch concludes.

This concern to shape the story of Numbers in such a way that it becomes the reader's own story is demonstrated and accomplished in a number of ways. The two census lists in chapters 1 and 26 divide the book into two different generations and thereby define the basic framework of the book as the movement from one generation to another. The reapplication of the past to a new generation is most clearly evident in the narrative of Numbers 32 in which Moses recalls the spy story and its consequences as a warning to the new generation. Many laws in Numbers are expressly given as perpetual statutes "throughout your generations." The flexibility and adaptability of God's laws as they encounter new questions and circumstances (Numbers 9, 15, 27, 36) provides a model for the ongoing interpretation of the traditions of the past for the sake of the present. The movable tent of meeting which reappears at the beginning of Numbers after the people leave the immovable mountain of Sinai (Num 1:1; cf. Lev. 27:34) illustrates the need for both a fixed tradition (Mount Sinai) and a means by which to actualize the tradition as the people march through time (the mobile tent of meeting). The God of Israel is not a dead idol but a living God who moves with and wrestles with his people as they walk toward the promised land.

The concern with issues of continuity and discontinuity between generations is also apparent. The entire rebellious generation of the wilderness must die with two exceptions, Caleb and Joshua. They remain to help and guide the new generation into the land. Moses himself remains for a time with the new generation and provides the necessary warrant for reinterpreting past traditions and applying them to the new people of God. In the end, however, Moses must die outside the land as his generation had done (Num 20: 12; Deut 34:4-6). The theme of generational continuity and discontinuity is also portrayed in the orderly succession of leadership offices. The Mosaic office is passed on to Joshua and the priestly office from Aaron to Eleazar and to Phinehas.

The Balaam oracles provide a climactic message of God's blessing which is oriented to a distant future (Num 24:17). This strikingly eschatological note thrusts the horizon of the book far beyond the time of Moses to the time of future generations. That future remains unresolved and open-ended for the new generation at the end of Numbers and the Pentateuch. The remainder of the story needs to be written anew for each succeeding generation. Promises remain unfulfilled and so invite the reader to take them up as promises directed to the reader in his or her own time and circumstance.

Such an interpretation of the intention of the writers and editors of the book of Numbers in some ways goes against the opinion of many other critical scholars. We have seen that the definitive structure of Numbers was most probably established by the early layer of the Priestly tradition. Later Priestly and perhaps even post-Priestly editors enhanced and enriched this basic structure and theme of the book through a number of redactions and additions. Commentators typically assign this Priestly tradition to the time of the exile or the post-exilic period in Israel's history, a position we would support as probable. These same commentators, however, often understand the Priestly portion of the book of Numbers as intended to address specifically and only the historical time of Israel's exile in Babylon, a time of crisis and despair.[5] There is no doubt that Israel's exile to Babylon and the theological issues connected with it made a profound impact on the biblical writers and redactors of that time and the shape of the literature which they produced. We must remember, however, that the members of the early Priestly tradition who definitively shaped the book of Numbers already had before them a long history of tradition which had served to nourish the faith of numerous generations. The growth of the book reflects this struggle of previous generations as they sought to appropriate past traditions for their time and for generations to come.

Furthermore, the book of Numbers contains many later additions and redactions which occurred after the definitive Priestly structure of the book had been completed. Thus, the book itself provides evidence that it continued to be read and edited far into the post-exilic period. The book was understood not only as directed to the specific exilic period of the sixth century B.C. or even only one generation after the exile. In other words, the book was understood as a word for more than one generation or one historical moment. The experience of the generation of the exile did not exhaust the meaning of the book. The book's editors expressly designed the book, as we have indicated, in such a way that it continued to function as model and paradigm for generation after generation.

Now it cannot be denied that the experience of the exile with the people of God awaiting a return to the land and the fulfillment of God's promises in many ways corresponds to the portrait of the new generation in Numbers as it stands on the edge of the promised land. But that same experience of living between promise and fulfillment has characterized every generation of God's people.[6] Heaven has never come to earth. The life of God's people in the world has never ended with them living happily ever after. The

promises of God have always lain ahead of his people, urging them
ever forward into the future. The stance of the new generation on
the verge of entering the long-awaited land of promise has continued
to be the definitive portrait of the community of God's people
throughout its history.

THE THEME OF NUMBERS AND THE PENTATEUCH

Our brief discussion of the relation of the structure and
theme of Numbers to the Pentateuch and the wider context of the
Old Testament will be by no means exhaustive. We will attempt only
to summarize a few of the implications of our study in light of the
larger biblical setting of the book of Numbers. In Chapter Five,
we saw that the toledot formulae and the genealogies of Genesis
along with the toledot formula and census lists in Numbers provided
an overarching editorial framework for all of Genesis through
Numbers. This overarching framework relates the succession of the
death of one generation and the birth of a new generation of God's
people. In every generation, the promise of innumerable descendants
and the inheritance of the land of Canaan is given. God's promise
of land and descendants is passed from Abraham (Gen 12:1-3; 15:5,
18-21; 17:4-8) to Isaac (Gen 17:19-21; 25:11) and Jacob (Gen 28:3-4,
13-15; 35:9-12) and Joseph (Gen 48:3). The promise is further
extended to the toledot of Jacob, that is, the twelve tribes of
Israel (Exod 1:7; 6:2-9; 23:23-33; 34:11).

Every generation experiences some obstacle which threatens the
existence of the people and so puts the continuance of the promise
in question. Examples include the childlessness of Abraham and
Sarah (Genesis 15-16), the near-sacrifice of Isaac (Genesis 22),
Jacob's wrestling with the angel (Genesis 32), the sale of Joseph
into slavery and his imprisonment in Egypt (Genesis 37-40), the
bondage of Israel in Egypt and Pharaoh's command to kill all the
sons of the Hebrews (Exodus 1), the harsh conditions of the wilderness wandering (Exodus 16-17), the murmurings of the people in the
wilderness including the incident of the golden calf (Exodus 32),
the climactic rebellion of the spy story (Numbers 13-14), and the
attempt of Balak to curse Israel through Balaam (Numbers 22-24).
For the new generation in the second half of Numbers, the potential
crisis of Reuben and Gad's request for territory in the Transjordan
instead of Canaan again threatens the fulfillment of the promise
(Numbers 32).

In the end, however, God rescues every generation from the
threat of oblivion and so ensures the continuation of his promises.
The promise of innumerable descendants is partially fulfilled in

each generation. The genealogies, birth stories and census lists record the arrival of new generations of descendants whose multitude grows increasingly larger from Abraham and Sarah to the seventy members of the family of Jacob (Gen 46:27 ; Exod 1:5) to the 600,000 plus people who are twenty years and older and are counted in the censuses (Exod 38:26; Num 1:46; Num 26:51). Balaam's oracles also proclaim the fulfillment of the promise of descendants in Num 23:10: "Who can number the dust of Jacob, or number the fourth part of Israel?"

The promise of the land is likewise proleptically fulfilled for each generation. The fulfillment of the land's possession begins with Abraham's purchase of the plot of land near Hebron in Canaan as a burial site for Sarah (Gen 23:1-20) and the subsequent burial of each of the patriarchs there (Abraham--Gen 25:7-10; Isaac-- Gen 35:27-29; Jacob--Gen 50:12-13; Joseph--Gen 50:24-26; Exod 13:19; cf. Josh 34:22). Representatives of all twelve tribes of Israel enter the land of Canaan as spies after the exodus out of Egypt. They search out the land from north to south and center on the area near Hebron (Num 13:22). This is the location of the patriarchs' burial site. It is also the place where Abraham had received the promise of the land and from which he himself had "spied out" the length and breadth of the land.[7] The LORD said to Abraham,

> "Lift up your eyes, and look from the place you are, north-
> ward and southward and eastward and westward; for all the
> land which you see I will give to you and to your descendants
> forever. I will make your descendants as the dust of the
> earth, so that if one can count the dust of the earth, your
> descendants also can be counted. Arise, walk through the
> length and breadth of the land, for I will give it to you."
> So Abram moved his tent and came and dwelt by the oaks of
> Mamre, which are at Hebron; and there he built an altar to
> the LORD (Gen 13:14-18).

In the book of Numbers, the Israelite spies return to the same place of promise. However, the people refuse to enter the land and so bring a judgment of death upon themselves (Numbers 13-14). After forty years of wandering, God raises up a new generation after them (Numbers 26). The members of this new generation become the carriers of the promise as they are again brought to the border of the land of Canaan. The promise of the land, reiterated by numerous laws pertaining exclusively to life in the land, is partially fulfilled as Gad, Reuben and the half-tribe of Manasseh receive an inheritance in the already conquered territory of the Transjordan. The book of Numbers as well as the whole of Genesis-Numbers ends with this new generation of hope whose final destiny remains undecided. Thus, the unifying theme of Genesis-Numbers may be seen as the faithful- ness of God in extending the promise of land and descendants to his

people from generation to generation. The overarching editorial
structure of these books is established by the toledot formulae,
genealogies and census lists which mark the succession of generations, each of which experience a partial accomplishment of what
God has promised. This definitive structure of the Tetrateuch, as
we saw in Chapter Five of our study, was probably formed by one or
more layers of the Priestly tradition.

The addition of the book of Deuteronomy as the final member
of the Pentateuch, whether by a Priestly or a Deuteronomic or simply
an unknown editor, poses a potential problem. Deuteronomy comes
from a tradition which is different from the Priestly tradition of
the Tetrateuch. Thus, does the addition of the book of Deuteronomy
seriously disrupt the definitive generational structure and theme
of the Priestly Tetrateuch? We would argue that it does not. In
fact, the addition of Deuteronomy serves to enhance the basic
generational framework of the preceding books. First of all,
Deuteronomy retains the same setting as Numbers of a new generation
on the edge of the promised land. The first prominent theme in
Deuteronomy 1 and throughout the book is the death of the old
rebellious generation and the birth of the new generation in connection with the spy story, a theme which we have seen to be central
to the book of Numbers. The fate of this generation remains undecided at the conclusion of Deuteronomy as it did at the end of
Numbers. Deuteronomy stands as Moses' last words to this new
generation. Moses' death at the end of Deuteronomy marks the death
of the last of the eyewitnesses of the Exodus and Sinai events and
the definitive personal mediation of God's words through Moses
(Deuteronomy 34). The book of the law of Moses will now come to
replace the person of Moses as the source of God's guidance and
revelation for the new generation (Josh 1:7-8). In this way,
Deuteronomy and the whole Pentateuch retains the perspective of the
new generation at the end of Numbers as a hermeneutical paradigm
for all succeeding generations.

Secondly, our analysis of the theological function of law in
Numbers in Chapter Eight above showed how the laws and other material in Numbers (e.g., the image of the movable tent of meeting)
evoked a sense of flexibility which is amenable to reinterpretations
of past traditions. In particular, the inclusion of the account of
the daughters of Zelophehad at the very end of Numbers ensures an
openness within the tradition. This openness to reinterpretation
provides a literary and theological warrant for the inclusion of
the book of Deuteronomy in the Pentateuch. In its present form,
Deuteronomy represents a summary and reapplication of past tradition

for a new generation. On critical grounds, we know that Deuteronomy
stems from a different tradition within Israel's history. Deuteronomy's interpretations of key events also related to Numbers are
sometimes different in details or emphases (e.g., the spy story--
Deut 1:19-46, or the rebellion of Korah, Dathan and Abiram--Deut
11:6). Additional laws not found in Numbers are included in
Deuteronomy. Nevertheless, the present shape of Numbers allows a
degree of flexibility and thus invites Deuteronomy to be heard as
a legitimate commentary upon itself.

Obviously, much more could be said about the relationship of
Numbers and the wider context of the Pentateuch. Comparisons and
contrasts could be drawn between much similar material in Numbers
and Exodus as well as Numbers and Deuteronomy. We have attempted,
however, to present only a broad overview of the ways in which the
unifying structure and theme of Numbers corresponds to and affects
the larger structure and theme of the Pentateuch. A few final
remarks are in order concerning an insightful study of the theme
and structure of the Pentateuch by David J. A. Clines.[8] Clines
sets out to describe the unifying theme of the Pentateuch which he
defines as "the partial fulfillment--which implies also the partial
non-fulfillment--of the promise to or blessing of the patriarchs."[9]
This promise has three elements: the promise of posterity which is
dominant in Genesis 12-50, the promise of a divine-human relationship which is dominant in Exodus and Leviticus, and the promise of
land which is dominant in Numbers and Deuteronomy.[10] Specifically
in relation to Numbers, Clines observes the inability of many
commentators to detect any coherent structure to the book. He
proposes as an alternative that Numbers is unified by a concern for
the promised land:

> Numbers establishes from its very beginning the thematic
> element of the land as the end to which everything drives,
> and its matter and movement are consistently oriented toward
> that goal.[11]

The unifying theme of Numbers, according to Clines, is concern for
the promised land.

Much of Clines' analysis is very helpful and illuminating.
His interpretation of the central theme of the book of Numbers,
however, requires some correction in light of our study. First of
all, the theme of concern for the land is not as pervasive in
Numbers as Clines suggests. Material related to the land is
concentrated in the second half of Numbers, chapters 26-36. The
first half in Numbers 1-25 involves the organization of the holy
people of God on the move in the wilderness after leaving Mount
Sinai. It then depicts the rebellions of the generation of the

Exodus and Sinai and the judgment of death in the wilderness which
God imposes upon its members. Much of this first half of Numbers
has little to do specifically with the land.[12]

Secondly, the basis of the structure of Numbers which we have
discerned, namely, the census lists in Numbers 1 and 26, signal a
partial actualization of the promise of innumerable descendants.
The family of Jacob is increased from the census total of seventy
persons in Exod 1:5 to census totals of over 600,000 fighting men
in Numbers 1 and 26. The Balaam oracles also allude to a fulfillment of the promise of progeny (Num 23:10). Now one might respond
by arguing that the censuses in Numbers depict the mustering of an
army and so presuppose a concern for conquering the land. We would
grant the validity of such a position, especially for the second
census list (cf. Num 26:52-56), as long as one also concedes that
a concern for the fulfillment of the promise of a multitude of
descendants is also evident.[13] In fact, we would argue that the
book of Numbers is concerned with the continuation of all three
elements of the promises to the patriarchs: the land, descendants,
and the divine-human relationship. The concern for the latter
reaches a dramatic turning point in the spy story as God threatens
to disinherit the people and to dissolve any relationship with them
(Num 14:11-12). Therefore, the concern for the land is not the
only element of the promise which is clearly carried forward in
Numbers.

A third problem with Clines' approach is a methodological one.
He has assembled all the references to the promises to the patriarchs throughout the Pentateuch and extrapolated a general impression of the dominant theme of each Pentateuchal book. Genesis is
concerned with progeny, Exodus-Leviticus with the divine-human
relationship and Numbers-Deuteronomy with land. Such a method has
the potential for subjectivity and lack of controls. In contrast,
our methodology has sought to determine the editorial framework of
Numbers and the Pentateuch by which later redactors have intentionally structured the material. Such a method provides a more
verifiable basis for proposing a given structure or theme as definitive since it deals with specific evidence of editorial activity
and intentionality. Evidence of such redactional intentionality
has been presented in Chapter Five of our study. This approach has
led us to uncover the central structural foundation of the present
form of the Pentateuch as the succession of generations, climaxing
in Numbers with the death of the generation of the Exodus and Sinai
and the birth of a new and paradigmatic generation. This structural
foundation has been marked by specific redactional devices which

include the toledot formulae, the genealogies and the census lists
throughout the Pentateuch. Such specific redactional markers are
not evident in Clines' presentation of the structure and theme of
the Pentateuch.

THE THEME OF NUMBERS BEYOND THE PENTATEUCH

The theme of the death of the old generation and the birth of
the new generation of hope is one which continues far beyond Numbers
and the Pentateuch. The Deuteronomistic History from Joshua through
Kings is structured on the basis of a series of generations which
is marked by a succession of judges and kings who are born, reign
for a time, die and are then replaced by a new generation of leadership. Judges 2, for example, provides a paradigmatic example of
the cycle of generations. After the generation of Joshua dies, a
rebellious generation arises. Their rebellion threatens their
existence. God sends a deliverer who saves the people. When the
deliverer dies, a new generation again acts rebelliously and the
generational cycle begins anew. The book of Kings, after recounting
the succession of the generations of kings in Israel's history, ends
with a note of subdued hope as Jehoiachin, the exiled king of Judah
and the last member of the line of David who had been promised an
eternal dynasty (2 Samuel 7), is released from prison and treated
kindly by the Babylonian monarch (2 Kgs 25:27-30). The generations
of the people of God continue to live in a time between promise and
fulfillment.

The book of Psalms also provides examples of the theme of the
death of the old and the birth of the new, the movement from hope-
lessness to hope, from confession to forgiveness, from death to life.
Psalms 95 and 96 specifically recall the wilderness generation of
rebellion, exhorting the future generations not to follow the ways
of their fathers:

> "For forty years I loathed that generation
> and said, 'They are a people who err in heart
> and they do not regard my ways.'
> Therefore I swore in my anger
> that they should not enter my rest" (Ps 95:8-11).

Psalm 96 follows immediately with a call for a new song for a new
generation:

> "O sing to the LORD a new song;
> sing to the LORD, all the earth!
> Sing to the LORD, bless his name;
> tell of his salvation from day to day (Ps 96:1-2).

The theme of the death of the old and the birth of the new
which is the central theme of Numbers is also a prevalent theme and

image among the pre-exilic and exilic prophets. The prophet Hosea
depicts God's judgment whereby God "will put an end to the kingdom
of the house of Israel" as well as the people of Judah (Hos 1:4, 11).
The people will be called "Not Pitied" and "Not My People" (Hos 1:6,
9). Despite the harlotry and unfaithfulness of his people, however,
God will raise up a new generation of children whom he will plant
in the promised land:

> "And I will have pity on Not Pitied, and I will say to Not
> My People 'You are my people;' and he shall say, 'Thou art
> my God'" (Hos 2:23).

The last chapter of the book of Hosea contains an exhortation to
return to the LORD "for you have stumbled because of your iniquity"
and a promise of the rebirth of God's people:

> "They will return and dwell beneath my shadow, they shall
> flourish as a garden; they shall blossom as the vine, their
> fragrance shall be like the wine of Lebanon" (Hos 14:1, 7).

The oracles of the prophet Jeremiah include a word of judgment
on the generation past but also a profound word of hope for rebirth:

> "Behold, the days are coming, says the LORD, when I will sow
> the house of Israel and the house of Judah with the seed of
> man and the seed of beast. And it shall come to pass that
> as I have watched over them to pluck up and break down, to
> overthrow, destroy and bring evil, so I will watch over them
> to build and to plant, says the LORD" (Jer 31:27-28).

These words are followed by the promise of a new covenant for a new
generation, a covenant unlike the covenant which their fathers had
broken:

> "Behold, the days are coming, says the LORD, when I will make
> a new covenant with the house of Israel and the house of
> Judah, not like the covenant which I made with their fathers
> when I took them by the hand to bring them out of the land of
> Egypt, my covenant which they broke, though I was their hus-
> band, says the LORD. But this is the covenant which I will
> make with the house of Israel after those days, says the
> LORD: I will put my law within them, and I will write it
> upon their hearts; and I will be their God, and they shall
> be my people" (Jer 31:31-33).

For Jeremiah, the people of God continue to look forward to the
accomplishment of God's promises. The rebellious generation of the
fathers is gone, and a new generation of hope will arise. The book
of Jeremiah ends on the same note of subdued hope as does the
Deuteronomistic History: Jehoiachin, the exiled king of Judah and
the last member of the line of David, continues to live under the
good graces of the Babylonians (Jer 52:31-34). The hope remains
that someday God may reinstate the line of David in Jerusalem and
again plant his people in the promised land (Jer 30:18-22; 33:6-11,
25-26).

The book of the exilic prophet Ezekiel uses the image of the
death of the old and the birth of the new as a recurrent motif.
God promises that he will again assemble his people and bring them
into the land with a new heart and spirit (Ezek 11:17-20). God will
increase the numbers of the people (Ezek 36:37-38). But a warning
is also given: "But as for those whose heart goes after detestable
things . . . I will requite their deeds upon their heads" (Ezek 11:
21; cf. also Ezek 18:30-32). Ezekiel 20 recounts the history of
Israel from its beginnings as a story of rebellions which extended
from generation to generation. The time of the wilderness wandering
is presented as the paradigm of Israel's wrestling with God. The
wilderness was the time when God's law occasioned the rebellion of
the people and thus their death (Ezek 20:21-26). The exile into
Babylon is portrayed as a new wilderness experience in which the
old generation of rebels is condemned and forbidden to enter the
land. God proclaims,

> "I will bring you into the wilderness of the people, and
> there I will enter into judgment with you face to face. As
> I entered into judgment with your fathers in the wilderness
> of the land of Egypt, so I will enter into judgment with you,
> says the LORD God. I will make you pass under the rod, and I
> will let you go in by number. I will purge out the rebels
> from among you, and those who transgress against me; I will
> bring out of the land where they sojourn, but they shall not
> enter the land of Israel" (Ezek 20:35-38).

A new generation of hope will be raised up once again in the land.

> "For on my holy mountain, the mountain height of Israel,
> says the LORD God, there all the house of Israel, all of
> them, shall serve me in the land . . . And you shall know
> that I am the LORD, when I bring you into the land of Israel,
> the country which I swore to give to your fathers" (Ezek
> 20:40,42

The most striking use of the imagery of death and rebirth is
Ezekiel's vision of the valley of dry bones which are given life by
God. God speaks to Ezekiel,

> "Son of man, these bones are the whole house of Israel.
> Behold, they say, 'Our bones are dried up and our hope is
> lost; we are clean cut off.' Therefore prophesy and say to
> them, Thus says the LORD God: Behold I will open your graves,
> and raise you from your graves, O my people; and I will bring
> you home into the land of Israel" (Ezek 37:11-12).

God makes it clear that this rebirth of his people involves all
Israel, north and south. It is God who will do this, and it will
be done for the sake of God's name and glory among the nations
(Ezek 37:15-28). Ezekiel 39 is a variation on this theme of the
death of the old and the birth of the new (cf. especially Ezek
39:21-29). Like the book of Numbers, the book of Ezekiel concludes

with ordinances for the boundaries and division of the land which
function as words of promise as the people await future entry into
the land.[14]

Second Isaiah is likewise pervaded by images of the passing of
the old and the birth of the new in a return through the wilderness
toward the promised land:

> "Behold, the former things have come to pass, and new things
> I now declare; before they spring forth I tell you of them"
> (Isa 42:9).

> "Behold, I am doing a new thing; now it springs forth, do
> you not perceive it? I will make a way in the wilderness
> and rivers in the desert" (Isa 43:19; cf. also Isa 41:17-19;
> 44:26-28).

The promise of a multitude of descendants (Isa 54:1-3) and a return
to the promised land (Isa 49:8-9) is repeated and addressed to a
new generation. The vision of the book of Isaiah expands beyond
the rebirth of a people to a bold promise of the rebirth of the
entire cosmos in a new creation:

> "For behold I create new heavens and a new earth; and the
> former things shall not be remembered or come into mind . . .
> For behold I create Jerusalem a rejoicing and her people
> a joy" (Isa 65:17).

Even with this strong note of discontinuity with the past, however,
the promises and warnings of the people and traditions of the past
will not be forgotten. They will remain as a guide for the future:

> "For as the new heavens and the new earth which I will make
> shall remain before me, says the LORD; so shall your descen-
> dants and your name remain. From new moon to new moon, and
> and from sabbath to sabbath, all flesh shall come to worship
> before me, says the LORD. And all shall go forth and look on
> the dead bodies of the men that have rebelled against me, for
> their worm shall not die, their fire shall not be quenched,
> and they shall be an abhorrence to all flesh" (Isa 66:22-24).

The theme of the death of the old and the birth of a new
generation of hope is further developed by later post-exilic
prophets like Zechariah who speaks of the past judgment and rejection
of the people as well as the LORD's promise that their children will
again enter the land and that their numbers will increase:

> "Their children shall see it and rejoice,
> their hearts shall exult in the LORD.
> I will signal for them and gather them in,
> for I have redeemed them,
> and they shall be as many as of old.
> Though I scattered them among the nations,
> yet in far countries they shall remember me,
> and with their children they shall live and return"
> (Zech 10:7-9).

As the prophetic style and imagery moves into an apocalyptic mode
in Israel's tradition, the theme of the death of the old and the
birth of the new is radicalized. Concepts of the resurrection of
the dead, the succession or world ages or eras, and cosmic and
mythic symbols of evil and divine powers are combined to form
graphic depictions of the death of the old and the birth of the
new people of God and the future fulfillments of God's promises to
them. The latter chapters of the book of Daniel are perhaps the
best examples of such apocalyptic reinterpretations of the theme of
the death of the old and the birth of the new (e.g., Dan 7:24-27;
9:24-27; 11:40-12:3).

Our brief look at the wider Old Testament context of the theme
of the death of the old and the birth of the new is by no means
exhaustive. We hope simply to have shown that the theme is not an
imposition of a concept which is foreign to Israel's religious
tradition. The theme is not peculiar or unique to the book of
Numbers. In fact, it appears as an important part of Israel's
self-understanding in several traditions and is applied to several
periods of her history. The experience of Israel in the wilderness
is presented as a paradigm by which succeeding generations may
understand and interpret their present experience and future hope
in their life before God.

Of course, the theme of the wilderness generation and the death
of the old and the birth of the new continued to be appropriated by
the religious traditions of Judaism and Christianity in various
forms. The most thorough source for the history of interpretation
of individual pericopes in Numbers is the commentary on Numbers by
de Vaulx who traces the history of exegesis through Jewish sources
as well as through the New Testament and Church Fathers.[15] The
commentary by Binns provides a helpful list of New Testament references to the book of Numbers.[16] Examples of recent studies which
analyze the New Testament interpretation of the wilderness wandering
and themes related to Numbers include Albert Vanhoye's study of the
book of Hebrews, Ulrich Mauser's treatment of the Gospel of Mark,
and David Moessner's study of the structure of the Gospel of Luke.[17]
Robert Funk and Shemaryahu Talmon have written surveys of the
interpretation of the experience of God's people in the wilderness
in the Bible and in the Qumran literature.[18] Yigael Yadin has
pointed to an interesting Qumran text in which a new census of all
the people of Israel will inaugurate the new eschatological age.[19]
The Qumran interpretation is clearly dependent on the function of
the census list in Numbers 26 as a marker of the birth of a new
generation of God's people in the wilderness on the edge of the

promised land. Noteworthy treatments of the spy story in Numbers
13-14 and the larger theme of the death of the old generation and
the birth of the new have been offered from the perspective of the
rabbinic and more modern Jewish traditions.[20] The continuing importance of the paradigm in Numbers of God's people standing in hope
on the edge of the promised land in the history of Judaism and
Christianity has been well documented by W. D. Davies' study of the
function of the promised land in early Judaism and Christianity.[21]
A full treatment of this history of interpretation would carry us
well beyond the boundaries of this study. Nevertheless, this brief
sampling of reinterpretations of the book of Numbers illustrates
the repeated application of the themes of Numbers to new situations
and historical moments in the history of the people of God. This
capacity for reapplication testifies to the power and continued
relevance of the book and to the skillful art of the writers and
editors of Numbers and the Pentateuch as they intended to make
Israel's experience of the wilderness an ongoing paradigm for
generations to come.

CONCLUSION TO PART THREE

This final part of our study has attempted to illustrate the theological implications of the unifying framework of the census lists in Numbers 1 and 26 for interpreting the book of Numbers and the Pentateuch. The spy story in Numbers 13-14 (Chapter Six) has been clearly integrated into this framework by means of a series of explicit verbal connections which run through Numbers 1, 13, 14, 26, 32 and 34. The fact that the spy story was firmly embedded in the editorial framework led to a number of specific theological implications for understanding the nature of the sin and punishment of the first generation and the ongoing threat and promise to the new generation of God's people.

The literary connection of the Balaam cycle (Chapter Seven) and the selected legal material (Chapter Eight) was of a different nature than that of the spy story. The connection to the framework of the census lists was not achieved by virtue of direct verbal links as much as by literary positioning within the overarching framework and within the immediate literary context of the individual passages. The Balaam cycle which had a long history of transmission with roots early in Israel's history was strategically placed at the end of the first generation and functioned as words of promise to a future generation. The legal materials in Numbers 15 along with Numbers 27 and 36 which were probably later in date than the Balaam oralces likewise were assigned certain theological functions by virtue of their placement within the larger structure of Numbers. Thus, Numbers 15 functioned as words of assurance and promise to the new generation because of its subject matter and its position immediately after the debacle of the rebellion in Numbers 13-14. Similarly, the case of the daughters of Zelphehad in chapters 27 and 36 had a significant role in setting the tone for the second generation which was introduced by the census list in Numbers 26. These two chapters formed an inclusio for all the material relating to the new generation of the people of God. The content of these chapters which dealt with the inheritance of the promised land provided a theological warrant for a posture of hope and expectation in relation to God's promises for the future. Moreover, the new questions and circumstances which forced the reinterpretation of past traditions provided a precedent of flexibility and openness in interpreting the past for the sake of the present.

The theology of Numbers as a whole and its literary and theological function within the Pentateuch were the subjects of our final chapter (Chapter Nine). The theme of the death of the old and the birth of the new generation of God's people on the verge of entering the promised land was established by the two census lists in Numbers 1 and 26 which divide the book into two halves. We argued that the second generation of hope functioned as a model or paradigm for every succeeding generation of the community of God's people as they struggled to appropriate the promises and warnings of theological traditions inherited from the past. This paradigmatic portrait of God wrestling with his people in every generation, always ensuring that his promises continue from generation to generation, characterizes not only the structure of Numbers but the structure of the entire Pentateuch. God's promise to the patriarchs is passed on to the generation of the Exodus and Sinai and to every succeeding generation who receives the challenge and commission to be God's holy people. The book of Deuteronomy takes up this same theme of the concern for the faithful transmission of God's covenant to a new generation as an ultimate matter of life and death (Deut 30:15-20). This theme of the death of the old generation and the birth of the new generation of hope was also found beyond the Pentateuch in other parts of the Old Testament. The theme definitively shaped much of Israel's religious tradition and literature. Its influence continued to shape the theological understanding of generations of God's people beyond the boundaries of the Old Testament itself.

We began our study with a problem: the inability of modern commentators on Numbers to propose a coherent, convincing and meaningful structure for the book. We offer this study as a proposed remedy for the problem in hopes that it will better enable the book of Numbers to be read as an intelligible literary work in its present form. Its important role within the larger structure of the Pentateuch will also hopefully be greater appreciated. Even more than its literary intelligibility, it is hoped that this study will lead to a greater appreciation and use of the theological insight which the book of Numbers offers to this and future generations of the people of God.

NOTES

MODERN STUDY OF NUMBERS

[1]Julius Wellhausen, Die Composition des Hexateuchs (Berlin:
W. de Gruyter, 1963, first edition 1885); and Prolegomena to the
History of Israel, tr. J. S. Black and A. Menzies (New York:
Meridan Books, 1957, first edition 1883). The latter work is an
English translation of the second edition of Wellhausen's history
of Israel. His first edition was entitled Geschichte Israels I
(Marburg: n. p., 1878).

[2]The commentary by August Knobel, Die Bücher Numeri,
Deuteronomium und Joshua (Leipzig: S. Hirzel, 1861), was the last
critical commentary to reflect a thoroughly pre-Wellhausen view of
literary sources within Numbers. The Priestly source, according to
Knobel, was the oldest literary layer, not the latest as Wellhausen
would suggest. Knobel's work was absorbed with source-critical
divisions, devoting an extensive introduction and appendix to
source-critical issues alone. Knobel was also concerned to uncover
details of the text which were historically problematic. The other
end of the spectrum of German scholarship was best represented by
the conservative commentaries of Johann Peter Lange, Numbers, or
the Fourth Book of Moses, tr. Samuel Lowrie and A. Gosman (New York:
Charles Scribner's Sons, 1879, original German edition, 1864), and
above all, Karl Friedrich Keil, The Pentateuch, Numbers and Deuteronomy, Volume 3, tr. James Martin (Edinburgh: T & T Clark, 1870,
original German edition, 1870). Both Lange and Keil endeavored to
support the historicity of the narratives of Numbers as well as the
Mosaic authorship and unity of the book and the entire Pentateuch.
Two conservative commentators from the United States in this period
before Wellhausen included George Bush, Notes, Critical and Practical, on the Book of Numbers (New York: Ivison, Phinney, Blakeman
and Co., 1868), and T. E. Espin, "Numbers," The Holy Book with
Commentary, Leviticus-Deuteronomy, ed. F. C. Cook (London: John
Murray, 1871). Although coming after Wellhausen's major work had
appeared, the commentary by the American scholar Daniel Steele,
Leviticus and Numbers, Wheadon's Commentary, Volume 2 (New York:
Hunt and Eaton, 1891), followed much the same line as Keil and was
at points dependent on him.

[3]August Dillmann, Die Bücher Numeri, Deuteronomium und Joshua
(Leipzig: S. Hirzel, 1886).

[4]Dillmann represented a position somewhere between the earlier
reconstruction of the sequence of literary sources by Knobel and
Wellhausen's later view which came to prevail in critical circles.
Knobel held the Priestly source (P) to be the earliest, followed
by the Elohist (E), the Yahwist (J), and finally the Deuteronomist
(D). Thus, he posited the sequence of P, E, J and D. Cf. Knobel,
Die Bücher Numeri, Deuteronomium und Joshua, 489-606. Dillmann
retained the D source as the latest literary strand as well as the
sequence of the Elohist and Yahwist relative to each other. His
major break from Knobel was to place the Priestly source as later,
not earlier, than E and J. Thus, Dillmann's view of the sequence

of sources ran E, J, P, and D with the Elohist as the earliest
layer. Dillmann maintained, however, that the basic Priestly source,
although later than E and J, was still essentially pre-exilic.
Furthermore, the Deuteronomist was the last layer to be incorporated
into the Hexateuch. Cf. Dillmann, Die Bücher Numeri, Deuteronomium
und Joshua, 591-690. Wellhausen argued that the Yahwist and not
the Elohist was the earliest layer of the Hexateuch. Moreover, the
Priestly source was not pre-exilic but post-exilic. P was also the
final layer of the whole work, not the Deuteronomist. Among his
contemporaries, Dillmann remained one of the few critical scholars
who continued to oppose Wellhausen's scheme with any degree of
sophistication.

[5]H. Holzinger, Numeri (Tübingen: J. C. B. Mohr, 1903).

[6]Bruno Baentsch, Exodus-Leviticus-Numeri, HKAT (Göttingen:
Vandenhoeck & Ruprecht, 1903).

[7]George B. Gray, A Critical and Exegetical Commentary on
Numbers, ICC (New York: Scribner, 1903).

[8]Ibid., xlii.

[9]Ibid., xliii.

[10]Ibid., xlvii.

[11]Ibid., li.

[12]Cf. George F. Genung, Leviticus-Numbers-Deuteronomy, An
American Commentary on the Old Testament (Philadelphia: American
Baptist Publication Society, 1906). Genung was a conservative
American commentator who acknowledged the strength of the source-
critical analysis of the Pentateuch and yet completely ignored it
in his actual exegesis. The commentaries by A. R. S. Kennedy,
Leviticus and Numbers, The New Century Bible (New York: Oxford
University Press, 1910), and A. H. McNeile, The Book of Numbers,
The Cambridge Bible for Schools and Colleges (Cambridge: Cambridge
University Press, 1911), were popular distillations by English
scholars of the results of source-critical exegesis on the book of
Numbers. A representative of Jewish scholarship in this period was
an article by George Barton and Max Seligsohn, "Numbers, Book of,"
The Jewish Encyclopedia, ed. Isidore Singer et al. (New York: Funk
and Wagnalls Co., 1905), 343-6. Seligsohn provided a thoroughly
traditional view while Barton gave a thoroughly source-critical
analysis of the book with no attempt to integrate the two approaches.
Finally, Robert A. Watson was the author of a commentary on Numbers
in The Expositor's Bible, Leviticus-Numbers, ed. W. Robertson Nicoll
(New York: A. C. Armstrong and Son, 1903). Watson accepted the
broad outlines of the source-critical theory, but his primary
interest involved theological reflections on the text in homiletical
style. While sometimes straying from the text, Watson remained one
of the few in this period to have studied Numbers from a primarily
theological perspective. The commentary's fault was its failure to
engage the critical exegesis of its day and its failure to provide
a compelling theological interpretation of the book as a whole.

[13]Hermann Gunkel, Genesis, übersetz und erklärt (Göttingen:
Vandenhoeck & Ruprecht, 1901). Cf. also Gunkel, The Legends of
Genesis, tr. W. H. Carruth (New York: Schocken Books, 1964).

[14]Hugo Gressmann, Mose und seine Zeit (Göttingen: Vandenhoeck
& Ruprecht, 1913).

[15]Hugo Gressmann, Die Schriften des Alten Testaments, Die Anfange Israels (von 2 Mosis bis Richter und Ruth) (Gottingen: Vandenhoeck & Ruprecht, 1914). Most of Gressmann's commentary was taken verbatim from his analyses of passages in Numbers in his Mose und seine Zeit, although in condensed form. The commentary provided little which was new and original in relation to Gressmann's earlier work.

[16]L. Elliott Bins, The Book of Numbers (London: Methuen and Co., 1927).

[17]Ibid., xix.

[18]Ibid., xli.

[19]Ibid., xliii.

[20]Bonaventura Ubach, Els Nombres-El Deuteronomi, Lu Biblia, III (Montserrat: Monestir, 1928).

[21]Paul Heinisch, Das Buch Numeri (Bonn: Peter Hanstein, 1936), and Heinrich Schneider, "Numeri," in Zweites bis Funftes Buch Moses, Echter Bibel, ed. Heinrich Schneider and Hubert Junker (Würzberg: Echter Verlag, 1952).

[22]Karl F. Krämer, Numeri und Deuteronomium, Herders Bibel-kommentar (Freiburg: Herder, 1955).

[23]A. Clamer, La Sainte Bible, Lévitique-Nombres-Deutéronome, ed. L Pirot (Paris: Letouzey et Ane, 1940).

[24]H. Cazelles, Les Nombres, La Sainte Bible (Paris: Les Éditions du Cerf, 1952).

[25]A. Drubbel, Numeri uit de grondtekst vertaald en uitgelegd, De Boeken van het Oude Testament, Deel II, Boek II (Roermond en Maaseik: Romen und Zonen, 1963).

[26]Cf. R. J. Thompson, Moses and the Law in a Century since Graf (Leiden: E. J. Brill, 1970), 127ff. Other papal encyclicals issued in 1950 and 1961 again tended to discourage the free use of historical-critical tools in biblical study. This was the case up until the Second Vatican Council when critical study on the Bible was again encouraged.

[27]The Jewish commentary by J. H. Hertz, The Pentateuch and Haftorahs, Numbers, Volume IV (London: Oxford University Press, 1934), combined a conservative brand of critical exegesis with excerpts from traditional rabbinic and medieval Jewish commentaries. The commentary by S. Fisch, "The Book of Numbers," The Soncino Chumash, The Five Books of Moses with Haphtaroth, ed. A. Cohen (Hindhead: The Soncino Press, 1947), 793-987, presented an exposition of Numbers based only on medieval Jewish commentaries. Another Jewish work of this period should also be mentioned, namely, the German translation of the entire Midrash Sifre, the classical rabbinic commentary on Numbers, by Karl Georg Kuhn, Sifre zu Numeri, Der tannaitische Midrasch, Volume 3 (Stuttgart: W. Kohlhammer, 1959). An English translation of selections from the Midrash Sifre was made by Paul Levertoff, Midrash Sifre on Numbers (London: Society for Promoting Christian Knowledge, 1926).

[28]Julius H. Greenstone, Numbers, with Commentary (Philadelphia: Jewish Publication Society, 1939, second edition 1948).

[29]Ibid., xxiii.

[30]Several brief commentaries of little independent significance
from this period included Charles R. Erdman, The Book of Numbers,
An Exposition (Westwood, N.J.: Fleming H. Revell Co., 1952); J.
Marsh, "The Book of Numbers--Exegesis," and A. G. Butzer, "Exposition," IB (New York: Abingdon Press, 1953), vol. 2, 137-308; and
R. C. Dentan, "Numbers, Book of," IDB, ed. George Arther Buttrick
(Nashville: Abingdon Press, 1962), vol. 3, 567-713. Dentan was
noteworthy for his very negative view of Numbers, emphasizing the
book's disunity, lack of structure, absence of historical value,
and the theological insignificance of much of the book's contents.

[31]B. D. Eerdmans, "The Composition of Numbers," OTS 6 (1949),
101-216.

[32]Willem H. Gispen, Het boek Numeri (Kampen: J. H. Kok, 1959,
1964), 2 volumes.

[33]Ibid., vol. 1, 13.

[34]Cf. Keil, The Pentateuch, Volume 3. The book was published
in 1870.

[35]James L. Mays, The Book of Leviticus, The Book of Numbers,
The Layman's Bible Commentary (Atlanta: John Knox Press, 1963).

[36]Martin Noth, Numbers, A Commentary, OTL, tr. James Martin
(Philadelphia: Westminister Press, 1968). The German edition
appeared as Das vierte Buch Mose, Numeri, ATD (Göttingen: Vandenhoeck & Ruprecht, 1966).

[37]For a more systematic treatment of Noth's perspective, cf.
Martin Noth, A History of Pentateuchal Traditions, tr. Bernhard W.
Anderson (Chico, California: Scholars Press, 1981).

[38]Noth, Numbers, 5.

[39]Ibid., 4. Noth did make use of the results of source criticism but only as one small stage in the larger process of the growth
of the tradition. Furthermore, Noth reduced the E source in Numbers
to an insignificant portion. E was confined almost entirely to the
Balaam cycle in Numbers 22-24.

[40]Ibid., 6.

[41]Ibid., 9.

[42]Ibid., 4.

[43]Ibid., 11.

[44]N. H. Snaith, "Numbers," PCB (London: Thomas Nelson and
Sons, 1962), 254-268; and Snaith, Leviticus and Numbers, The Century
Bible (Thomas Nelson and Sons, 1967).

[45]Arnold Goldberg, Das Buch Numeri (Dusseldorf: Patmos Verlag,
1970). Another short commentary by I. Caine, "Numbers, Book of,"
EncJud (New York: Macmillan Co., 1971), vol. 12, 1249-54, followed
Goldberg's tendency to adopt Noth's view of tradition-themes in
Numbers. Like Goldberg, however, Caine detected more of a pattern
or coherence in the development of the final form of the book than
Noth did.

[46]Ibid., 15.

[47]Ibid., 136.

[48]Baruch A. Levine, "Numbers, Book of," IDBSup (Nashville: Abingdon, 1976), 631-635.

[49]W. Gunther Plaut, "Numbers," The Torah, A Modern Commentary (New York: Union of American Hebrew Congregations, 1981), 1009-1286; including an essay by William W. Hallo, "Numbers and Ancient Near Eastern Literature," 1014-1023. Hallo argued, as we will do, that "in spite of its electic character, the book of Numbers does constitute some kind of literary unity."

[50]Two brief studies of the book may be found in two one-volume Roman Catholic commentaries. Cf. F. L. Moriarty, "Numbers," JBC (Englewood Cliffs, New Jersey: Prentice-Hall, Inc., 1968), 86-100; and P. P. Saydon, "Numbers," NCCHS (London: Thomas Nelson and Sons, 1969), 242-255.

[51]J. de Vaulx, Les Nombres (Paris: J. Gabalda, 1972).

[52]Ibid., 29.

[53]Ibid., 40.

[54]Giuseppe Bernini, Il Libro dei Numeri (Rome: Marietti, 1972).

[55]Ibid., 31-32.

[56]Walter Riggans, Numbers, The Daily Study Bible (Philadelphia: Westminster Press, 1983). Other conservative Protestant commentaries include J. A. Thompson, "Numbers," The New Bible Commentary, Revised, ed. D. Guthrie et al. (Grand Rapids, Michigan: Eerdmans, 1970), 168-200; and John Joseph Owens, "Numbers," Leviticus-Ruth, The Broadman Bible Commentary, Volume 2, ed. C. J. Allen et al. (Nashville: Abingdon, 1970), 75-174. Two brief and more critical commentaries by Protestant scholars also emerged in this period: Harvey H. Guthrie, "The Book of Numbers," The Interpreter's One-Volume Commentary, ed. Charles M. Laymon (Nashville: Abingdon, 1971), 85-99; and John Sturdy, Numbers (Cambridge: Cambridge University Press, 1976).

[57]Riggans, Numbers, 2

[58]Gordon Wenham, Numbers, Tyndale Old Testament Commentaries (Downers Grove, Illinois: Inter-Varsity Press, 1981).

[59]Rolf Rendtorff, Das überlieferungsgeschichtliche Problem des Pentateuch (Berlin: Walter de Gruyter, 1977). Cf. also Rendtorff, "The Yahwist as Theologian: The Dilemma of Pentateuchal Criticism," JSOT 3 (1977), 2-45, with several replies to Rendtorff's proposal in the same volume; and Rendtorff, "Traditio-historical Method and the Documentary Hypothesis," Proceedings of the World Congress of Jewish Studies 5 (1969), 5-11.

[60]JSOT 3 (1977) devoted the entire issue to a debate of Rendtorff's position. Cf. also Robert North, "Can Geography Save J from Rendtorff?" Bib 63 (1982), 47-55.

[61]Wenham, Numbers, 14-18.

[62]Ibid., 21.

[63]Ibid., 21.

[64]For a more complete discussion, cf. G. B. Gray, Numbers, 128-134, and Chapter Six of our study.

[65]Cf. G. B. Gray, Numbers, 307, and the discussion in Chapter Seven of our study.

[66]Wenham, Numbers, 24.

[67]One of the latest commentators who claims to focus on the present form of the text in his interpretation is Gordon Wenham (1981) who states that "it is the final form of the text that has canonical authority for the church, and that is the focus of interest in the chapters that follow" (p. 25). W. Gunther Plaut (1981) writes, "While reference is made repeatedly to critical analysis as an important aid to understanding of the Torah, the text is generally treated as a literary unit, not because it always was of one piece (it was not), but because in the final editing process it was so treated and because ever since the readers of the Torah have approached it in this fashion" (p. 1012). Likewise, J. de Vaulx (1972) describes his task in this way: "This work attempts to study the pericopes in their entirety while striving to disclose the various stages of their redaction and while extricating the religious teaching and the interpretation given over the course of the ages" (p. 1). The goal, however, is not always successfully reached. The work of de Vaulx often fails to connect his critical exegesis with his theological interpretation as derived from the text's history of interpretation. Plaut's commentary tends to present several options in the interpretation of a given passage, many of which are not close readings of the final form of the text (whether midrashic or modern critical and historical readings). Wenham's analysis of the basic structure of Numbers ignores the book of Numbers as a separate literary unit in its final form.

[68]Aelred Cody, A History of the Old Testament Priesthood (Rome: Pontifical Biblical Institute, 1969); Frank M. Cross, Canaanite Myth and Hebrew Epic (Cambridge, Massachusetts: Harvard University Press, 1973), 195-215; A. H. J. Gunneweg, Leviten und Priester (Göttingen: Vandenhoeck & Ruprecht, 1965); K. Mohlenbrink, "Die levitischen Uberlieferungen des Alten Testaments," ZAW 52 (1934), 184-231; J. Milgrom, "Levitical ʿabodā," JQR 61 (1970), 132-54; and E. Nielsen, "The Levites in Ancient Israel," Annual of the Swedish Theological Institute, 3 (Leiden: E. J. Brill, 1964), 17-20.

[69]Frank M. Cross, "The Tabernacle: A Study from an Archaeological and Historical Approach," BA 10 (1947), 45-68; Frank M. Cross, "The Priestly Tabernacle in the Light of Recent Research," Temples and High Places, Proceedings of the Colloquium in Honor of the Centenniel of Hebrew Union College-Jewish Institute of Religion (Jerusalem: The Nelson Glueck School of Biblical Archaeology, 1981), 170-172; M. Haran, "Nature of the ʿohel môʿedh in Pentateuchal Sources," JSS 5 (1960), 50-65; M. H. Segal, "The Tent of Meeting" (Hebrew) Tarbiz 25 (1956), 231ff.; Roland de Vaux, "Ark of the Covenant and Tent of Reunion," The Bible and the Ancient Near East, tr. Damian McHugh (Garden City, New York: Doubleday, 1971), 136-151; and Baruch A. Levine, In the Presence of the Lord, A Study of Cult and Some Cultic Terms in Ancient Israel (Leiden: E. J. Brill, 1974).

[70]Yohanan Aharoni, The Land of the Bible, A Historical Geography, tr. A. F. Rainey (Philadelphia: Westminster Press, 1967); Denis Baly, The Geography of the Bible (New York: Harper and Row, 1957); H. Bar-Deroma, "Kadesh-Barnea," PEQ 96 (1964), 101-34; P. Buis, "Qadesh un lieu maudit?" VT 24 (1974), 268-85; G. I. Davies,

The Way of the Wilderness (New York: Cambridge University Press, 1979); G. I. Davies, "The Wilderness Itineraries and the Composition of the Pentateuch," VT 33 (1983), 1-13; G. I. Davies, "The Wilderness Itineraries: A Comparative Study," Tyndale Bulletin 25 (1974), 46-81; Martin Noth, "Der Wallfahrtsweg zum Sinai," PJ 36 (1940), 5-28, reprinted in Aufsätze zur biblischen Landes- und Altertumskunde, I, ed. H. W. Wolff (Neukirchen-Vluyn: Neukirchener Verlag, 1971), 55-74; J. Simon, The Geographical and Topographical Texts of the Old Testament (Leiden: E. J. Brill, 1959), 233-66; M. Wüst, Untersuchungen zu den siedlungsgeographischen Texten des Alten Testaments, I, Ostjordanland (Wiesbaden: Reichert, 1975); William F. Albright, "The List of Levitic Cities," Louis Ginzburg Jubilee Volume, I (New York: American Academy for Jewish Research, 1945), 49-73; Moshe Greenberg, "Levitical Cities," EncJud, vol. 11, 136-7; M. Haran, "Studies in the Account of the Levitical Cities," JBL 80 (1961), 45-54, 156-65; and B. Mazar, "The Cities of the Priests and Levites," VTSup 7 (Leiden: E. J. Brill, 1960), 193-205. Cf. also the standard histories of Israel for more extensive discussions and references to secondary literature.

71A. Kuschke, "Die Lagervorstellung der priestschriftlichen Erzählung," ZAW 63 (1951), 74-105.

72Again, one may refer to the standard histories of Israel for extensive discussions. Cf. also Manfred Weippert, The Settlement of the Israelite Tribes in Palestine (Naperville, Illinois: Alec R. Allenson, Inc., 1971); Yohanan Aharoni, "Nothing Early and Nothing Late: Re-writing Israel's Conquest," BA 39 (1976), 55-76; John R. Bartlett, "Conquest of Sihon's Kingdom: A Literary Reexamination," JBL 97 (1972), 182-197; John van Seters, "Once Again--the Conquest of Sihon's Kingdom," JBL 99 (1980), 117-124; J. Simon, "Two Connected Problems Relating to the Israelite Settlement in Transjordan," PEQ 79 (1949), 27-39, 87-101.

73William F. Albright, "Midianite Donkey Caravans," Translating and Understanding the Old Testament, Essays in Honor of Herbert Gordon May, ed. H. Frank and W. Reed (Nashville: Abingdon, 1970), 197-205; and Otto Eissfeldt, "Protektorat der Midianiter über ihre Nachbarn im letzen viertel des 2 Jahrtausends v. Chr. mit Beiträgen von William F. Albright," JBL 87 (1968), 383-93.

74Norman Gottwald, The Tribes of Yahweh (Maryknoll, New York: Orbis Books, 1979); A. Malamat, "UMMATUM in Old Babylonian Texts and Its Ugaritic and Biblical Counterparts," UF 11 (1979), 527-36; and J. Milgrom, "Priestly Terminology and the Political and Social Structure of Pre-Monarchic Israel," JQR 69 (1978), 65-81.

75The classical text-critical study of a text in Numbers is by William F. Albright, "The Oracles of Balaam," JBL 63 (1944), 207-33. Others include Norman H. Snaith, "Numbers XXVII 9, 11, 13 in the Ancient Versions," VT 19 (1969), 374; Harry Orlinsky, "Numbers XXVII 9, 12, 13," VT 20 (1970), 500; P. W. Skehan, "4QLXX Num.: A Pre-Christian Reworking of the Septuagint," HTR 70 (1977), 39-50; and Wilhelm Rudolph, "Zum Texte des Buches Numeri," ZAW 11 (1934), 113-20.

76B. D. Eerdmans, "The Composition of Numbers," OTS 6 (1949), 101-216; Robert North, "Can Geography Save J from Rendtorff?" Bib 63 (1982), 47-55; Rolf Rendtorff, "The Yahwist as Theologian: Dilemma of Pentateuchal Criticism," JSOT 3 (1977), 2-10, with replies and rebuttals by other scholars on pp. 11-45; Wilhelm Rudolf, Der "Elohist" von Exodus bis Josua (Berlin: A. Töpelmann, 1938); Hans H. Schmid, Der sogannante Jahwist: Beobachtungen und Fragen zur Pentateuchforschung (Zürich: Theologisches Verlag, 1976); Werner H. Schmidt, "Ein Theologie in salomischer Zeit? Plädoyer für den

Jahwisten," BZ 25 (1981), 82-102; and Horst Seebass, "Num. 11, 12
und die Hypothese des Jahwisten," VT 28 (1978), 214-223. A summary
of the contours of the source-critical debate over the last century
is provided by Robert John Thompson, Moses and the Law in a Century
of Criticism since Graf, VTSup 19 (Leiden: E. J. Brill, 1970).

[77]The classic and most thorough form-critical study of material
related to Numbers remains the study by Hugo Gressmann, Mose und
seine Zeit.

[78]R. Bach, Die Erwählung Israels in der Wüste, Nachwirkungen
der unpentateuchischen "Fundtradition," Dissertation (Bonn: 1952);
George W. Coats, "Conquest Traditions in the Wilderness Theme,"
JBL 95 (1976), 177-190; George W. Coats, Rebellion in the Wilderness,
The Murmuring Motif in the Wilderness Tradition of the Old Testament
(Nashville: Abingdon, 1968); Ivan Engnell, "The Wilderness Wandering"
and "The Pentateuch," A Rigid Scrutiny, tr. John T. Willis (Nashville:
Vanderbilt University Press, 1969), 50-68, 207-214; Volkmar Fritz,
Israel in der Wüste, Traditionsgeschichtliche Untersuchung der
Wüstenüberlieferung des Jahwisten (Marburg: N. G. Elwert Verlag,
1970); Diether Kellermann, Die Priesterschrift von Numeri 1,1 bis
10,10, literarkritisch und traditionsgeschichtlich untersucht
(Berlin: W. de Gruyter, 1970); Martin Noth, A History of Pentateuchal
Traditions; Martin Noth, Überlieferungsgeschichtliche Studien
(Tübingen: Max Niemeyer Verlag, 1957), 180-217; Rolf Rendtorff,
"Traditio-Historical Method and the Documentary Hypothesis,"
Proceedings of the World Congress of Jewish Studies 5 (1969), 5-11;
Rolf Rendtorff, Das überlieferungsgeschichtliche Problem des Penta-
teuch; John van Seters, "Recent Studies on the Pentateuch: A Crisis
in Method," JAOS 99 (1979), 663-672; John van Seters, "Tradition
and Social Change in Ancient Israel," Perspectives in Religious
Studies 7 (1980), 96-113; Roland de Vaux, "Reflections on the Pres-
ent State of Pentateuchal Criticism," The Bible and the Ancient
Near East, tr. Damian McHugh (Garden City, New York: Doubleday,
1971), 31-48; and F. W. Winnett, The Mosaic Tradition (Toronto:
University of Toronto Press, 1949).

[79]For example, cf. David Jobling, "A Structural Analysis of
Numbers 11-12," The Sense of Biblical Narrative (Sheffield, England:
Journal for the Study of the Old Testament, 1978).

[80]Cf. Norman Gottwald, The Tribes of Yahweh; Gordon Wenham,
Numbers, 25-39, 82-85, 202-205; Robert R. Wilson, Genealogy and
History in the Biblical World (New Haven, Connecticut: Yale
University Press, 1977).

[81]For example, Katherine Doob Sakenfeld, "Old Testament Perspectives: Methodological Issues," JSOT 22 (1982), 13-20, studies
the narratives of the daughters of Zelophehad in Numbers 27 and 36
from such a standpoint.

[82]For example, George W. Coats, "The Way of Obedience: Tradition-
Historical and Hermeneutical Reflections on the Balaam Story," Old
Testament Interpretation from a Process Perspective, Semeia 24
(Chico, California: Society of Biblical Literature, 1982), 53-79,
with a response in the same volume by Lewis S. Ford, "The Divine
Curse Understood in Terms of Persuasion," 81-87.

NOTES TO CHAPTER TWO: PROBLEM OF THE STRUCTURE OF NUMBERS

[1]Noth, Numbers, 1.

[2]Ibid., 4, 11.

[3]R. C. Dentan, "Numbers, Book of," 567. Similar comments on
the "haphazard and disjointed" character of Numbers have been made
by Walter Riggans, Numbers, 2; Harvey Guthrie, "The Book of Numbers,"
85; John Owens, "Numbers," 75; H. Cazelles, Les Nombres, 13; Bruno
Baentsch, Exodus-Leviticus-Numeri, v; George B. Gray, Numbers, xxii;
and H. Holzinger, Numeri, x.

[4]It should be noted that apart from the 46 commentaries
mentioned here, eight other commentaries which we studied did not
propose any outline or overall structure for the book for various
reasons. For example, Hugo Gressmann's form-critical approach had
no interest in the book of Numbers as a whole. He was only interested in the smaller form-critical units which he detected within
the book. Several of the Jewish commentaries which presented
traditional midrashic or medieval interpretations simply proceeded
on a verse by verse basis without regard to the overall structure
of the book.

[5]Owens, "Numbers," 75, 80-83.

[6]Barton and Seligsohn, "Numbers, Book of," 343-6.

[7]Riggans, Numbers, 1-2.

[8]Dillmann, Numeri, 1ff.; Baentsch, Exodus-Leviticus-Numeri, v;
Mays, Leviticus, Numbers, 8; Gray, Numbers, xxiii-xxiv; Noth,
Numbers, 11; Wenham, Numbers, 14-16.

[9]Gray, Numbers, xxiii-xxiv.

[10]The rejection of the book of Numbers as a separate literary
unit is also expressed by Barton, "Numbers, Book of," 345; Dentan,
"Numbers, Book of," 568; Goldberg, Das Buch Numeri, 11-12; Moriarty,
"Numbers," 86; and Guthrie, "The Book of Numbers," 85.

[11]Eight of the 46 commentaries used the chronological notations
in formulating an outline for Numbers.

[12]Cf. Gray, Numbers, xlv.

[13]Geographical notations are used in determining the outline
of Numbers in 33 out of the 46 commentaries surveyed.

[14]These three sample outlines are taken from de Vaulx, Les
Nombres, 11-13; Holzinger, Numeri, v-x; and Gray, Numbers, xxvi-xxix.

[15]Num 1:1; 9:1; 9:5; 10:12; 11:3; 11:34; 12:16; 13:3; 13:17;
13:24; 13:25; 14:45; 20:1; 20:13; 20:14; 20:21; 20:22; 21:1-3; 21:4;
21:10; 21:21f.; 22:1; 25:1; 26:1; 26:3; 26:63; 27:12; 31:1; 32:1;
32:33f.; 34:2; 35:1; 35:9; and 36:13. Whatever functions the
etymologies or place name associations which appear in Numbers had
in the course of their development, they seem to function in the
present narrative to highlight the significance of the narrative
with which they are now associated.

[16]Cf. Noth, A History of Pentateuchal Traditions, 272-275;
Holzinger, Numeri, xiv-xvii; Baentsch, Exodus-Leviticus-Numeri.
These provide a more detailed breakdown of proposed literary source
divisions. Some scholars now deny the existence of such literary
sources in favor of independent blocks of tradition which have been
subsequently joined end to end. Cf. Wenham, Numbers, 18-21; and
Rendtorff, Das überlieferungsgeschichtliche Problem des Pentateuch.

[17]Diether Kellermann, Die Priesterschrift von Numeri 1,1 bis
10,10, 2-3. We will discuss Kellermann's work in more detail in
our treatment of the census lists in Numbers 1 and 26 in Chapter
Five.

[18]Noth, Numbers, 4-12. Cf. also Noth, A History of Pentateuchal
Traditions.

[19]Bernini, Il Libro dei Numeri, 5-8.

[20]Wenham, Numbers, 14-21. Cf. also our discussion of Wenham's
commentary in Chapter One.

[21]Noth, Numbers, 11.

NOTES TO CHAPTER THREE: NUMBERS AS A LITERARY UNIT

[1]Mays, Baentsch, Dillmann, and in some ways Wenham, Noth and
Gray, are examples of scholars who disregard the present division
of Numbers as the fourth of five parts of the Pentateuch in their
analysis of the book's structure. The fact that several scholars
assume such a position suggests that the shape of Numbers as an
independent book is not as immediately self-evident as it may be for
other books of the Pentateuch. Genesis and Deuteronomy, for example,
provide such clear evidence of cohesiveness that it is difficult to
find anyone who would deny their status as separate literary entities. We will argue, however, that a careful analysis of the evidence will show that Numbers also forms a separate literary unit
within the Pentateuch.

[2]Guthrie, "The Book of Numbers," 85.

[3]Dentan, "Numbers, Book of," 568.

[4]For other references, cf. Ludwig Blau, Zur Einleitung in die
Heilige Schrift (Budapest: n.p., 1894), 41; and Wilhelm Bacher, Die
exegetische Terminologie der Jüdischen Traditionsliteratur, I
(Leipzig: J. C. Hinrich, 1905), 63-64.

[5]Yoma 7:1; Sotah 7:9; and Menahoth 4:3.

[6]Tosefta Megillah 4:7.

[7]Sifre II, 127; Sifra to 16:5 (80d 4, 6); Sifra to 23:18 (101b
4); and Sifra to 23:20 (101c).

[8]The designation continued to be used in later rabbinic traditions. Examples include the Jerusalem Talmud, Sota 1:10 (17c 9),
and the Midrash Rabbah on Numbers, II (11a 5). For other references,
cf. Blau, Zur Einleitung, 44.

[9]Josephus, LCL (Cambridge, Massachusetts: Harvard University
Press, 1966), vol. 1, 179.

[10]Tractate Soferim 35b, in The Minor Tractates of the Talmud (London: Soncino Press, 1965), vol. 1, 218. Cf. also Josef M. Oesch, Petucha und Setuma, Untersuchungen zu einer überlieferten Gliederung im hebräischen Text des Alten Testaments (Göttingen: Vandenhoeck & Ruprecht, 1979), 22. The same regulation is found also in the Babylonian and Jerusalem Talmuds.

[11]Cf. Christian D. Ginsburg, Introduction to the Massoretico-Critical Edition of the Hebrew Bible (London: Trinitarian Bible Society, 1897), 1; Herbert Edward Ryle, The Canon of the Old Testament (London: Macmillan, 1895), 291-292; and more recently, Sid Z. Leiman, The Canonization of Hebrew Scripture (Hamden, Conn.: Archon Books, 1976), 165, n. 264; and Oesch, Petucha und Setuma, 18.

[12]On the recent trends in scholarship on the Samaritan Pentateuch, cf. Frank M. Cross, "Aspects of Samaritan and Jewish History in Late Persian and Hellenistic Times," HTR 59 (1966), 201-211; J. D. Purvis, The Samaritan Pentateuch and the Origin of the Samaritan Sect (Cambridge, Massachusetts: Harvard University Press, 1968). The article on the "Samaritan Pentateuch" in IDBSup provides a helpful summary and bibliography.

[13]Henry Barclay Swete, An Introduction to the Old Testament in Greek (Cambridge: Cambridge University Press, 1914), 201-2; cf. also Leiman, Canonization, 165, n. 264.

[14]The Codex Alexandrinus in Reduced Photographic Facsimile, Old Testament, Part I (London: The British Museum, 1915).

[15]Otto Eissfeldt, The Old Testament, An Introduction, tr. Peter Ackroyd (New York: Harper and Row, 1965), 156.

[16]Leiman, Canonization, 165, n. 264.

[17]Sidney Jellicoe, The Septuagint and Modern Study (Oxford: Clarendon Press, 1968), 55-6; selected essays in Studies in the Septuagint: Origins, Recensions, and Interpretations, ed. Sidney Jellicoe (New York: KTAV Publishing House, 1974), 158-224; and Ralph Klein, Textual Criticism of the Old Testament, The Septuagint after Qumran (Philadelphia: Fortress Press, 1974).

[18]Leiman, Canonization, 26-29, 131.

[19]Patrick Skehan, "The Biblical Scrolls from Qumran and the Text of the Old Testament," BA 28 (1965), 87-100. Skehan writes that "the recognized authority of the Torah and the Latter (Writing) Prophets at Qumran is beyond dispute on the basis of the formal citations and commentary in addition to the copies of the text" (p. 89).

[20]Otto Kaiser, Introduction to the Old Testament, tr. John Sturdy (Minneapolis, Minn.: Augsburg Publising House, 1975), 408.

[21]Oesch, Petucha und Setuma, 18. Oesch only raises the possibility of this date and provides a number of suggestive biblical citations.

[22]Jacob Milgrom, in his article on "Leviticus" in IDBSup, 541, aptly acharacterizes the essential distinctiveness between Exodus and Leviticus when he writes that Leviticus "is thematically an independent entity. In Exodus, the P code describes the construction of the cultic implements. . . ., whereas Leviticus converts this static picture into scenes from the living cult."

[23]The only exception is Lev 7:38 which mentions the "wilderness of Sinai" but only in connection with a law commanded on Mount Sinai: "This is the law of the burnt offering . . . which the LORD commanded Moses on Mount Sinai, on the day he commanded the people of Israel to bring their offerings to the LORD, in the wilderness of Sinai."

[24]Noth, Überlieferungsgeschichtliche Studien.

[25]Engnell, "The Pentateuch," 50-67.

[26]Cross, Canaanite Myth and Hebrew Epic, 317.

[27]Rudolf Smend, Die Entstehung des Alten Testaments (Stuttgart: Verlag W. Kohlhammer, 1978), 46.

[28]Kellermann, Die Priesterschrift, 1ff.

[29]This is true of commentators like Baentsch, Holzinger, Gray, and more recently, Marsh and Snaith.

[30]Noth, Überlieferungsgeschichtliche Studien, 190-205, 217.

[31]Smend, Entstehung, 46, 63.

[32]Rendtorff, Pentateuch, 166-8.

[33]A. Graeme Auld, Joshua, Moses and the Land (London: T. & T. Clark, 1980).

[34]Ibid., 98-100, 111-2.

[35]Goldberg, Das Buch Numeri, 11.

[36]Nahum Sarna, "Bible," EncJud, vol. 4, 820. Otto Eissfeldt makes the same assumption in his book, The Old Testament, An Introduction: "As far as the Pentateuch is concerned, it is in any case clear that its division into five books took place only when the whole of the material now united within it had already been incorporated, and that this division was aimed at producing sections of approxomately equal length, corresponding to the normal length of the scrolls of the time" (p. 135). Later, however, Eissfeldt acknowledges that "the dividing lines between the individual books of the Pentateuch are in general meaningful" (p. 156). In regard to Numbers, he writes that "there is something new with the beginning of Numbers" and that "Deuteronomy stands out sharply from the end of Numbers" (pp. 156-7). Yet Eissfeldt concludes that "for our understanding of the Pentateuch, this five-fold division must not be in any case determinative, and a division undertaken with reference to the contents themselves would appear differently" (p. 157).

[37]Oesch, Petucha und Setuma, 22.

[38]The numbers of verses are taken from the Massoretic data. Genesis contains 1,534 verses, Exodus 1,209 verses, Leviticus 859, Numbers 1288 and Deuteronomy 955 verses.

NOTES TO CHAPTER FOUR: INTERPRETATIONS OF NUMBERS 1 AND 26

[1]Some scholars have proposed that the order of the list of
spies in Num 13:4-15 has been altered in the course of transmission
which has caused Ephraim and Manasseh, the two tribes of Joseph, to
be separated. They argue that vv. 10-12 should be placed before
v. 8 so that the list would have the following order: Reuben, Simeon,
Judah, Issachar, Zebulun, Manasseh, Ephraim, Benjamin, Dan, Asher,
Naphtali, Gad. The order of the preceding lists in Numbers places
Ephraim before Manasseh. Jack Sasson has recently proposed that the
seventh position in these lists was sometimes used to draw attention
to a noteworthy individual. In the list in Num 13:4-15, Ephraim
was given the preferred slot of seventh place because "that tribe's
delegate to the scouting mission was Hosea, son of Nun, better
known after v. 16, as Joshua, son of Nun." Cf. Jack Sasson, "A
Genealogical 'Convention' in Biblical Chronography?" ZAW 90 (1978),
171-185. Of course, this suggestion depends on a reconstruction
rather than the present form of the text.

[2]Martin Noth, Das System der zwölf Stämme Israels (Darmstadt:
Wissenschaftliche Buchgesellschaft, 1930, reprinted 1966), 7-28,
122-32.

[3]The tribal list in Num 34:16-29 is usually thought to be
secondary and late. The order involved is at least in part due to
the preceding narrative in which Reuben, Gad and the half-tribe of
Manasseh have settled in the Transjordan and so are not included in
the list of tribal leaders who will supervise the division of the
land of Canaan. Judah thereby leads the list.

[4]Noth, Das System, 14ff., 23ff.

[5]Ibid., 24ff.

[6]Ibid., 126ff.

[7]A. D. H. Mayes, Israel in the Period of the Judges (Naperville,
Ill.: Alec R. Allenson, 1974), 8-11, 16-31.

[8]Ibid., 18-20.

[9]Noth, Das System, 24-28.

[10]Mayes, Israel, 27, 31.

[11]Ibid., 24-26.

[12]Ibid., 28-29.

[13]Ibid., 20-21.

[14]Norman Gottwald, The Tribes of Yahweh, 358-375.

[15]Robert R. Wilson, Genealogy and History in the Biblical World
(New Haven: Yale University Press, 1977), esp. 183-198. Cf. also
Wilson, "The Old Testament Genealogies in Recent Research," JBL 94
(1975), 169-189; and Wilson, "Between 'Azel' and 'Azel,' Interpreting the Biblical Genealogies," BA 42 (1979), 11-22.

[16]Ibid., 193-195. Cf. also M. Cohen, "The Shilonite Priesthood in the United Monarchy of Ancient Israel," HUCA 36 (1965),
94-98. Cohen provides evidence that the northern Ephraimite tribe
played a major role in the rise of Saul to power.

[17] Wilson, Genealogy, 193.

[18] Ibid., 188; cf. n. 110.

[19] Perhaps the most significant alteration from Genesis 46 within the list in Numbers 26 is the expanded enumeration of a depth of seven generations for the tribe of Joseph via Manasseh as recorded in Num 26:28-34. All the other tribes in Numbers 26 barely reach beyond the second or third generation. Jack Sasson is perhaps correct when he observes that "the reason for extending Joseph's line via Manasseh is obvious. The genealogist was eager to link this eponymous ancestor to the well-known and juridically important incident of Zelophehad's daughters (cf. Num 27:1-11). Thus, he shows the following: Joseph-Manasseh-Machir-Gilead-Hepher-Zelophehad-five daughters" (Sasson, "A Genealogical 'Convention,'" 182).

[20] Noth, Numbers, 203. Cf. also Noth, Das System, 122-132.

[21] Noth, Numbers, 205-208.

[22] John Skinner, A Critical and Exegetical Commentary on Genesis, ICC (Edinburgh: T & T Clark, 1930), 492-493; E. A. Speiser, Genesis, AB (Garden City, New York: Doubleday and Co., 1964), 344-347; Gerhard von Rad, Genesis, OTL (Philadelphia: Westminster Press, 1972), 403.

[23] Gottwald, The Tribes of Israel, 268.

[24] Baentsch, Exodus-Leviticus-Numeri, ad loc.; and Otto Procksch, Genesis, KAT (Leipzig: Gütersloh, 1924), ad loc.

[25] Cross, Canaanite Myth and Hebrew Epic, 308.

[26] Cited in M. Barnounin, "Remarques sur les tableaux numériques de livre des Nombres," RB 76 (1969), 351.

[27] John Calvin, Calvin's Commentaries (Grand Rapids, Michigan: Baker Book House, 1979), vol. 3, 442: "If any disputatious person should contend that one family could not increase in 250 years to so great an amount, and thus should reject as fabulous what surpasses the ordinary rule of nature, we must bear in mind what I have already stated, that, inasmuch as this increase depended on the power of God, nothing is more absurd than to measure it by ordinary rules. For the intention of the Spirit is to represent to our eyes the incredible power of God in a conspicuous and signal miracle."

[28] Julius Wellhausen, Prolegomena to the History of Ancient Israel (Gloucester, Massachusetts: Peter Smith, 1883, reprinted 1973), 348.

[29] Commentators like Knobel, Dillmann, Baentsch, Gray and Heinisch all dismissed the census figures as unhistorical. The figures implied a total population of over two million people, including women and children. The Sinai peninsula, they argued, could never have sustained such a mass of people for any period of time. Keil, a conservative commentator, maintained that the Sinai peninsula was more fertile in ancient times and that God provided for the large numbers of Israelites through miracles (Keil, The Pentateuch, Numbers and Deuteronomy, 5ff.). Gispen (1959) is the most recent commentator to accept the authenticity of the census figures for the period of the wilderness wandering (Gispen, Het Boek Numeri, vol. 1, 29-34).

[30]W. M. Flinders Petrie, Egypt and Israel (New York: The Macmillan Co., 1923), 42-46. Cf. also Petrie, Researches in Sinai (New York: E. P. Dutton and Co., 1906).

[31]W. F. Albright, "The Administrative Divisions of Israel and Judah," JPOS 5 (1925), 20, n. 10. The earlier commentaries of Dillmann and Knobel had suggested that the census lists were from a later period, that is, late in the period of the judges. H. L. Strack attempted to defend the historical validity of the large numbers for the period of the wilderness wandering by suggesting that the two million or more people had left Egypt in several different groups at different times. Cf. Strack, Die Bücher Genesis, Exodus, Leviticus, und Numeri, Kurzgefasster Kommentar zu den heiligen Schriften Alten und Neuen Testamentes sowie zu den Apokryphen (Nordlingen: C. H. Beck, 1894), 213. However, in his article, "The Number of Israelites at the Exodus," PEQ 76 (1944), 164-168, A. Lucas argued that the rates of population growth in modern Egypt suggest that the 70 Israelites mentioned in Genesis 46 and Exodus 1 could have grown at the most to 10,363 people in a period of 430 years (Exod 12:40). For another treatment of the problem, cf. Martin Noth, Numbers, 22; and Noth, The History of Israel, 2nd ed. (New York: Harper and Brothers, 1960), 84f.

[32]Albright, "Administrative Divisions," 20. A. Bentzen, Introduction to the Old Testament, 5th ed. (Copenhagen: n. p., 1959), vol. 2, ad loc.; Holzinger, Numeri, ad loc.; and Georg Fohrer, Introduction to the Old Testament, ed. Ernst Sellin, tr. David Green (Nashville: Abingdon, 1965), 184, represent scholars who have argued for the origin of the numbers in the census lists in gematria or numerological speculations. The notion of gematria involves assigning numerical values to the letters of the alphabet in order to express some additional relation or meaning to a phrase. The first ten letters of the alphabet stand for ones, the eleventh through twentieth letters for tens and the rest stand for thousands. Thus, the numerical value of the phrase which is found in Numbers 1, בני ישראל, is equal to 2 + 50 + 10 / 10 + 300 + 200 + 1 + 30 = 603. The number 603 is the first part of the total of the census in Numbers 1 which 603,550. The number 550 is then also derived from another set of phrases which occurs in the same chapter. There are several objections to such an application of the principle of gematria to the census lists in Numbers 1 and 26. Gematria has been used to account for only one number, 603,550, while all the other numbers in Numbers 1 and 26 are left unexplained. Moreover, the numerical correspondences sometimes appear arbitrary or contrived. Nor is it clear that the principle of gematria was even operative until a much later date in Israel's history, namely, the second century B.C. For a more thorough critique, cf. Kellermann, Die Priesterschrift, 161-162.

[33]Claus Schedl, "Biblische Zahlen--unglaubwürdig?" Theologisch-praktische Quartalschrift 107 (1959), 58-62. R. Zimmermann calculated that the greatest extent of the kingdom of Israel included a land area which would have accomodated a total population of at most 100,000-120,000 people. Thus, Israel could never have attained the size of population implied by the census lists in their present form (over 600,000 people) as Albright had suggested. Cf. R. Zimmermann, Bevolkerungsdichte und Heererzählen in Alt-Palästina (Klio: 1927), 340-343. More recently, Roland de Vaux has also argued that the census figures are too large, even for the population under the united monarchy. Cf. R. de Vaux, Ancient Israel (New York: McGraw-Hill, 1965), vol. 1, 65-67. A recent study by M. Razin focuses on the census and genealogical material in 2 Samuel 24 and 1 Chronicles 5-12 and 21. Razin concludes that, apart from a few remnants in regard to the relative positions of

some tribes, the census lists in Numbers 1 and 26 reflect little of the actual population of Israel under the reigns of Saul and David. Cf. M. Razin, Census Lists and Genealogies and Their Historical Implications for the Times of Saul and David (Hebrew) (Haifa: The School of Education of the Kibbutz Movement, 1977). Zimmermann, de Vaux and Razin would all concur with Schedl in discounting Albright's claim that the census figures in Numbers represent the total population of Israel in the time of David.

[34]George Mendenhall, "The Census Lists in Numbers 1 and 26," JBL 77 (1958), 52-66.

[35]Ibid., 66. Variations of Mendenhall's interpretations have been proposed by R. E. D. Clark, "The Large Numbers of the Old Testament," Journal of the Transactions of the Victoria Institute 87 (1955), 82-92; and J. W. Wenham, "Large Numbers in the Old Testament," Tyndale Bulletin 18 (1967), 19-53. Their results differ only slightly from Mendenhall's conclusions and introduce an unnecessary amount of complexity.

[36]Mendenhall takes note of the ubiquity of census taking in the ancient world, from Rome and Greece to Egypt and Babylon to Japan and China. For further demonstration of this fact, cf. Hyman Alterman, Counting People: The Census in History (New York: Harcourt, Brace and World, 1969). However, Mendenhall is most dependent on the Mari and Alalakh texts for his argument since they are some of the few which deal with military mustering of troops on the basis of villages or tribes. Cf. J.-R. Kupper, "Les recensement dans les textes de Mari," Studia Mariana, ed. A. Parrot (Leiden: E. J. Brill, 1950), 99-110; Kupper, Les nomades en Mésopotamie au temps de rois de Mari (Paris: 1957), 47-81; J. D. Wiseman, The Alalakh Texts (London: 1953); E. A. Speiser, "The Alalakh Tablets," JAOS 74 (1954), 18-25.

[37]Mendenhall, "Census Lists," 63; cf. also 63, n. 52.

[38]Ibid., 63, n. 53.

[39]George Mendenhall, "Social Organization in Early Israel," Magnalia Dei: The Mighty Acts of God, In Memorium G. E. Wright, ed. Frank M. Cross et al. (New York: Doubleday, 1976), 148-149: "The 'great wars' of the Israelite 'conquest' cannot have been much more than guerilla skirmishes involving little more than a few hundred peasant militia in most instances. As Orlinsky, among others, has pointed out, there is hardly a case before Saul in which there was a complete mobilization of the entire Twelve Tribe Federation. In fact, it seems to me now very probable that the 'census lists' of Numbers 1 and 26 reflect the very early military organization inherited by King Saul and continued by David, prior to the complete bureaucratization of the kingdom under the impact of the old Jebusite political structure that he took over: the Davidic 'census'. . . . The traditional tribal recruiting district, the 'eleph, is the fundamental structure of the military organiza-tion--and well illustrated in the early stories of David. It is this that David's census destroyed forever--and the plague that broke out was evidently regarded as the divine punishment that ensued."

[40]George Mendenhall, "The Hebrew Conquest of Palestine," BA 25 (1962), 79-80. Cf. also M. Weippert, The Settlement of the Israelite Tribes in Palestine (Naperville, Illinois: Alec R. Allenson, 1971), 60.

[41]Gottwald, The Tribes of Yahweh, 51, 242-291. Gottwald writes: "Numbers 1 reports, therefore, a situation at some point in the premonarchic federation of shivṭē (= maṭṭōth) Israel when they collectively committed themselves to field an army of 5,500 men mustered by small quotas from the secondary organization units, averaging almost fifty 'alāphīm per tribe, with each tribe's 'eleph averaging a little more than nine men per unit. The averages for Numbers 26 vary only fractionally from those of Numbers 1 . . . Taken together, the modesty of the numbers interpreted as composite sums of units and of men, the grouping of the tribal contingents into hundreds which vary in total from tribe to tribe, and the unstylized numbers for the 'alāphīm in each tribe--all these features seem to reflect authentic information which can only make sense under a premonarhic military organization in which mishpāḥōth/ 'alāphīm contributed small quotas of warriors who were integrated into larger tribal tactical units."

[42]Ibid., 274: "If it is conjectured that mishpāḥāh and 'eleph (in the extended sense of the social unit from which the military unit of the same name was drawn) refer to the same organizational entity, we have at least the outlines of an answer to our earlier question about the approximate number of 'alāphīm per shēvet. The lists of Numbers 1 and 26 yield an average of about fifty 'alāphīm per tribe, ranging from a low of twenty-two for Simeon to a high of seventy-six for Judah . . . Since less than one-tenth of the enumerated 596 mishpāḥōth/'alāphīm of Numbers 26 are given by name, it is obvious how incomplete P's information was."

[43]Noth, Numbers, 22. Cf. also Gottwald's recognition of this fact, The Tribes of Yahweh, 272.

[44]Mendenhall, "Social Organization," 148-149.

[45]M. Barnouin, "Remarques sur les Tableaux Numériques du Livre des Nombres," RB 76 (1969), 351-364; and Barnouin, "Les Recensements du Livre des Nombres et L'Astronomie Babylonienne," VT 27 (1977), 280-303. Interestingly, Gottwald cites Barnouin's earlier article in his treatment of the census lists as "another way of reducing the numbers drastically" (Tribes of Yahweh, 742, n. 185). Despite the fact that Barnouin's thesis would undermine much of his reconstruction which is based on Mendenhall's work, Gottwald fails to engage or refute Barnouin's position.

[46]Barnouin, "Remarques," 362.

[47]The complexity of Barnouin's system of generating the census numbers from astronomical periods, the failure to account for all the numbers in the census lists, and the question of the degree of intentionality in relating the census numbers to astronomical calculations represent possible objections to Barnouin's analysis. For a more thorough response, cf. Wenham, Numbers, 64-66.

[48]Cf., for example, Beno Jacob, Der Pentateuch (Leipzig: Verlag Von Veit, 1905), 98-113. Jacob proposes a series of mathematical calculations based on the tribes' order of birth in the Genesis narratives and the relative positions within the tribal lists. His calculations, he argues, would account for the numbers as they now stand in the text. The complexity of some of the calculations, however, does not compel assent.

[49]Gray, Numbers, 14. Gray suggests that the number of fighting men assigned to the tribe of Judah implies a total population of about 250,000 people for that tribe. He correctly acknowledges the possibility that this may be a rough approximation of the actual

population of the Southern Kingdom at some point in its history. However, in its present context, the primary function of the census numbers of Judah is not historical but literary: Judah has the largest number and so is the tribe of highest status. This is also in accordance with the favorable blessing of Jacob on Judah in Genesis 49.

[50]Cf. Cazelles, Les Nombres, 8.

[51]In his article on the census lists, Mendenhall also applied his thesis to the list of numbers from each tribe who came to David's coronation in 1 Chronicles 12. Ralph W. Klein has argued against Mendenhall that the numbers in 1 Chronicles 12 are not historical but symbolic. The northern and most remote tribes bring the largest delegations to David's coronation at Hebron in the south. The delegation of Ephraim and Manasseh from the north are more numerous than David's own tribe of Judah. Such a situation seems historically very improbable. The numbers are then best interpreted as symbolic expressions of the enormous enthusiasm of even the most remote tribes for David and his kingship. A similar tendency may be operative, at least to some extent, in the census lists in Numbers. Cf. Ralph W. Klein, "How Many in a Thousand?" a seminar paper presented at the annual meeting of the Society of Biblical Literature, New York (December 1982).

[52]Exod 12:37 and Num 11:21 are typically assigned to J, but some scholars argue that a later Priestly editor has replaced the original number in these J passages with the number 600,000 in order to correspond roughly to the numbers of the census lists in Numbers 1 and 26. Cf. Gray, Numbers, 14; and Kellermann, Die Priesterschrift, 159. Such a position is possible but difficult to prove one way or the other.

[53]This multiplication may also be what is in part expressed by the reference to a census in Exodus 38. Exod 38:25ff. gives a total of 603,550 persons which is the same total of the census in Numbers 1:46. The contexts of the two Priestly passages, however, are quite different. In Exodus, a tax of half a shekel is being levied for construction and maintenance of the sanctuary. The census in Numbers 1 does not mention such a tax and involves a census of men who are 20 years or older who are able to go to war. Some have argued that the two passages are actually two stages of the same census. A more probable assumption is that Exodus 38 and Numbers 1 are intended as two separate events in the desert since they are clearly set on different days of the month (cp. Exod 40:17 and Num 1:1). Cf. J. Liver, "The Half-Shekel Offering in Biblical and Post-Biblical Literature," HTR 56 (1963), 177.

NOTES TO CHAPTER FIVE: CENSUS LISTS AS FRAMEWORK

[1]Gray, Numbers, xxii.

[2]The reason for the slight change in order of Ephraim and Manasseh is not immediately evident. Jack Sasson has proposed one plausible explanation on the basis of his thesis that the seventh position in the genealogical and tribal lists was often given to tribes or members in order to highlight them in some way. In Numbers 26, Manasseh is the only tribe with a depth of seven generations (from Joseph and Manasseh to the five daughters of Zelophehad) and serves to forge a link between one of the twelve tribes and the following narratives concerning the daughters of Zelophehad in Numbers 27 and 36. Thus, Manasseh was given the seventh position

in the list instead of Ephraim who occupied that position in the
list in Numbers 1. Cf. Jack Sasson, "A Genealogical 'Convention,'"
182. Note also our discussion of the extended genealogies in
Numbers 26 in Chapter Four.

[3]The names of the majority of sub-clans in Numbers 26 are
derived from the expanded genealogy in Genesis 46 which lists the
twelve sons of Jacob and their immediate offspring. The writer may
have simply taken the Genesis 46 list and added another generation
to it. For example, the list in Gen 46:14 reads, "The sons of
Zebulun: Sered, Elon, and Jahleel." Num 26:26 expands this by one
generation: "The sons of Zebulun, according to their families:
of Sered, the family of the Seredites; of Elon, the family of the
Elonites; of Jahleel, the family of the Jahleelites." Most of the
names of the second generation in Numbers 26 have apparently been
constructed by taking the names of the last generation mentioned in
Genesis 46 and adding the phrase, "the family of" plus the gentilic
form of the name, e.g., "the family of the Seredites." Names from
other sources, some unknown to us, also appear, but the great
majority of the material in Numbers 26 is related to the list in
Genesis 46 in this manner. Cf. our discussion of the list of
sub-clans in Numbers 26 in Chapter Four.

[4]Kellermann, for example, argues that the core of the census
list in Numbers 1 belongs to Pg (the Grundschrift of the Priestly
tradition) while the chronological and geographical notes in Numbers
1:1 belong to another stage of the tradition. Cf. Kellermann, Die
Priesterschrift, 14.

[5]The arrangement of the tribes in chapter 2 resembles a military
camp, albeit of a special kind. Cf. Wenham, Numbers, 66-67; and
Y. Yadin, The Art of Warfare in Biblical Lands (New York: McGraw-
Hill, 1963), 236ff., 292-293, 396-397.

[6]The superscription which precedes the census in Num 26:4--"The
people of Israel who came forth out of the land of Egypt were:"--
seems to contradict Num 26:63-65 which states that none of those
numbered in the first census (except Caleb and Joshua) were included
in this second census in Numbers 26. Yet in the final understanding
of the census, the statement in 26:63-65 clearly predominates since
it is "the last word" regarding the purpose of the census. Thus,
26:4 in its present context may be simply understood as referring
to the twelve tribes that came out of Egypt rather than the actual
individuals for thay have all perished, according to 26:63-65.

[7]Scholars have often failed to interpret the Balaam cycle
within its present context in Numbers and have analyzed it in
isolation from its narrative surroundings. We will present a more
detailed discussion of the Balaam cycle in Chapter Seven.

[8]Cf. de Vaulx, Les Nombres, 30; J. Fichter, "Die etymologische
Ätiologie in den Namengebungen," VT 6 (1956), 372-396.

[9]A. Jaubert, "Le calendrier des Jubilés et de la secte de
Qumrân, ses origines bibliques," VT 3 (1953), 250-264, esp. 259-260.

[10]Cf. A. C. Tunyogi, "The Rebellions of Israel," JBL 81 (1962),
388.

[11]Cf. de Vaulx, Les Nombres, 40.

[12]The literature on the structure and theology of the Priestly tradition is extensive and reaches into a large number of issues. For further literature and a sample of recent representative views, cf. K. Elliger, "Sinn und Ursprung der priesterliche Geschichtserzählung," Zeitschrift für Theologie und Kirche 49 (1952), 121-143; reprinted in Elliger, Kleine Schriften zum Alten Testaments, ed. H. Gese and O. Kaiser (Munich: Chr. Kaiser Verlag, 1966), 174-198; P. Grelot, "La derniere étape de la rédaction sacerdotale," VT 6 (1956), 174-189; Sean E. McEvenue, The Narrative Style of the Priestly Writer (Rome: Biblical Institute Press, 1971); Walter Brueggemann, "The Kerygma of the Priestly Writers," ZAW 84 (1972), 397-417; reprinted in The Vitality of Old Testament Traditions, ed. W. Brueggemann and H. W. Wolff (Atlanta: John Knox Press, 1975); Frank M. Cross, Canaanite Myth and Hebrew Epic, 293-325; Enzo Cortese, La Terra di Canaan nella Storia Sacerdotale del Pentateuco, Suppl. alla Rivista Biblica (Italiana), Volume 5 (Brescia: Paideia, 1972); E. Cortese, "Dimensioni Letterarie e Elementi Structurali de Pg: Per una Teologia del Documento Sacerdotale," Rivista Biblica (Italiana) 28 (1980), 59-77; Joseph Blenkinsopp, "The Structure of P," CBQ 38 (1976), 275-292; Norbert Lohfink, "Die Priesterschrift und die Geschichte," Supplements to Vetus Testamentum, Congress Volume (Gottingen, 1977) (Leiden: E. J. Brill, 1978), 189-225; and Richard Elliott Friedman, The Exile and Biblical Narrative, HSM (Chico, California: Scholars Press, 1981). On the date of the Priestly tradition, cf. J. G. Vink, The Date and Origin of the Priestly Code in the Old Testament (Leiden: E. J. Brill, 1969); A. S. Kapelrud, "The Date of the Priestly Code," Annual of the Swedish Theological Institute in Jerusalem 3 (1964), 58-64; A. Hurvitz, "Evidence of Language in Dating the Priestly Code, a Linguistic Study in Technical Terms and Terminology," RB 81 (1974), 24-56; R. Polzin, Late Biblical Hebrew, Toward an Historical Typology of Biblical Hebrew Prose (Missoula, Montana: Scholars Press, 1976); and Gary Rendsburg, "Late Biblical Hebrew and the Date of P," JANESCU 12 (1980), 65-80.

[13]For a more thorough description of the forms and functions of linear and segmented genealogies, cf. Wilson, Genealogy, 9-55.

[14]Walther Eichrodt, Die Quellen der Genesis von neuem untersucht (Giessen: A. Töpelmann, 1916), 20-23, 52-54.

[15]Cf. Josef Scharbert, "Der Sinn der Toledot-Formel in der Priesterschrift," Wort-Gebot-Glaube, Beiträge zur Theologie des Alten Testaments, ed. Hans Joachim Stoebe (Zurich: Zwingli Verlag, 1970), 45; and Otto Eissfeldt, "Biblos Geneseos," Kleine Schriften, III, ed. R. Sellheim and Fritz Maass (Tübingen: J. C. B. Mohr, 1966), 459.

[16]Scharbert, "Der Sinn der Toledot-Formel," 56.

[17]Lohfink, "Die Priesterschrift und die Geshichte," 204, n. 38.

[18]Eissfeldt, "Biblos Geneseos," 461; Gerhard von Rad, Genesis, 70; Cross, Canaanite Myth and Hebrew Epic, 308; Marshall D. Johnson, The Purpose of the Biblical Genealogies, with Special Reference to the Setting of the Genealogies of Jesus (Cambridge: Cambridge University Press, 1969), 14ff.

[19]Peter Weimar, "Die Toledot-Formel in der priesterschriftlichen Geschichtsdarstellung," BZ 18 (1974), 65-93, esp. 84-87. Weimar provides a helpful summary of the debate and concludes that no full toledot book existed. Only a few of the toledot formulae existed in the prior tradition which Pg used for his work. The other toledot superscriptions were creations of Pg. Of course,

others of a more conservative bent have argued that the toledot
formulae are not products of a later tradition but form the original
basis for the whole book of Genesis which was written at one time
by one author in its entirety. Cf. S. R. Külling, Zur Datierung
der "Genesis" P-Stücke (Kampen: J. H. Kok, 1964), 216-226; and
M. H. Woudstra, "The Toledot of the Book of Genesis and Their
Redemptive-Historical Significance," Calvin Theological Journal
5 (1970), 184-189. Such a position, however, ignores the evidence
of various oral and literary layers and the long history of the
growth of the literature.

[20]For a brief review of the discussion, cf. Eissfeldt, "Biblos
Geneseos," 459-460.

[21]Lohfink, "Die Priesterschrift und die Geschichte," 204,
n. 38; 209, n. 53. Cf. also Kellermann, Die Priesterschrift, 46-48;
and Cortese, "Dimensioni Letterarie," 135.

[22]Otto Eissfeldt, "Toledot," Kleine Schriften, IV, 1-7; von
Rad, Genesis, 70.

[23]Eissfeldt, "Biblos Geneseos," 468-470; Eissfeldt, "Toledot,"
3-7. Cf. also Johnson, The Purpose of the Biblical Genealogies,
14ff.

[24]We will discuss the redactional history of Num 3:1 in more
detail below.

[25]Lohfink, "Die Priesterschrift und die Geschichte," 204, n.
38.

[26]Other attempts have been made to fix the original number of
toledot at seven which, it is argued, represents a significant
number for the Priestly tradition (the creation in seven days in
Genesis 1). Thus, Johnson, The Purpose of the Biblical Genealogies,
27, counts seven toledot from Abraham to Aaron. This seems to
ignore arbitrarily the toledot preceding Abraham. Sven Tengström,
Die Toledotformel und die literarische Struktur der priesterlichen
Erweiterungsschicht im Pentateuch (Lund: GWK Gleerup, 1981), 54ff.
counts only the toledot which trace the central genealogical line
in Genesis in connection with the vertical genealogies. Thus, the
toledot of the heavens and the earth, Adam, Noah, Shem, Terah,
Isaac and Jacob form the seven-fold scheme which Tengström detects.
Apart from ignoring the other toledot which are associated with
the horizontal or segmented genealogies, Tengström arbitrarily
ignores the toledot of Aaron (and Moses) in Num 3:1, a verse which
he suggests is part of P's original toledot series. This is done
in order to attain the number seven. These varied attempts to fix
the original number of the toledot series demonstrate the arbitrary
nature of such a procedure. We would not rule out the possibility
that the toledot series consisted of some significant number at
some earlier stage. The present form of the series, however, seems
to have obscured any such numerical significance.

[27]Weimar, "Die Toledot-Formel," 65-93.

[28]Ibid., 84-87.

[29]Ibid., 87-93.

[30]Ibid., 90-91, n. 110. Cf. also P. Weimar, "Aufbau und
Struktur der priesterschriftlichen Jakobgeschichte," ZAW 86 (1974),
178-179. Weimar relies to some extent on Diether Kellermann's
treatment of Num 3:1-4 in his monograph, Die Priesterschrift von

Numeri 1,1 bis 10,10, 46-48, in which he detects more than one later redactional layer within the verses in question. Noth, Numbers, 31, comes to a similar conclusion. On this question, see below.

[31]Kellermann, Die Priesterschrift, 46-48. We cannot attempt to comment on all of Kellermann's detailed redactional analysis of Numbers 3. Only a broad outline will be presented as a backdrop to the more detailed analysis of the toledot formula in Num 3:1.

[32]Ibid., 4-32, 49-62; cf. also 145-151.

[33]Ibid., 32-49.

[34]Ibid., 46-49.

[35]Ibid., 45-46.

[36]We cannot here consider the complex but important question of the actual historical relationship of the Aaronic priesthood and the Levites in the history of Israelite religion. We are concerned here with the stages of reflection on the relationship of priests and Levites within the later Priestly tradition as portrayed in Numbers 3.

[37]Eleazar came to be the chief priest. This is reflected in the later additions of Num 3:32 and 4:16 and stated explicitly in the formal succession of the priesthood from Aaron to Eleazar in Num 20:25-28.

[38]Kellermann, Die Priesterschrift, 46-48.

[39]Scharbert, "Der Sinn der Toledot-Formel," 49, n. 13; Eissfeldt, "Biblos Geneseos," 462, n. 1; Kellermann, Die Priesterschrift, 46-48; and Tengström, Die Toledotformel, 55.

[40]This is also borne out by the tradition of the relative ages of both men. Aaron was the older brother. Num 33:39 states that "Aaron was a hundred and twenty-three years old when he died on Mount Hor." Deut 34:7 recounts the later death of Moses who was only "a hundred and twenty years old when he died."

[41]Lohfink, "Die Priesterschrift und die Geschichte," 204, n. 38.

[42]Cf. the discussion of Eissfeldt, "Toledot," 3-7, where he leaves the question open. Eissfeldt's primary concern is to show that Num 3:1, whatever its original location, is part of P's original toledot series (Pg) and not a secondary addition. Weimar has subsequently argued that Exod 6:14-25 is a late redactional insertion. Thus, even if the toledot formula of Aaron and Moses was originally found in Exodus 6, that would not prove that it belonged to the earliest layer of the Priestly tradition as Eissfeldt argued. Cf. Weimar, "Die Toledot-Formel," 91, n. 110.

[43]A third option would also be possible, even if less probable. Marshall Johnson has argued that an original and independent Toledot Book existed. This toledot series ran from Adam to Aaron and was the source of the formula in Num 3:1. Given the difficulties which we cited above in positing the existence of an independent Toledot Book in any form, this option is the least viable.

[44]In one of the most recent studies on the toledot formulae entitled Die Toledotformel und die literarische Struktur der priesterlichen Erweiterungsschicht im Pentateuch, Sven Tengström analyzes the toledot formulae in order to show that the Priestly stratum was not an independent literary source but a revision and expansion of an earlier Hexateuchal narrative tradition. In the course of his argument, Tengström argues that Num 3:1 is part of this early Priestly stratum. His reasons are its similarities to the preceding toledot formulae. These similarities, as we have noted, include the chronological note in Num 3:1 and the name formula ("these are the names of the sons of Aaron") which follows in Num 3:2. Tengström maintains that these features are the conscious stylistic marks of the compositional technique of the author of the basic P-stratum. However, he fails to consider the possibility that a later Priestly redactor has consciously imitated the style of the previous toledot formulae in constructing and placing a new toledot formula in Num 3:1. Such literary capabilities of later redactors cannot be dismissed out of hand. Tengström's earlier work, Die Hexateucherzählung (Lund: GWK Gleerup, 1976), likewise endeavors to show that P is not an independent source but presupposes throughout an earlier Hexateuchal narrative. The thesis is similar to that of Frank Cross, Canaanite Myth and Hebrew Epic, 301-320. The argument, however, may pose a false dichotomy. The Priestly source shows evidence at times of being a redactional layer, and at other times it seems to exhibit characteristics of an independent source. Cf. Brevard Childs, Introduction to the Old Testament as Scripture (Philadelphia: Fortress Press, 1979), 122-123. Moreover, as our study of Num 3:1 indicates, one must reckon with the possibility of more than one layer of Priestly redaction. This Tengström apparently does not do. For a more thorough overview and evaluation of Tengström's thesis, cf. A. Graeme Auld, Joshua, Moses and the Land, 92-93, 113-114; and Auld's review of Tengström's Die Hexateucherzählung in JSOT 8 (1978), 71-74.

[45]Scharbert, "Der Sinn der Toledot-Formel," 52.

[46]Eissfeldt, "Biblos Geneseos," 461.

[47]Scharbert, "Der Sinn der Toledot-Formel," 52.

[48]To the extent that these two forms of genealogies may have existed in oral form in an actual sociological setting in Israel's history, their original functions were quite different from their present literary function within the book of Genesis. Linear genealogies typically function in a society to legitimate a leader's claim to authority by demonstrating his descent from a renowned ancestor. Segmented genealogies typically function to register the political and social relationships among groups by adjusting their lineages to reflect the realities of the existing social order. Cf. Wilson, Genealogy, 189-202. The present literary functions of the genealogies in Genesis are now quite different from their original use in Israelite society.

[49]Cf. Exod 28:9-12 (a Priestly passage): "And you shall take two onyx stones, and engrave on them the names of the sons of Israel, six of their names on the one stone, and the names of the remaining six on the other stone, in the order of their birth . . . And you shall set the two stones upon the shoulder-pieces of the ephod, as stones of remembrance for the sons of Israel; and Aaron shall bear their names before the LORD upon his two shoulders for remembrance."

[50]Eissfeldt, "Biblos Geneseos," 462; Scharbert, "Der Sinn der Toledot-Formel," 49-50.

[51]Lohfink, "Die Priesterschrift und die Geschichte," 204, n. 38.

[52]Weimar, "Die Toledot-Formel," 87-93.

[53]John Skinner, Genesis, ICC (New York: Scribner's Sons, 1910). 40-41.

[54]Beno Jacob, Der Pentateuch, 92-98, 113, maintained that there exists an intentional correspondence in the number of people at three important junctures in the Pentateuch: Genesis 10, Genesis 46/Exodus 1, and Numbers 26. In each case, one counts 70 members in the family or group which is mentioned. Genesis 10 lists 70 members of the generation of the sons of Noah and marks the transition from all humanity to the father of Israel, Abraham. Genesis 46/Exodus 1 likewise has 70 members who represent the family of the sons of Jacob as well as the movement from a family history to a history of the people of Israel. Numbers 26 does not list 70 individuals but 70 family groups or clans, if one includes the five daughters of Zelophehad and the Levites in the following census. It represents the transition from the generation of the exodus to a new generation of Israelites. Jacob's observations are intriguing, although the probability that these numerical correspondences are intentional is difficult to establish.

[55]We wish to avoid at this point the issue of how the present shape of the Pentateuch originated, whether from an original Hexateuch or a Tetrateuch plus Deuteronomy. Our concern here is to discern the overarching editorial structure of the present shape of the Pentateuch and to show its correspondence to the overarching editorial structure of the book of Numbers.

[56]One possible objection which might be raised is that our view of the structure of the Pentateuch implies a disproportionately large section for the toledot of Jacob in comparison to the other toledot. The toledot of Jacob begins at Gen 37:2 and extends on into Numbers. As Lohfink points out, however, the sections introduced by the toledot formulae already consist of varying lengths even before Gen 37:2. Cf. Lohfink, "Die Priesterschrift und die Geschichte," 204, n. 38. Furthermore, the length of the section for the toledot of Jacob is an indication that the events and fate of the offspring of Jacob form the core and center of the Pentateuch in its present form.

[57]For a recent survey of traditional and modern attempts to locate the places named in Exodus-Numbers, cf. G. I. Davies, The Way of the Wilderness (New York: Cambridge University Press, 1979). For other summaries from a modern perspective, cf. Roland de Vaux, "L'Itinéraire des Israéliens de Cadès aux Plaines de Moab," Hommages à André Dupont-Sommer (Paris: Librairie d'Amerique et d'Orient, 1971), 331-342; and Wenham, Numbers, 216-230.

[58]The article which has formed the basis for subsequent discussions is by Martin Noth, "Der Wallfahrtsweg zum Sinai," PJ 36 (1940), 5-28. Cf. more recently, Cross, Canaanite Myth and Hebrew Epic, 308-317; J. Simons, Geographical and Topographical Texts of the Old Testament, 234ff.; G. I. Davies, "The Wilderness Itineraries and the Composition of the Pentateuch," VT 33 (1983), 1-13.

[59]On source criticism, cf. Jerome T. Walsh, "From Egypt to Moab, A Source Critical Analysis of the Wilderness Itinerary," CBQ 39 (1977), 20-33; and G. I. Davies, "The Wilderness Itineraries and the Composition of the Pentateuch," 1-13. The only recent

form-critical study is by G. I. Davies, "The Wilderness Itineraries:
A Comparative Study," Tyndale Bulletin 25 (1974), 46-81.

[60]Cross, Canaanite Myth and Hebrew Epic, 308. Cf. also Weimar,
"Die Toledot-Formel," 91, n. 110: "Genealogies and lists--just
like the toledot introductions--are limited to the first part of
Pg's presentation of history which ends with Ex. 1:7. In this
connection, it is relevant to note that in the second part of the
Priestly work the itinerary notes (the category of expansion in
space) become the major elements of structural division in place of
the toledot formulae (the category of extension in time)."

[61]Walsh, "From Egypt to Moab," 20-33.

[62]Davies, "The Wilderness Itineraries and the Composition of
the Pentateuch," 1-13.

[63]Cf. George Coats, "The Wilderness Itinerary," CBQ 34 (1972),
135-152. Coats argues that the itinerary notices serve to link
together certain traditions which were once independent and separate.
Thus, they do play a role in structuring the material.

[64]On the notices of change in geographical location as a means
of distinguishing and organizing smaller narrative sections in the
book of Genesis, cf. D. W. Baker, "Diversity and Unity in the
Literary Structure of Genesis," Essays on the Patriarchal Narratives, ed. A. R. Millard and D. J. Wiseman (Leicester, England:
Inter-Varsity Press, 1980), 194-195. Baker correctly perceives
the use of the itinerary or settlement notices in Genesis as
markers of structural subdivisions within the narrative. His
article provides a helpful survey of the wide range of structural
and framework devices in Genesis. His final conclusion, however,
that the unity of the book's structure necessitates a reappraisal
of the theory of source documents, does not necessarily follow.
Baker fails to take into account the artfulness of later redactors
in amalgamating and shaping older traditional material. For other
discussions of the use of geographical movement or location to
structure material in Genesis, cf. George Coats, From Canaan to
Egypt (Washington, D.C.: Catholic Biblical Association of America,
1976), 9; I. L. Seeligmann, "Hebraische Erzählung und biblische
Geschichtsschreibung," Theologische Zeitschrift 18 (1962), 307-310;
Claus Westermann, Genesis 12-50 (Darmstadt: Wissenschaftlische
Buchgesellschaft, 1977), 49-51, 159.

[65]Gen 12:8-10; 13:1-3; 13:12; 13:18; 14:5, 8; 14:11-13; 14:17;
17:22; 18:16; 19:1; 19:23; 19:30; 20:1; 21:14; 21:20-21; 21:33-34;
22:8-9; 22:19; 24:10; 24:61-62; 25:11 (within the toledot of Terah).

[66]It should also be noted that the toledot formulae in Genesis
and Numbers are almost always accompanied by another means of
marking structural divisions, whether a geographical note, a
chronological indicator or other transitional device. Baker lists
the following types of division markers which accompany the toledot
formulae in Genesis: chronological indicator--Gen 2:4; 5:1; change
in subject--Gen 6:9; 10:1; 11:10, 27; 25:19; 35:1; chronological
indicator and geographical note--Gen 25:12; change of subject and
geographical note--Gen 36:9; change in subject, chronological
indicator and geographical note--Gen 37:2. Cf. Baker, "Diversity
and Unity," 196; 205, n. 61. The toledot formula in Num 3:1 is
likewise additionally marked by a change of subject and a chronological notation.

[67]Cf. G. I. Davies, "The Wilderness Itineraries and the
Composition of the Pentateuch," 1-13. For a suggestive analysis

of other secondary material which may have been added to the latter
part of the book of Numbers in the process of later editing after
the definitive Priestly generational structure had been established,
cf. Auld, Joshua, Moses and the Land. Of course, the addition of
the book of Deuteronomy, however it was done, materially affected
the shape of the emerging Torah. Nevertheless, it did not substantially violate the overarching framework which had already been
established by the Priestly tradition for Genesis-Numbers.

[68]For other examples of recent attempts to describe the
structure of the Priestly tradition or the Pentateuch, cf. Casper
J. Labuschagne, "The Pattern of the Divine Speech Formulas in the
Pentateuch, The Key to Its Literary Structure," VT 32 (1982), 268-
296; or Blenkinsopp, "The Structure of P," 275-292. These attempts
to describe the structure of the Pentateuch discern, at best, only
a secondary means of structuring the material, whether divine
speech formulas (Labuschagne) or the formulaic reports of the
completion of a work or fulfillment of a divine command (Blenkinsopp).

NOTES TO CHAPTER SIX: THE SPY STORY

[1]Noth, Numbers, 101. George Coats, Rebellion in the Wilderness, 138-139, follows much of Noth's analysis except in assigning
the secondary material in 14:11b-23a to an addition within the J
source iteself rather than to a Deuteronomistic hand as Noth
proposed. The source analyses of de Vaux, The Early History of
Israel, 524, W. Beltz, Die Kaleb-Traditionen im Alten Testament
(Stuttgart: W. Kohlhammer, 1974), 11-46; James Flanagan, "History,
Religion and Ideology: The Caleb Tradition," Horizons 3 (1976),
177, and J. Maxwell Miller, "The Israelite Occupation of Canaan,"
Israelite and Judaean History, ed. John Hayes and J. Maxwell Miller
(Philadelphia: Westminster Press, 1977), 222, all follow Noth's
division with minor exceptions. Even the earlier source analysis
by G. B. Gray, Numbers, 129ff., agrees in large measure with Noth,
except that Gray labels the earlier tradition JE rather than J and
includes 13:32-33 and 14:8-9 in this earlier JE source.

[2]Sean McEvenue, "A Source-Critical Problem in Nm 14, 26-38,"
Bib 50 (1969), 453-465. Cf. also McEvenue, The Narrative Style of
the Priestly Writer (Rome: Biblical Institute Press, 1971), 90-91.
Much of McEvenue's source analysis of Pg (the earliest layer of P)
depends on the work by Karl Elliger, "Sinn und Ursprung der
Priesterlichen Geschichtserzählung, ZTK 49 (1952), 121-143.

[3]JE = 13:3b-16, 17b-20, 22-24, 26b-31, 33; 14:1b, 4, 8-9, 25,
29b.

[4]This is consistent with the analysis of Noth and most others.

[5]Pg = 13:1-3a, 17a, 21, 25, 26a, 32; 14:1a, 2, 5-7, 10,
26-29a, 35-38.

[6]McEvenue, "A Source-Critical Problem in Nm 14,26-38," 456-
458, argues that the use of the verbal root nw', "to oppose,
frustrate," in Num 13:34 is "an ironical reflection on Nm 13-14 in
conjunction with a late text in Nm 32." In particular, Num 32:6-15
is late by virtue of its dependence on the completed story of
Numbers 13-14 and Josh 14:6-14. The dependence suggests a time
when the Pentateuch was already joined to the Deuteronomistic
History. The other reverberation of the spry story in Num 26:64,
according to McEvenue, is also a late supplement which arose at the

same time as Num 32:6-15. On the theological conundrum in the
history of exegesis which was occasioned by the use of the root
nw', "to be frustrated," in connection with God in this context,
cf. Raphael Loewe, "Divine Frustration Exegetically Frustrated--
Numbers 14:34, תנואתי," Words and Meanings, Essays Presented to
David Winton Thomas, ed. Peter Ackroyd and Barnabas Lindars
(Cambridge: Cambridge University Press, 1968), 137-158.

[7]McEvenue, "A Source-Critical Problem," 127.

[8]Ibid., 127-144.

[9]Ibid., 128.

[10]Ibid.

[11]Wenham, Numbers, 124-126. Cf. our summary and critique of
Wenham in Chapter One.

[12]McEvenue, The Narrative Style, 94.

[13]Ibid., 125.

[14]Wenham concludes that his observations "do not of themselves
demand that the source critical analysis be abandoned." He admits
that the narrative's "present form may be the result of subsequent
expansion by a later editor," but it is not the result of "the
combination of two independent sources" (126). Still, he argues
that "it would seem safer to assume that it is a basic unit as it
stands" (126). We would concede that the present form of the spy
story certainly can be read as a unified story. The tensions in
the story are such that they do not simply cause the story to fly
apart. Moreover, the work of later redactors has bound the story
together in significant ways through various key words and explicit
correspondences. For example, an ironic correspondence exists
between what the people say they want to do (e.g., 14:1-4) and the
punishment which God later actually visits upon them (14:20-38).
There is a correspondence between the forty days of the spy mission
(13:25) and the forty years of wandering in the wilderness (14:34).
And the literary effect of placing the two traditions concerning
the territory covered by the spies, one of the whole land (P) and
the other only of the area around Hebron (J) is to make the account
of what the spies saw around Hebron a specific illustration of
what they otherwise saw in the whole land. But this question of
the literary effect of the present form of the story is a different
one from the question of the origin of the traditions.

[15]Gressmann, Mose und seine Zeit, 291-300; cf. also Gressmann,
Die Schriften, vol. 2, 109-113.

[16]Caleb was a Kenizzite, and Kenizzites were associated with
the Edomite tribes. Cf. Num 32:12 and Gen 36:11, 42.

[17]Gressmann, Mose und seine Zeit, 295.

[18]Ibid.

[19]Ibid., 298.

[20]Siegfried Wagner, "Die Kundschaftergeschichten im Alten
Testament," ZAW 76 (1964), 255-269.

[21]Ibid., 261-262.

[22]McEvenue, The Narrative Style, 96-97.

[23]Wagner, "Die Kundschaftergeschichten," 264.

[24]Noth, A History of Pentateuchal Traditions, 130-136; cf. also Noth, Numbers, 97-112.

[25]Noth, A History of Pentateuchal Traditions, 122-130; cf. also Noth, Numbers, 84-91.

[26]George Coats, Rebellion in the Wilderness, 249-251.

[27]Ibid., 137-156.

[28]Ibid., 251.

[29]Simon de Vries, "The Origin of the Murmuring Tradition," JBL 87 (1968), 51-58.

[30]Ibid., 58.

[31]Ibid., 52-54.

[32]Ibid., 54.

[33]Ibid.

[34]Ibid., 58.

[35]Volkmar Fritz, Israel in der Wüste, Traditionsgeschichtliche Untersuchung der Wüstenüberlieferung des Jahwisten (Marburg: N. G. Elwert Verlag, 1970), esp. 19-24, 79-86.

[36]Cf. Roland de Vaux, "The Settlement of the Israelites in Southern Palestine and the Origins of the Tribe of Judah," Translating and Understanding the Old Testament, ed. Harry Frank and William Reed (Nashville: Abingdon, 1970), 108-134; de Vaux, The Early History of Israel, 523-550; Mayes, Israel in the Period of the Judges, 100, 107-108; Miller, "The Israelite Occupation of Canaan," 222-225; Beltz, Die Kaleb-Traditionen; and Flanagan, "History, Religion and Ideology: The Caleb Tradition," 175-185. Cf. also the standard histories of ancient Israel on this issue.

[37]Ant. Jirku, "Wo stand ursprünglich die Notiz über Hebron im Num. 13,22?" ZAW 39 (1921), 312; S. Mowinckel, "Die Gründung von Hebron," Orientalia Suecana 4 (1955), 67-76; N. Na'aman, "Hebron was built seven years before Zoan in Egypt," VT 31 (1981), 488-492.

[38]Gray, Coats, Noth and others all assign 14:29 to P. McEvenue, "A Source-Critical Problem," 463, does likewise. McEvenue, however, assigns the following verses, 14:30-33, to a source which is after J and before P.

[39]Of course, the emphases on the LORD's presence in the midst of the camp, on the priests and Levites around the tent of meeting at the camp's center, and on the fact that the LORD commanded the census suggest that this is a military venture within a highly theological context.

[40]McEvenue, "A Source-Critical Problem," 456, argues that Num 26:64 was written at the time the Pentateuch was joined to the Deuteronomistic History. Cf. Noth, Numbers, 204. This editorial addition serves to make evident what was already implied in the earlier Priestly structure of the book which contained the two census lists and the spy story. The supplements of later editors (e.g., Num 26:63-65; Num 32:6-15) did not significantly alter but

rather enhanced the overall structure of the book which had already been established. These later supplements, along with the census lists and the spy story, serve to clearly bind the book together into a meaningful whole.

[41]McEvenue, The Narrative Style, 142-144.

[42]Ibid., 144.

[43]It is interesting to note that God's initial offer to Moses (14:11-12) is not prefaced by a binding oath formula. In contrast, the judgment on the old generation and the promise to the new generation is introduced by such a formula, "As I live . . ." (14:21, 28). God again binds himself to a people, the children of the wilderness generation.

[44]Cf. McEvenue, "A Source-Critical Problem," 456-459. McEvenue notes the play on the root nw', "oppose, discourage, frustrate," in Num 32:7, 9 and Num 14:34. Cf. also Gray, Numbers, 426; and Noth, Numbers, 237-238. For a recent suggestive treatment of Numbers 32 from a structuralist standpoint, cf. David Jobling, "The Jordan a Boundary: A Reading of Numbers 32 and Joshua 22," Society of Biblical Literature, 1980 Seminar Papers, ed. Paul J. Achtemeier (Chico, California: Scholars Press, 1980), 183-207.

[45]An obvious parallel to this chapter is found in the description of the future boundaries and division of the land in Ezekiel 47-48. Like Numbers 34, these chapters come at the end of the book of Ezekiel and function as statements of future promise which constitute a promising "last word" in the book.

[46]Coats, Rebellion in the Wilderness, 146.

[47]Goldberg, Numeri, 66.

[48]McEvenue, The Narrative Style, 142-144; see our discussion above.

[49]John Sturdy, Numbers, 94, for example, understands the theme of faithlessness as the central theme of Numbers when he writes, "These two chapters (Numbers 13-14) have a key position in the book, and set out in classic form the theme of faithlessness and its punishment . . . This strongly theological theme, the great theme of Numbers, underlies the whole narrative, and is responsible for the form it takes." McEvenue's reconstruction of the early layer of the Priestly work (Pg) presents a similarly pessimistic picture (McEvenue, The Narrative Style, 123): "Hope there is, but it is obscure. The events at Paran, together with sin at Meriba, forn in Pg a rather tragic last chapter in his story. Pg has not written a spy story in Num. 13-14. Rather he has written a story which can only be called 'Israel's self-condemnation at Paran.'"

[50]Coats, Rebellion in the Wilderness, 148.

[51]Katherine Sakenfeld, "The Problem of Divine Forgiveness in Numbers 14," CBQ 37 (1975), 317-330.

[52]We will discuss this latter aspect in more detail in Chapter Eight when we consider the function of law in Numbers.

[53]Andrew Tunyogi, "The Rebellions of Israel," JBL 81 (1962), 385-390, esp. 388, has an interesting discussion of Israel's history in the wilderness as an "exemplar history" which provides "archetypes" for all successive generations.

NOTES TO CHAPTER SEVEN: THE BALAAM CYCLE

[1]Noth, Numbers, 171.

[2]For differing views on the source-critical analysis of the
Balaam cycle, cf. Wilhelm Rudolph, Der Elohist von Exodus bis Joshua
(Berlin: A. Töpelmann, 1938), 97ff.; Otto Eissfeldt, "Die Komposition der Bileam-Erzählung, Eine Nachprüfung von Rudolphs Beitrag
zur Hexateuchkritik," ZAW 57 (1939), 212-241' Sigmund Mowinckel,
"Der Ursprung der Bil'amsage," ZAW 48 (1930), 233-271; Noth, A
History of Pentateuchal Traditions, 76; and de Vaulx, Les Nombres,
255-264. Several scholars have disputed the conventional criteria
for the division of at least some portions of the cycle into J and
E sources. These include L. M. Pakozdy, "Theologische Redaktionsarbeit in der Bileam-Perikope," Von Ugarit nach Qumran, ed. J.
Hempel and L. Rost (Berlin: A. Töpelmann, 1961), 161-176; Walter
Gross, Bileam: Literar- und formkritische Untersuchung der Prosa
in Num. 22-24 (Munich: Kösel, 1974); Alexander Rofé, The Book of
Balaam (Hebrew) (Jerusalem: Simor Ltd., 1979); Ludwig Schmidt, "Die
alttestamentliche Bileamüberlieferung," BZ 23 (1979), 234-261; and
Hedwige Rouillard, "L'ânesse de Balaam," RB 87 (1980), 5-36, 211-
241.

[3]For example, Holzinger, Numeri, 109-111, argued that the
oracles did not belong to J or E but were much later products of
the postexilic period.

[4]Gressmann, Die Schriften, vol. 3, 52-70.

[5]Cf. S. Daiches, "Balaam--A Babylonian Baru," Bible Studies
(London: Edward Goldston, 1950), 110-119; René Largement, "Les
oracles de Bileam et las mantique suméro-akkadienne," Travaux de
l'Institut Catholique de Paris, École des Langues Orientales
Anciennes de l'Institut Catholique de Paris: Mémorial du Cinquan-
tenaire (Paris: Bloud and Gay, 1964), 37-50; R. Castellino, "Un
'giudizio divino' con rituale in Mesopotamia?" JCS 9 (1977), 3-6,
32-36; Aelrud Cody, "The Phonecian Ecstatic in Wenamūn, a Professional Oracular Medium," JEA 65 (1979), 99-106; and L. Rost, "Fragen
um Bileam," Beiträge zur Alttestamentlichen Theologie, Festschrift
für Walther Zimmerli, ed. H. Donner et al. (Göttingen: Vandenhoeck
& Ruprecht, 1977).

[6]On the Deir 'Allā texts and Balaam, cf. J. Hoftijzer and G.
van der Kooij, Aramaic Texts from Deir 'Alla (Leiden: E. J. Brill,
1976), 173-192, 268-282; A. Caquot and A. Lemaire, "Les textes
araméens de Deir 'Alla," Syria 54 (1977), 193-202; J. Hoftijzer,
"Prophet Balaam in a 6th Century Aramaic Inscription," BA 39 (1976),
11-17; G. Rinaldi, "Balaam al suo paese," BeO 20 (1978), 51-59;
H. P. Muller, "Einige alttestamentliche Probleme zur aramäischen
Inschrift von Deir 'Alla," ZDPV 94 (1978), 56-67; Robert R. Wilson,
Prophecy and Society in Ancient Israel (Philadelphia: Fortress
Press, 1980), 132-133; and Jo Ann Hackett, The Balaam Text from
Deir 'Allā, HSM (Chico, California: Scholars Press, 1984).

[7]The most thorough analysis of the "seer speech" is by Dieter
Vetter, Seherspruch und Segensschilderung: Ausdruckabsichten und
Sprachliche Verwinklungen in den Bileam-Sprüchen von Numeri 23 und
24 (Stuttgart: Calwer, 1974). Other studies of formulae within the
oracles include E. Zenger, "Funktion und Sinn der ältesten Herausführungsformel," ZDMG, Supplement (1969), 334-342; and O. Loretz,
"Die Herausführungsformel in Num 23:22 und 24:8," Ugarit-Forschung
7 (1975), 571-572. The most comprehensive form-critical study of
the prose sections of Numbers 22-24 is by Walter Gross, Bileam:
literar- und formkritische Untersuchung der Prosa in Num. 22-24.

[8]Cf. Noth, A History of Pentateuchal Traditions, 74-79; Joseph Coppens, "Les oracles de Biléam: leur origine littéraire et leur portée prophétique," Melanges Eugène Tisserant, ed. P. Hennequin et al. (Vatican City: Biblioteca Apostolica Vaticana, 1964), 67-78; and George W. Coats, "The Way of Obedience: Traditio-Historical and Hermeneutical Reflections on the Balaam Story," Semeia 24 (1982), 53-79.

[9]W. F. Albright, "The Oracles of Balaam," JBL 63 (1944), 207-233. For refinements of Albright's work, cf. S. Gevirtz, Patterns in the Early Poetry of Israel (Chicago: University of Chicago Press, 1963), 48-71; David A. Robertson, Linguistic Evidence in Dating Early Hebrew Poetry (Missoula, Montana: Society of Biblical Literature, 1972), 145, 150; Angelo Tosato, "The Literary Structure of the First Two Poems of Balaam," VT 29 (1979), 98-106; and P. C. Craigie, "The Conquest and Early Hebrew Poetry," Tyndale Bulletin 20 (1969), 76-94.

[10]Albright, "The Oracles of Balaam," 210, 226.

[11]Ibid., 208; cf. Mowinckel, "Der Ursprung der Bil'amsage," 250-259, 271.

[12]Pakozdy, "Theologische Redaktionsarbeit," 161-176.

[13]Ruth Mackensen, "The Present Literary Form of the Balaam Story," The Macdonald Presentation Volume, ed. W. G. Shellabear et al. (Princeton: Princeton University Press, 1933), 276-291.

[14]Robert Alter, The Art of Biblical Narrative (New York: Basic Books, Inc., 1981), 104-107.

[15]Ibid., 106-107.

[16]For a summary of the history of interpretation, cf. de Vaulx, Les Nombres, 263-265, 289-294; H. Karpp, "Bileam," RAC ed. T. Klauser (Stuttgart: Hiersemann Verlag, 1954), vol. 2, 362-373; Karl G. Kuhn, "Balaam," TDNT (Grand Rapids, Michigan: Wm. B. Eerdmans, 1964), vol. 1, 524-525; Geza Vermes, "The Story of Balaam, The Scriptural Origin of Haggadah," Scripture and Tradition in Judaism (Leiden: E. J. Brill, 1955), 127-177; and Judith Baskin, Pharaoh's Counsellors: Job, Jethro and Balaam in Rabbinic and Patristic Tradition (Chico, California: Scholars Press, 1984). Other studies on the messianic significance of the Balaam oracles include G. J. Brooke, "The Amos-Numbers Midrash (CD 7,136-8,1a) and Messianic Expectation," ZAW 92 (1980), 397-404; Marilyn F. Collins, Messianic Interpretation of the Balaam Oracles, dissertation, Yale University, New Haven, Conn., 1978 (on the targums and ancient versions of Numbers 24:7, 17); K. Seybold, "Das Herrscherbild des Bileamorakels, Num. 24:15-19," Theologische Zeitschrift 29 (1973), 1-19; S. Cypriani, "Il senso messianico degli oracoli di Balaam," Il Messianismo (Bresci: Paideia, 1966), 58-63; and G. H. Guyot, "The Prophecy of Balaam," CBQ 2 (1940), 330-340.

[17]On the figure of Balaam, cf. Gerhard von Rad, "Balaam," God at Work in Israel, tr. John Marks (Nashville: Abingdon Press, 1974), 36-39; Arthur E. Zannoi, "Balaam: International Wizard Prophet," The St. Luke's Journal of Theology 22 (1978), 5-19; George W. Coats, Balaam: Sinner or Saint?" Biblical Research 18 (1973), 21-29; and M. L. Digges, "Balaam: A Man in a Corner," Bible Today 13 (1964), 869-874. On the episode of Balaam and the ass, cf. Z. Sousek, Bileam und seine Eselin; exegetisch-theologische Bemerkungen zu Num. 22," Communio Viatorum 10 (1967), 183ff.; and D. M. Stanley, "Balaam's Ass, or a Problem of New Testament Hermeneutics," CBQ

20 (1958), 50-56. Other theological overviews of the Balaam cycle
include J. A. Wharton, "Command to Bless, an Exposition of Numbers
22," Int 13 (1959), 37-48; Ronald B. Allen, "The Theology of the
Balaam Oracles," Tradition and Testament: Essays in Honor of
Charles Lee Feinberg, ed. J. S. and P. D. Feinberg (Chicago: Moody
Press, 1981), 79-119; and George W. Coats, "The Way of Obedience:
Traditio-Historical and Hermeneutical Reflections on the Balaam
Story," 53-79, with a response from the perspective of process
theology by Lewis Ford, "The Divine Curse in Terms of Persuasion,"
Semeia 24 (1982), 80ff.

[18]Ruth Mackenson, "The Present Literary Form of the Balaam
Story," 276.

[19]M. Margaliot, "The Connection of the Balaam Narrative with
the Pentateuch," Proceedings of the Sixth World Congress of Jewish
Studies (1973), ed. A. Shinan (Jerusalem: World Union of Jewish
Studies, 1977), vol. 1, 279-290.

[20]Ibid., 279, 284.

[21]Ibid., 285-289.

[22]The issue of the relation of the positive and negative depictions of Balaam in the Bible has been a source of traditional and
scholarly interest. Cf. Vermes, "The Story of Balaam, The Scriptural Origin of Haggadah," 173ff.; Coats, "Balaam: Sinner or Saint?"
1-9; H. Donner, "Balaam pseudopropheta," Beiträge zur Alttestamentlichen Theologie, Festschrift für Walther Zimmerli, ed. H. Donner
et al. (Göttingen: Vandenhoeck & Ruprecht, 1977), 112-123; and
de Vaulx, Les Nombres, 263-265.

[23]As we noted above, Robert Alter has shown that the verb,
"to see," functions as a unifying Leitwort in the Balaam cycle in
Numbers 22-24. We would propose that this function extends into
Numbers 25 where the contrast between what Balaam saw in his visions
is in stark contrast with the present reality which the Israelites
see in Num.25:6-7: "And behold, one of the people of Israel came
and brought a Midianite woman to his family, in the sight of Moses
and in the sight of the whole congregation of the people of Israel,
while they were weeping at the door of the tent of meeting. When
Phinehas . . . saw it, he rose and left the congregation, and took
a spear in his hand and went after the man of Israel into the inner
room, and pierced both of them, the man of Israel and the woman,
through her body. Thus the plague was stayed from the people of
Israel."

[24]Cf. de Vaulx, Les Nombres, 289-294. We would not deny the
validity of a messianic or eschatological interpretation of the
Balaam oracles within a larger interpretive framework (e.g., the
New Testament presentation of Jesus as Messiah). Such an interpretation, however, should first seek to understand the role of the
oracles within their present literary framework in Numbers before
proceeding too quickly to a wider hermeneutical context.

[25]Noth, A History of Pentateuchal Traditions, 79.

[26]Margaliot, "The Connection of the Balaam Narrative with the
Pentateuch," 288.

NOTES TO CHAPTER EIGHT: SELECTED LEGAL MATERIAL

[1]Thus, Noth observes that "all kinds of material were added in
5:1-9:14, material which can no longer be regarded as belonging to
the various 'sources.' This material consists of numerous individual units, having no connection with one another and in whose
sequence no factual arrangement can be discerned" (Noth, Numbers,
9). The same is true of the bulk of Numbers 25-36, according to
Noth. Holzinger likewise writes that Numbers "lacks a smooth
literary flow and sense of unity. One particularly notes the
absence of any inherent connection between the history or narrative
and the legal material; this is especially true in the second and
third sections of the book" (Holzinger, Numeri, x). R. C. Dentan
describes the arrangement of the legal and other non-narrative
material as "largely fortuitous" (Dentan, "Numbers, Book of," 568).

[2]So Noth, Numbers, 6, 9.

[3]For an initial summary and bibliography, cf. W. Malcolm Clark,
"Law," Old Testament Form Criticism, ed. John Hayes (San Antonio:
Trinity University Press, 1974), 99-140; W. J. Harrelson, "Law in
the Old Testament," IDB, vol. 3, 77-89; S. Greengus, "Law in the
Old Testament," IDBSup, 532-537. The classic articles of Albrecht
Alt, "The Origins of Israelite Law," Essays on Old Testament History
and Religion, tr. R. A. Wilson (Oxford: Basil Blackwell, 1966), 79-
132; and Martin Noth, "The Laws of the Pentateuch," The Laws of the
Pentateuch and Other Studies, tr. D. R. Ap-Thomas (Philadelphia:
Fortress Press, 1967), should also be mentioned.

[4]Noth, Numbers, 6, 9; The History of Pentateuchal Traditions,
9-10.

[5]Besides the standard commentaries, cf. Roland de Vaux, Les
Sacrifices de l'Ancien Testament (Paris: J. Gabalda, 1964), 34-37,
44-48. De Vaux emphasizes the Canaanite background of the sacrifices, especially in light of the Krt text from Ugarit. René
Dussaud provided an earlier treatment in his Les Origines Cananéenes
du Sacrifice Israél (Paris: Ernest Leroux, 1921). For a summary
and bibliography on the laws of sacrifice, cf. J. Milgrom, "Sacrifices and Offerings," IDBSup, 631-635.

[6]So P. Grelot, "La Derniere Étape de la Rédaction Sacerdotale,"
VT 6 (1956), 174-189, esp. 177, 185. Grelot argues that these
texts reflect the attempt in the Persian empire to simplify and
unify legislation in the different parts of the empire. On the
basis of parallels from the papyri from Elephantine, he dates this
material to c. 419 B.C.

[7]J. Weingreen, "The Case of the Woodgatherer (Numbers XV 32-
36)," VT 16 (1966), 361-364. Weingreen's suggestion provides one
possible explanation of the original significance of the case, but
other options are available to explain why this case necessitated
a divine ruling. One alternative is that the proper mode of
execution needed to be clarified; cf. Levertoff, Midrash Sifre on
Numbers, 104. Another explanation might be that it was not clear
whether gathering wood was actually a violation of the general
prohibition against doing work on the sabbath; cf. Noth, Numbers,
117. All of these possibilities, however, are conjectural and
ignore the function of the pericope in its present literary context.

[8]Gnana Robinson, "The Prohibition of Strange Fire in Ancient
Israel, A New Look at the Case of Gathering Wood and Kindling a
Fire on the Sabbath," VT 28 (1978), 316.

[9]Ibid., 313, 317. Cf. also Gray, Numbers, 182.

[10]Ferris J. Stephans, "The Ancient Significance of Ṣiṣith," JBL 50 (1931), 59-71.

[11]Gershon Brin, "Numbers XV 22-23 and the Question of the Composition of the Pentateuch," VT 30 (1980), 349-354.

[12]Ibid., 353.

[13]The Hebrew word order in Num 15:22-23 is essentially the following: conjunction + verb ("not observe") + subject ("you") + object ("all these commandments . . ., all that the LORD has commanded you by Moses") + the formula ("from the day the LORD gave commandment and onward throughout your generations"). The same word order is apparent in 1 Sam 18:9 which uses the same chronological formula: "And Saul eyed David from that day and onward" (conjunction + verb + subject + object + the formula "from that day and onward"). Here the chronological formula clearly does not modify the object, David, but defines the duration of the clause's verbal action, "eyed." Ezek 39:22 provides another example of the use of the same formula to define the duration of the clause's main verbal action and not to modify the object of the clause: "And the house of Israel shall know that I am the LORD their God from that day and onward." Again, the chronological formula does not define when the LORD was Israel's God (that had always been true) but when the people of Israel will know that the LORD is their God (i.e., the main verbal action of the clause). Therefore, Brin's interpretation which assumes that the chronological formula somehow modifies the object in the clause rather than the main verbal action of the clause appears questionable.

[14]J. Weingreen, "The Case of the Daughters of Zelophehad," VT 16 (1966), 518-522. The other two examples are Lev 24:10-16 and Num 15:32-36.

[15]Ibid., 521-522. Bernard Jackson, "Reflections on Biblical Criminal Law," Essays in Jewish and Comparative Legal History (Leiden: E. J. Brill, 1975), 25-63, also uses Numbers 27 as evidence of the existence of such a law in early Israel.

[16]Eryl W. Davies, "Inheritance Rights and the Hebrew Levirate Marriage," VT 31 (1981), 138-144.

[17]Cyrus H. Gordon, "Paralleles Nouziens aux Lois et Coutumes de l'Ancien Testament," RB 44 (1935), 38; and more recently, Z. Ben Barak, "The Case of the Daughters of Zelophehad in Light of a New Document from Nuzi," (Hebrew with English summary), Shnaton/Annual 3 (1978), 116-123.

[18]Andre Lemaire, "Galaad et Makir, Remarques sur la Tribu de Manasse a l'Est du Jourdain," VT 31 (1981), 37-61.

[19]N. H. Snaith, "The Daughters of Zelophehad," VT 16 (1966), 124-127.

[20]David Jobling, "The Jordan a Boundary: A Reading of Numbers 32 and Joshua 22," 203-205.

[21]Ibid., 205.

[22]Katherine Doob Sakenfeld, "Old Testament Perspectives: Methodological Issues," JSOT 22 (1982), 13-20, esp. 15-16.

[23]Noth observes that Numbers 15 is "one of the very latest sections of the Pentateuch" but precise dating is difficult: "There is nothing definite to go by in order to date either the whole collection or the individual parts of it" (Noth, Numbers, 114). Numbers 27 and 36 are likewise secondary additions to P, according to Noth (Numbers, 211).

[24]Noth, Numbers, 114. In another context, Noth states that Numbers 15 was "inserted without apparent motivation" (Noth, A History of Pentateuchal Traditions, 9). James L. Mays agrees with Noth's assessment. The various sections of Numbers 15 "have no internal similarity to indicate why they are grouped together. Nor is there presupposed any connection with the story of Israel to show why the collection appears just after Israel's failure to enter Canaan in chapters 13-14" (Mays, Leviticus and Numbers, 98). Volkmar Fritz is of the same opinion: "A reason for the attachment of these ordinances to the spy story is not obvious" (Fritz, Israel in der Wüste, 24).

[25]Wenham, Numbers, 126. Such linking to surrounding material by means of key words occurs frequently in legal sections in Numbers. Cf. J. Cassuto, "The Sequence and Arrangement of Biblical Sections," Biblical and Oriental Studies, tr. Israel Abrahams (Jerusalem: The Magnes Press, 1973), vol. 1, 3-4.

[26]Quoted by S. Fisch, "The Book of Numbers," The Soncino Chumash, The Five Books of Moses with Haphtaroth, ed. A. Cohen (Hindhead: The Soncino Press, 1947), 870. Gordon Wenham, a modern commentator, also perceives the promissory effect of these laws after the spy story: "These laws reassert very plainly that the LORD will bring his people into Canaan" (Wenham, Numbers, 127).

[27]Cited in de Vaulx, Les Nombres, 189.

[28]Gray, Numbers, 396.

[29]Cf. Jobling, "The Jordan a Boundary," 204.

[30]As one commentator writes, "The law given (in Numbers) is usually case law, arising from the specific circumstances in the narrative. For instance, telling the story of the dedication of the Tabernacle occasions the statement of priestly obligations and privileges in general. From the law applicable to a particular event told in the book, the Torah proceeds to state the broader law valid for all time" (Plaut, "Numbers," The Torah, A Modern Commentary, 1011). Other laws also serve to supplement earlier laws in Exodus or Leviticus. The substitution of the Levites for the first-born of Israel in Numbers 3-4 is one example.

NOTES TO CHAPTER NINE: NUMBERS, THE PENTATEUCH AND BEYOND

[1]De Vaulx, Les Nombres, 28-40; and Bernini, Il Libro dei Numeri, 10-15.

[2]De Vaulx, Les Nombres, 40.

[3]Bernini, Il Libro dei Numeri, 15.

[4]Cf. our detailed treatment of the theology of the spy story in Chapter Six. This story is the key episode in the entire book.

[5]More conservative commentators sometimes date the Priestly
tradition to the pre-exilic period, but the majority suggest an
exilic or post-exilic date. Examples of scholars who believe the
Priestly tradition is designed to address the specific time of
Israel's exile in the sixth century B.C. include Elliger, "Sinn und
Ursprung der priesterlichen Geschichtserzählung," 121ff.;
Brueggemann, "The Kerygma of the Priestly Writers," 397-413; Rudolf
Kiliam, "Die Hoffnung auf Heimkehr in der Priesterschrift," BibLeb
7 (1966), 39-51; Sakenfeld, "The Problem of Divine Forgiveness in
Numbers 14," 329-330; and McEvenue, The Narrative Style, 144.

[6]Indeed, the exile itself, Israel's historical experience of
living between promise and fulfillment, was understood by many
groups within Judaism to have continued for centuries after the
exile had officially ended. Michael Knibb's interesting study of
the references to the exile in the intertestamental literature
concludes that "despite the many differences in presentation the
writings we have been considering all seem to share the view that
Israel remained in a state of exile long after the sixth century,
and that the exile would only be brought to an end when God
intervened in this world order to establish his rule (Michael Knibb,
"The Exile in the Literature of the Intertestamental Period," The
Heythrop Journal 17 (1976), 253-272). Our argument, of course, is
that this stance of hope and expectation has marked the people of
God throughout their history, biblical and post-biblical.

[7]Cf. Wenham, Numbers, 118-119.

[8]David J. A. Clines, The Theme of the Pentateuch (Sheffield,
England: Journal for the Study of the Old Testament, 1978).

[9]Ibid., 29.

[10]Ibid.

[11]Ibid., 87.

[12]This is also the conclusion of A. Graeme Auld, Joshua, Moses
and the Land, 114-115. It should be noted that Clines himself
recognizes that not everything in Numbers can be subsumed under the
concern for the land. Cf. Clines, The Theme of the Pentateuch, 86.

[13]That the concern for the promise of descendants also extends
into Deuteronomy is acknowledged by Clines, The Theme of the Pentateuch, 58-59. Cf. Deut 1:10-11 where Moses says to the people,
"The LORD your God has multiplied you, and behold, you are this
day as the stars of the heaven for multitude. May the LORD, the
God of your fathers, make you a thousand times as many as your are,
and bless you, as he has promised you!"

[14]For a recent study of the relation of judgment and hope in
Ezekiel and Jereimiah, cf. Thomas M. Raitt, A Theology of Exile,
Judgment/Deliverance in Jeremiah and Ezekiel (Philadelphia: Fortress
Press, 1977).

[15]De Vaulx, Les Nombres.

[16]Binns, The Book of Numbers, ixv.

[17]Albert Vanhoye, "Longue marche ou accès tout proche? Le
context biblique de Hebreux 3,7-4,11," Bib 49 (1968), 9-26; Ulrich
Mauser, Christ in the Wilderness (Naperville, Illinois: Alec R.
Allenson, Inc., 1963); and David Moessner, "Jesus and the 'Wilderness Generation,'" SBL Seminar Papers 1982, 319-340.

[18]Shemaryahu Talmon, "The 'Desert Motif' in the Bible and in Qumran Literature," Biblical Motifs, Origins and Transformations, ed. Alexander Altmann (Cambridge, Massachusetts: Harvard University Press, 1966), 31-63; and from a more New Testament orientation, Robert W. Funk, "The Wilderness," JBL 78 (1959), 205-214.

[19]Yigael Yadin, "A Crucial Passage in the Dead Sea Scrolls, 1QSa 2:11-17," JBL 78 (1959), 238-241.

[20]Cf. M. André Neher, "Ils S'Obstinerent . . .," and M. Emmanuel Levinas, "Terre Promise ou Terre Permise? Texte du Traite Sota 34b-35a," in Israël dans la Conscience Juive, Septième Colloque d'Intellectuels Juifs de Langue Francaise (1965), ed. E. Amado Lévy-Valensi and J. Halperin (Paris: Presses Universitaires de France, 1971), 151-185; Arnold Goldberg, Das Buch Numeri, 70-71; Ahad Ha-Am, "Moses," Selected Essays, tr. and ed. L. Simon (Philadelphia: Jewish Publication Society, 1912), 325; and Plaut, "Numbers," The Torah, A Modern Commentary, 1013.

[21]W. D. Davies, The Gospel and the Land, Early Christianity and Jewish Territorial Doctrine (Berkeley: University of California Press, 1974). Cf. also Eric M. Meyers and James F. Strange, "Jewish and Christian Attachment to Palestine," Archaeology, the Rabbis and Early Christianity (Nashville: Abingdon Press, 1981), 155-165.

BIBLIOGRAPHY

Aharoni, Yohanan. "Nothing Early and Nothing Late, Re-writing Israel's Conquest." _BA_ 39 (1976): 55-76.

Albright, W. F. "The Administrative Divisions of Israel and Judah." _JPOS_ 5 (1925): 17-54.

_____. "Midianite Donkey Caravans." _Translating and Understanding the Old Testament, Essays in Honor of Herbert Gordon May_. Edited by H. Frank and W. Reed. Nashville: Abingdon Press, 1970. Pp. 197-205.

_____. "The Oracles of Balaam." _JBL_ 63 (1944): 207-233.

Allegro, J. M. "Meaning of the phrase šetūm hā'ayin in Num XXIV 3, 15." _VT_ 3 (1953): 78-79.

Allen, Ronald B. "The Theology of the Balaam Oracles." _Tradition and Testament: Essays in Honor of Charles Lee Feinberg_. Edited by J. S. Feinberg and Paul D. Feinberg. Chicago: Moody Press, 1981. Pp. 79-119.

Alter, Robert. _The Art of Biblical Narrative_. New York: Basic Books, Inc., 1981.

Alterman, Hyman. _Counting People: The Census in History_. New York: Harcourt, Brace and World, Inc., 1969.

Arden, E. "How Moses Failed God." _JBL_ 76 (1957): 50-52.

Auld, A. Graeme. _Joshua, Moses and the Land_. Edinburgh: T & T Clark, 1980.

Bacher, Wilhelm. _Die Exegetische Terminologie der Jüdischen Traditionsliteratur_. Leipzig: J. C. Hinrich, 1905.

Baentsch, Bruno. _Exodus-Leviticus-Numeri_. Göttingen: Vandenhoeck & Ruprecht, 1903.

Baker, D. W. "Diversity and Unity in the Literary Structure of Genesis." _Essays on the Patriarchal Narratives_. Edited by A. R. Millard and D. J. Wiseman. Leicester, England: Intervarsity Press, 1980. Pp. 189-205.

Barnouin, M. "Les Recensements du Livre des Nombres et l'Astronomie Babylonienne." _VT_ 27 (1977): 280-303.

_____. "Remarques sur les Tableaux Numériques de Livre des Nombres." _RB_ 76 (1969): 351-364.

Baskin, Judith. _Pharaoh's Counsellors: Job, Jethro and Balaam in Rabbinic and Patristic Tradition_. Chico, California: Scholars Press, 1984.

Beltz, W. Die Kaleb-Traditionen im Alten Testament. Stuttgart: W. Kohlhammer, 1974.

Ben Barak, Z. "The Case of the Daughters of Zelophehad (Hebrew)," Shnaton/Annual 3 (1978): 116-123.

Bentzen, A. Introduction to the Old Testament. Copenhagen: G. E. C. Gad, 1959.

Bernini, Giuseppe. Il Libro dei Numeri. Rome: Marietti, 1972.

Binns, L. Elliott. The Book of Numbers, with Introduction and Notes. London: Methuen and Co., 1927.

Blau, Ludwig. Zur Einleitung in die Heilige Schrift. Budapest: n. p., 1894.

Blenkinsopp, Joseph. "Structure of P." CBQ 38 (1976): 275-292.

Brin, Gershon. "The Formulae 'From . . . and Onward/Upward." JBL 99 (1980): 351-354.

_____. "Numbers xv 22-23 and the Question of the Composition of the Pentateuch." VT 30 (1980): 351-354.

Brooke, G. J. "The Amost-Numbers Midrash (CD 7:13b-8:1a) and Messianic Expectation." ZAW 92 (1980): 397-404.

Brueggemann, Walter. "The Kerygma of the Priestly Writers." ZAW 84 (1972): 397-413; reprinted in The Vitality of Old Testament Traditions. Edited by W. Brueggemann and Hans Walter Wolff. Atlanta: John Knox Press, 1976. Pp. 101-113.

Buis, P. "Qadesh, un lieu maudit?" VT 24 (1974): 268-285.

Bush, George. Notes, Critical and Practical, on the Book of Numbers. New York: Ivison, Phinney, Blakeman, 1868.

Caine, I. "Numbers, Book of." EncJud. New York: Macmillan Co., 1971. Vol. 12. Pp. 1249-1254.

Calvin, John. Calvin's Commentaries. Translated by C. W. Bingham. Grand Rapids, Michigan: Baker Book House Co., 1979. Vol. 3.

Castellino, R. "Un 'giudizio divino' con rituale in Mesopotamia?" JCS 9 (1977): 3-6, 32-36.

Cazelles, Henri. Les Nombres. Paris: Éditions du Cerf, 1952.

Childs, Brevard S. Introduction to the Old Testament as Scripture. Philadelphia: Fortress Press, 1979.

Clamer, A. Lévitique, Nombres, Deutéronome. Edited by L. Pirot. Paris: La Sainte Bible, 1940. Vol. 2.

Clark, R. E. D. "The Large Numbers in the Old Testament." Journal of the Transactions of the Victoria Institute 87 (1955): 82-92.

Clark, W. Malcolm. "Law." Old Testament Form Criticism. Edited by John H. Hayes. San Antonio: Trinity University Press, 1974. Pp. 99-140.

Clines, David J. A. The Theme of the Pentateuch. Sheffield,
     England: Journal for the Study of the Old Testament, 1978.

Coats, George W. "Balaam: Sinner or Saint?" Biblical Research
     18 (1973): 21-29.

_____. "An Exposition of the Wilderness Traditions." VT 22
     (1972): 288-295.

_____. "Legendary Motifs in the Moses Death Reports." CBQ 39
     (1977): 34-44.

_____. Rebellion in the Wilderness. Nashville: Abingdon Press,
     1968.

_____. "A Structural Transition in Exodus 1:1-14." VT 22
     (1972): 129-142.

_____. The Way of Obedience: Traditio-Historical and Hermeneu-
     tical Reflections on the Balaam Story." Semeia 24 (1982):
     53-79.

_____. "Wilderness Itinerary." CBQ 34 (1972): 135-152.

Cody, Aelred. A History of the Old Testament Priesthood. Rome:
     Pontifical Biblical Institute, 1969.

_____. "The Phonecian Ecstatis in Wenamūn, a Professional
     Oracular Medium." Journal of Egyptian Archaeology 65 (1979):
     99-106.

Collins, Marilyn F. Messianic Interpretations of the Balaam Oracles.
     Ph.D. dissertation, Yale University, 1979.

Coppens, Joseph. "Les Oracles de Bileam: Leur Origine Littéraire
     et leur Portée Prophétique." Melanges Eugène Tisserant.
     Edited by P. Hennequin et al. Vatican City: Biblioteca
     Apostolica Vaticana, 1964. Pp. 67-78.

Cortese, Enzo. "Dimensioni Letterarie e Elementi Structurali de Pg:
     Per una Teologia del Documento Sacerdotale." Rivista Biblica
     (Italiana) 25 (1977): 113-141.

_____. "Num. 33:50-56 e la Teologia Sacerdotale della Terra."
     Rivista Biblica (Italiana) 28 (1980): 59-77.

_____. La Terra de Canaan nella Storia Sacerdotale del Penta-
     teuco. Brescia: Paideia, 1972.

Craigie, P. C. "The Conquest and Early Hebrew Poetry." Tyndale
     Bulletin 20 (1969): 76-94.

Cross, Frank M. Canaanite Myth and Hebrew Epic. Cambridge, Massa-
     chusetts: Harvard University Press, 1973.

_____. "The Priestly Tabernacle in the Light of Recent Research."
     Temples and High Places in Biblical Times, Proceedings of the
     Colloquium in Honor of the Centenniel of Hebrew Union College-
     Jewish Institute of Religion. Jerusalem: The Nelson Glueck
     School of Biblical Archaeology, 1981. Pp. 170-172.

_____. "The Tabernacle: A Study from an Archaeological and
     Historical Approach." BA 10 (1947): 45-68.

Cypriani, Settimio. "Il Senso Messianico degli Oracoli de Balaam."
Il Messianismo. Brescia: Paideia, 1966. Pp. 58-63.

Davies, Eryl. "Inheritance Rights and Hebrew Levirate Marriage."
VT 31 (1981): 138-144.

Davies, G. I. The Way of the Wilderness. New York: Cambrige
University Press, 1979.

_____. "The Wilderness Itineraries: A Comparative Approach."
Tyndale Bulletin 25 (1974): 46-81.

_____. "The Wilderness Itineraries and the Composition of the
Pentateuch." VT 33 (1983): 1-13.

Davies, W. D. The Gospel and the Land: Early Christianity and
Jewish Territorial Doctrine. Berkeley: University of
California Press, 1974.

Dentan, R. C. "Numbers, Book of." IDB. New York: Abingdon Press,
1962. Vol. 3. Pp. 567-571.

De Vries, S. J. "Origin of the Murmuring Tradition." JBL 87
(1968): 51-69.

Digges, M. L., Sr. "Balaam: A Man in a Corner." Bible Today 13
(1964): 869-874.

Dillmann, August. Die Bücher Numeri, Deuteronomium und Joshua.
Leipzig: S. Hirzel, 1886.

Donner, Herbert. "Balaam Pseudopropheta." Beiträge zur Alttestamentlichen Theologie, Festschrift für Walther Zimmerli zum
70 Geburtsdag. Edited by H. Donner et al. Göttingen:
Vandenhoeck & Ruprecht, 1977.

Drubbel, A. Numeri uit de Grondtekst Vertaald en Uitgelegd, De
Boeken van het Oude Testament, Deel II, Boek II. Roermond en
Maaseik: Romen and Zonen, 1963.

Edelkoort, A. H. Numeri. Groningen: Wolters, 1930.

Eerdmans, B. D. "The Composition of Numbers." Oudtestamentische
Studiën 6 (1949): 101-216.

Eising, H. "Balaams Eselin." Bibel und Kirche 13 (1958): 45-46.

Eissfeldt, Otto. "Biblos geneseos." Kleine Schriften. Tübingen:
C. B. Mohr, 1966. Vol. 3. Pp. 459-462.

_____. "Die Komposition der Bileam-Erzählung, Eine Nachprüfung
von Rudolphs Beitrag zur Hexateuchkritik." ZAW 57 (1939): 212ff.

_____. The Old Testament, An Introduction. Translated by Peter
Ackroyd. New York: Harper and Row, 1965.

_____. "Protektorat der Midianiter über ihre Nachbarn im Letzen
Viertel des 2 Jahrtausends v. Chr. mit Beiträgen von William
F. Albright." JBL 87 (1968): 383-393.

_____. "Sinai Erzählung und Bileam-Sprüche." HUCA 32 (1961):
179-190.

Elliger, Karl. "Sinn und Ursprung der Priesterliche Geschichts-
     erzählung." Zeitschrift für Theologie und Kirche 49 (1952):
     121-143; reprinted in Elliger. Kleine Schriften zum Alten
     Testaments. Edited by H. Gese and O. Kaiser. Munich: Chr.
     Kaiser Verlag, 1966. Pp. 174-198.

Enciso, J. "El Jahwismo de Balaam." Estudia Biblica 3 (1931):
     123-129.

Engnell, Ivan. "The Wilderness Wandering." A Rigid Scrutiny.
     Translated by John T. Willis. Nashville: Vanderbilt University
     Press, 1969. Pp. 207-214.

Erdman, Charles R. The Book of Numbers, an Exposition. Westwood,
     N. J.: Revell, 1952.

Erform, R. "Military Intelligence in the Bible." Dor le Dor 5
     (1976): 183-191.

Fichter, J. "Die Etymologische Ätiologie in den Namengebungen."
     VT 6 (1956): 372-396.

Fisch, S. "The Book of Numbers." The Soncino Chumash, The Five
     Books of Moses with Haphtaroth. Edited by A. Cohen.
     Hindhead: The Soncino Press, 1947. Pp. 793-987.

Flack, E. E. "Flashes of New Knowledge, Recent Study and the Book
     of Numbers." Int 13 (1959): 3-23.

Flanagan, James W. "History, Religion and Ideology: The Caleb
     Tradition." Horizons 3 (1976): 175-185.

Ford, Lewis S. "The Divine Curse Understood in Terms of Persuasion."
     Semeia 24 (1982): 81-87.

Friedman, Richard E. The Exile and Biblical Narrative, HSM. Chico,
     California: Scholars Press, 1981.

Fritz, Volkmar. Israel in der Wüste, Traditionsgeschichtliche
     Untersuchung der Wüstenüberlieferung des Jahwisten. Marburg:
     N. G. Elwert Verlag, 1970.

Genung, George F. The Book of Numbers. Philadelphia: American
     Baptist Publication Society, 1906.

Ginsburg, Christian D. Introduction to the Massoretico-Critical
     Edition of the Hebrew Bible. London: Trinitarian Bible
     Society, 1897.

Gispen, Willem H. Het Boek Numeri. Kampen: J. H. Kok, 1959, 1965.
     2 volumes.

Goldberg, Arnold Maria. Das Buch Numeri. Düsseldorf: Patmos-
     Verlag, 1970.

Görg, M. "Die 'Heimat Bileams.'" Biblische Notizen 1 (1976): 24-28.

Gottwald, Norman. The Tribes of Yahweh. Maryknoll, New York:
     Orbis Books, 1979.

Gray, George B. A Critical and Exegetical Commentary on Numbers,
     ICC. New York: Scribner, 1903.

Greenstone, Julius H. Numbers, with Commentary. Philadelphia: Jewish Publication Society, 1948.

Grelot, P. "La Derniere Étape de la Rédaction Sacerdotale." VT 6 (1956): 174-189.

Gressmann, Hugo. Mose und seine Zeit. Göttingen: Vandenhoeck & Ruprecht, 1913.

_____. Die Schriften des Alten Testaments. Göttingen: Vandenhoeck & Ruprecht, 1910, 1914. Volumes 2 and 3.

Gross, Walter. Bileam: Literar- und Formkritische Untersuchung der Prosa im Num. 22-24. Munich: Kösel, 1974.

Gunneweg, A. H. J. Leviten und Priester. Göttingen: Vandenhoeck & Ruprecht, 1965.

Guthrie, Harvey H. "The Book of Numbers." The Interpreter's One-Volume Commentary on the Bible. Edited by Charles M. Laymon. Nashville: Abingdon Press, 1971. Pp. 85-99.

Guyot, G. H. "The Prophecy of Balaam." CBQ 2 (1940): 330-340.

Hackett, Jo Ann. The Balaam Text from Deir ʿAllā, HSM. Chico, California: Scholars Press, 1984.

Haran, M. "Nature of the ʿōhel môʿēdh in Pentateuchal Sources." JSS 5 (1960): 50-65.

_____. "Studies in the Account of the Levitical Cities." JBL 80 (1961): 45-54.

Harrelson, W. "Guidance in the Wilderness, the Theology of Numbers." Int 13 (1959): 24-36.

Heinisch, P. Das Buch Numeri, Die Heilige Schrift des Alten Testament. Bonn: Peter Hanstein, 1936.

Hoftijzer, Jacob. "The Prophet Balaam in a 6th Century Aramaic Inscription." BA 39 (1976): 11-17.

Holzinger, Heinrich. Numeri. Tübingen: J. C. B. Mohr, 1903.

Hurvitz, A. "Evidence of Language in Dating the Priestly Code; a Linguistic Study in Technical Terms and Terminology." RB 81 (1974): 24-56.

Jackson, Bernard. "Reflections on Biblical Criminal Law." Essays in Jewish and Comparative Legal History. Leiden: E. J. Brill, 1975. Pp. 25-63.

Jacob, B. Der Pentateuch, Exegetisch-Kritische Forschungen. Leipzig: Verlag von Veit, 1905.

Jaubert, A. "Le Calendrier des Jubilés et de la Secte de Qumrân, Ses Origines Bibliques." VT 3 (1953): 250-264.

Jellicoe, Sidney. The Septuagint and Modern Study. Oxford: Clarendon Press, 1968.

Jirku, Ant. "Wo Stand Ursprünglich die Notiz über Hebron in Num. 13:22?" ZAW 39 (1921): 312.

Jobling, David. "The Jordan a Boundary: A Reading of Numbers 32
    and Joshua 22." Society of Biblical Literature, 1980 Seminar
    Papers. Edited by Paul J. Achtemeier. Chico, California:
    Scholars Press, 1980. Pp. 183-207.

Kaiser, Otto. Introduction to the Old Testament. Translated by
    John Sturdy. Minneapolis, Minnesota: Augsburg Publishing
    House, 1975.

Kapelrud, A. S. "The Date of the Priestly Code." Annual of the
    Swedish Theological Institute in Jerusalem 3 (1964): 58-64.

Karpp, H. "Bileam." Reallexicon für Antike und Christentum. Edited
    by T. Klausner. Stuttgart: Hiersemann Verlag, 1954. Volume
    2. Pp. 362-373.

Kaufmann, Y. "Der Kalendar und der Priester-Kodex." VT 4 (1954):
    307-313.

Keil, Karl Friedrich. The Pentateuch. Translated by James Martin.
    Edinburgh: T & T Clark, 1869, 1870.

Kellermann, Diether. Die Priesterschrift von Numeri 1,1 bis 10,10,
    Literarkritisch und Traditionsgeschichtlich Untersucht.
    Berlin: W. de Gruyter, 1970.

Kennedy, A. R. S. Leviticus and Numbers. New York: Oxford Univer-
    sity Press, 1910.

Kilian, R. "Die Hoffnung auf Heimkehr in der Priesterschrift."
    BibLeb 7 (1966): 39-51.

Kittel, R. History of the Hebrews. Edinburgh: Williams and Norgate,
    1895. Volume 1.

Klein, Ralph. "How Many in a Thousand?" A seminar paper read at
    the Society of Biblical Literature annual meeting, New York,
    December 20, 1982.

_____. Textual Criticism of the Old Testament, The Septuagint
    after Qumran. Philadelphia: Fortress Press, 1974.

Knobel, August. Die Bücher Numeri, Deuteronomium und Joshua.
    Leipzig: S. Hirzel, 1861.

Krämer, K. F. Numeri und Deuteronomium Übersetz und Erklärt.
    Frankfort: Herder, 1955.

Kuhn, Karl Georg. Sifre zu Numeri, Der Tannaitische Midrasch.
    Stuttgart: W. Kohlhammer, 1959. Volume 2.

Kupper, J. R. Les Nomades en Mésopotamie au Temps de Rois de Mari.
    Paris: Société d'Edition Les Belles Lettres, 1957.

_____. "Le Recensement dans les Texte de Mari." Studia Mariana.
    Edited by A. Parrot. Leiden: E. J. Brill, 1950. Pp. 99-110.

Kuschke, A. "Die Lagervorstellung der Priesterschriftlichen
    Erzählung." ZAW 63 (1951): 74-105.

Lange, Johann Peter. Numbers, or the Fourth Book of Moses. Trans-
    lated by Samuel Lowrie and A. Gosman. New York: Scribner's,
    1879.

Largement, René. "Les Oracles de Bileam de la Mantique Suméro-
    Akkadienne." Travaux de l'Institut Catholique de Paris,
    École des Langues Orientales Anciennes de l'Institut Catholique
    de Paris: Mémorial du Cinquanteraire. Edited by E. Tisserant
    et al. Paris: Bloud and Gay, 1964. Pp. 37-50.

Leiman, Sid Z. The Canonization of Hebrew Scripture. Hamden,
    Connecticut: Archon Books, 1976.

Lemaire, André. "Galaad et Makîr. Remarques sur la Tribu de
    Manassé à l'Est du Jourdain." VT 31 (1981): 39-61.

Levertoff, Paul. Midrash Sifre on Numbers. London: Society for
    Promoting Christian Knowledge, 1926.

Levinas, Emmanuel. "Terre Promise ou Terre Permise? Texte du
    Traité Sota 34b-35a." Israël dans la Conscience Juive,
    Septième Colloque d'Intellectuels Juifs de Langue Française
    (1965). Edited by E. Amado Lévy-Valensi and J. Halperin.
    Paris: Presses Universitaires de France, 1971. Pp. 151-185.

Levine, Baruch A. In the Presence of the Lord, A Study of Cult
    and Cultic Terms in Ancient Israel. Leiden: E. J. Brill, 1974.

_____. "Numbers, Book of." IDBSup. Edited by Keith Crim et
    al. Nashville: Abingdon Press, 1976. Pp. 631-635.

Liver, J. "The Half-Shekel Offering in Biblical and Post-Biblical
    Literature." HTR 56 (1963): 173-198.

Loewe, Raphael. "Divine Frustration Exegetically Frustrated--
    Numbers 14:34." Words and Meanings, Essays Presented to
    David Winton Thomas. Edited by Peter Ackroyd and Barnabas
    Lindars. Cambridge: Cambridge University Press, 1968. Pp.
    137-158.

Lohfink, Norbert. "Die Priesterschrift und die Geschichte."
    Supplements to Vetus Testamentum, Congress Volume, Göttingen
    1977. Leiden: E. J. Brill, 1978. Pp. 189-225.

Loretz, O. "Die Herausführungsformel in Num. 23:22 und 24:8."
    Ugarit-Forschungen 7 (1975): 571-572.

Lucas, A. "The Number of Israelites at the Exodus." PEQ (1944):
    164-168.

McEvenue, Sean E. The Narrative Style of the Priestly Writer.
    Rome: Biblical Institute Press, 1971.

_____. "A Source-Critical Problem in Num. 14:26-38." Biblica
    50 (1969): 453-465.

Mackensen, Ruth S. "The Present Literary Form of the Balaam Story."
    D. B. MacDonald Presentation Volume. Edited by W. G.
    Shellabear et al. Princeton, N. J.: Princeton University
    Press, 1933. Pp. 276-291.

Mackintosh, Charles. Notes on the Book of Numbers. New York:
    Loizeaux Brothers, 1882.

McNeile, A. H. The Book of Numbers in the Revised Version.
    Cambridge: Cambridge University Press, 1911.

Malamat, A. "UMMATUM in Old Babylonian Texts and its Ugaritic and
    Biblical Counterparts." Ugarit-Forschungen 11 (1979): 527-536.

Mann, Thomas. "Theological Reflections on the Denial of Moses."
    JBL 98 (1979): 481-494.

Margaliot, M. "The Connection of the Balaam Narrative with the
    Pentateuch." Proceedings of the Sixth World Congress of
    Jewish Studies (1973). Edited by A. Shinan. Jerusalem: World
    Union of Jewish Studies, 1977. Volume 1. Pp. 279-290.

Marsh, J. "The Book of Numbers (Exegesis)." IB. New York:
    Abingdon Press, 1953. Volume 2. Pp. 137-308.

Mauser, Ulrich. Christ in the Wilderness, The Wilderness Theme in
    the Second Gospel and its Basis in the Biblical Tradition.
    Naperville, Illinois: Alec R. Allenson, Inc., 1963.

Mayes, A. D. H. Israel in the Period of the Judges. Naperville,
    Alec R. Allenson, Inc., 1974.

Mays, James L. The Book of Leviticus, The Book of Numbers, Layman's
    Bible Commentary. Richmond, Virginia: John Knox Press, 1963.

Mazar, B. "The Cities of the Priests and the Levites." Supplements
    to Vetus Testamentum. Leiden: E. J. Brill, 1960. Volume 7.
    Pp. 193-205.

Mendenhall, George E. "The Census Lists of Numbers 1 and 26." JBL
    77 (1958): 52-66.

_____. "The Hebrew Conquest of Palestine." BA 25 (1962): 66-87.

_____. "Social Organization in Early Israel." Magnalia Dei:
    The Mighty Acts of God, In Memorium G. E. Wright. Edited by
    Frank M. Cross et al. New York: Doubleday, 1976.

Meyers, Eric M. and James F. Strange. "Jewish and Christian
    Attachment to Palestine." Archaeology, the Rabbis and Early
    Christianity. Nashville: Abingdon Press, 1981. Pp. 155-165.

Milgrom, Jacob. "Levitical ʿabodā." JQR 61 (1970): 132-154.

_____. "Priestly Terminology and the Political and Social
    Structure of Pre-Monarchic Israel." JQR 69 (1978): 65-81.

Mohlenbrink, K. "Die Levitischen Überlieferungen des Alten
    Testaments." ZAW 52 (1934): 184-231.

Moessner, David P. "Jesus and the Wilderness Generation." Society
    of Biblical Literature, 1982 Seminar Papers. Edited by Kent
    Harold Richards. Chico, California: Scholars Press, 1982.
    Pp. 319-340.

Moriarty, F. L. "Numbers." The Jerome Biblical Commentary. Edited
    by Raymond Brown et al. Englewood Cliffs, New Jersey: Prentice-
    Hall, Inc., 1968. Pp. 86-100.

Mowinckel, Sigmund. Tetrateuch, Pentateuch, Hexateuch. Die
    Berichte über die Landnahme. Berlin: A. Töpelmann, 1964.

_____. "Der Ursprung der Bil'amsage," ZAW 48 (1930): 233-271.

Müller, H. P. "Einige Alttestamentliche Probleme zur Aramäischen
    Inschrift von Deir ʿAllā." ZDPV 94 (1978): 56-67.

Na'aman, N. "Hebron Was Built Seven Years before Zoan in Egypt."
    VT 31 (1981): 488-492.

North, Robert. "Can Geography Save J from Rendtorff?" <u>Bib</u> 63
    (1982): 47-55.

Noth, Martin. <u>The History of Israel</u>. New York: Harper and
    Brothers, 1960. Second edition.

_____. <u>A History of Pentateuchal Traditions</u>. Translated by
    Bernhard W. Anderson. Chico, California: Scholars Press, 1981.

_____. <u>The Laws in the Pentateuch and Other Essays</u>. Translated
    by D. R. Ap-Thomas. Philadelphia: Fortress Press, 1967.

_____. <u>Numbers, A Commentary</u>, OTL. Translated by James D.
    Martin. Philadelphia: Westminster Press, 1968.

_____. <u>Der System der Zwölf Stämme Israels</u>. Darmstadt:
    Wissenschaftliche Buchgesellschaft, 1930, reprinted 1966.

_____. <u>Überlieferungsgeschichtliche Studien</u>. Tübingen: Max
    Niemeyer Verlag, 1957.

_____. "Der Wallfahrtsweg zum Sinai." <u>PJ</u> 36 (1940): 5-28.

Oesch, Josef M. <u>Petucha und Setuma, Untersuchungen zu einer</u>
    <u>Überlieferten Gliederung im Hebräischen Text des Alten</u>
    <u>Testaments</u>. Göttingen: Vandenhoeck & Ruprecht, 1979.

Origen, "Homily XXVII on Numbers." Origen, <u>The Classics of</u>
    <u>Western Spirituality</u>. Translation by Roland A. Greer.
    New York: Paulist Press, 1979.

Owens, John Joseph. "Numbers." <u>Leviticus-Ruth, The Broadman</u>
    <u>Bible Commentary</u>. Edited by C. J. Allen et al. Nashville:
    Abingdon Press, 1970. Volume 2. Pp. 75-174.

Pace, James H. <u>The Caleb Traditions and the Role of the Calebites</u>
    <u>in the History of Israel</u>. Ph.D. dissertation, Emory Univer-
    sity, 1976.

Pakozdy, L. M. "Theologische Redaktionsarbeit in der Bileam-
    Perikope." <u>Von Ugarit nach Qumran</u>. Edited by J. Hempel and
    L. Rost. Berlin: A. Töpelmann, 1961. Pp. 161-176.

Petrie, Sir W. M. Flinders. <u>Egypt and Israel</u>. New York: The
    Macmillan Co., 1923.

_____. <u>Researches in Sinai</u>. New York: E. P. Dutton and Co.,
    1906.

Plaut, W. Gunther and William Hallo. "Numbers." <u>The Torah, A</u>
    <u>Modern Commentary</u>. New York: Union of American Hebrew
    Congregations, 1981. Pp. 1009-1286.

Procksch, Otto. <u>Genesis</u>, KAT. Leipzig: Gutersloh, 1924.

Rad, Gerhard von. "Balaam." <u>God at Work in Israel</u>. Translated
    by John Marks. Nashville: Abingdon Press, 1980.

_____. <u>Genesis</u>, OTL. Philadelphia: Westminster Press, 1972.

Raitt, Thomas M. <u>A Theology of Exile, Judgment/Deliverance in</u>
    <u>Jeremiah and Ezekiel</u>. Philadelphia: Fortress Press, 1977.

Razin, M. Census Lists and Genealogies and their Historical
    Implications for the Times of David and Saul (Hebrew). Haifa:
    The School of Education of the Kibbutz Movement, 1977.

Rendtorff, Rolf. Die Gesetze in der Priesterschrift, Eine
    Gattungsgeschichtliche Untersuchung. Göttingen: Vandenhoeck
    & Ruprecht, 1954.

_____. Das Überlieferungsgeschichtliche Problem des Pentateuch.
    Berlin: W. de Gruyter, 1977.

_____. "Traditio-historical Method and the Documentary
    Hypothesis." Proceedings of the World Congress of Jewish
    Studies 5 (1969): 5-11.

_____. "The Yahwist as Theologian: Dilemma of Pentateuchal
    Criticism." JSOT 3 (1977): 2-45.

Riggans, Walter. Numbers, Daily Study Bible. Philadelphia:
    Westminster Press, 1983.

Rinaldi, G. "Balaam al suo Paese." BeO 20 (1978): 51-59.

Robinson, Gnana. "The Prohibition of Strange Fire in Ancient
    Israel, A New Look at the Case of Gathering Wood and Kindling
    Fire on the Sabbath." VT 28 (1978): 301-317.

Robertson, David A. Linguistic Evidence in Dating Early Hebrew
    Poetry. Missoula, Montana: Society of Biblical Literature,
    1972.

Rofé, Alexander. The Book of Balaam (Hebrew). Jerusalem: Simor
    Ltd., 1979.

Rost, Leonhard. "Fragen um Bileam." Beiträge zur Alttestament-
    lichen Theologie, Festschrift für Walther Zimmerli zum 70
    Geburtsdag. Edited by H. Donner et al. Göttingen:
    Vandenhoeck & Ruprecht, 1977. Pp. 377-387.

Rouillard, Hedwige. "L'ânesse de Balaam." RB 87 (1980): 5-36,
    211-241.

Rowley, H. H. From Joseph to Joshua. London: Oxford University
    Press, 1950.

Ryle, Herbert Edward. The Canon of the Old Testament. London:
    Macmillan, 1895.

Sakenfeld, Katherine Doob. "Old Testament Perspectives: Methodo-
    logical Issues." JSOT 22 (1982): 13-20.

_____. "Problem of Divine Forgiveness in Numbers 14." CBQ
    37 (1975): 317-330.

Sanders, James. Torah and Canon. Philadelphia: Fortress Press,
    1972.

Santos Olivera, B. "La Estrella de Jacob." Estudia Biblica 3
    (1931): 55-58.

Sarna, Nahum. "Bible." EncJud. New York: Macmillan, 1971.
    Volume 4. Pp. 814-969.

Sasson, Jack M. "A 'Genealogical Convention' in Biblical Chronography?" ZAW 90 (1978): 171-185.

Scharbert, J. "Der Sinn der Toledot-Formel in Priesterschrift." Wort-Gebot-Glaube. Edited by H. J. Stoebe. Zürich: Zwingli Verlag, 1970. Pp. 45-56.

Schedl, Claus. "Biblische Zahlen--unglaubwürdig?" Theologisch-praktische Quartalschrift 107 (1959): 58-62.

Schmid, Hans H. Der Sogennante Jahwist: Beobachtungen und Fragen zur Pentateuchforschung. Zurich: Theologisches Verlag, 1976.

Schmidt, Ludwig. "Die Alttestamentliche Bileamüberlieferung." BZ 23 (1979): 234-261.

Schmidt, Werner H. "Ein Theologie in Salomonischer Zeit? Plädoyer für den Jahwisten." BZ 25 (1981): 82-102.

Schneider, Heinrich. "Numeri." Zweites bis Funftes Buch Moses, Echter Bibel. Edited by Heinrich Schneider and Hubert Junker. Würzberg: Echter Verlag, 1952.

Seybold, K. "Das Herrscherbild des Bileamorakels, Num. 24:15-19." Theologische Zeitschrift 29 (1973): 1-19.

Skehan, Patrick. "The Biblical Scrolls from Qumran and the Text of the Old Testament." BA 28 (1965): 87-100.

Smend, Rudolf. Die Entstehung des Alten Testaments. Stuttgart: Verlag W. Kohlhammer, 1978.

Smick, Elmer B. "A Study of the Structure of the Third Balaam Oracle." Law and the Prophets, Festschrift for Oswald Thompson. Edited by J. H. Skilton. N. p.: Presbyterian and Reformed Publishing Co., 1974. Pp. 242-252.

Snaith, N. H. "Daughters of Zelophehad." VT 16 (1966): 124-127.

_____. Leviticus and Numbers, The Century Bible. London: Nelson, 1967.

_____. "Numbers." PCB. London: Thomas Nelson and Sons, 1962. Pp. 254-268.

Sousek, Z. "Bileam und seine Eselin, Exegetisch-theologische Bemerkungen zu Num 22." Communio Viatorum 10 (1967): 183-186.

Speiser, E. A. "The Alalakh Tablets." JAOS 74 (1954): 18-25.

_____. "Census and Ritual Expiation in Mari and Israel." Biblical and Oriental Studies. Philadelphia: University of Pennsylvania Press, 1967. Pp. 171-186.

_____. Genesis, AB. Garden City, New York: Doubleday and Co., 1964.

Steele, Daniel. Leviticus and Numbers. New York: Hunt and Eaton, 1891.

Stanley, D. M. "Balaam's Ass, or a Problem of New Testament Hermeneutics." CBQ 20 (1958): 50-56.

Strack, H. L. Die Bücher Genesis, Exodus, Leviticus und Numeri,
    Kurzgefasster Kommentar zu den Heiligen Schriften Alten und
    Neuen Testamentes sowie zu den Apokryphen. Nordlingen: C. H.
    Beck, 1894.

Sturdy, John. Numbers. New York: Cambridge University Press, 1976.

Swete, Henry Barclay. An Introduction to the Old Testament in
    Greek. Revised by R. R. Ottley. Cambridge: Cambridge
    University Press, 1914.

Tengström, Sven. Die Toledotformel und die Literarische Struktur
    der Priesterlichen Erweiterungsschicht im Pentateuch. Lund:
    GWK Gleerup, 1982.

Thompson, J. A. "Numbers." The New Bible Commentary, Revised.
    Edited by D. Guthrie et al. Grand Rapids, Michigan: Eerdmans,
    1970. Pp. 168-200.

Thompson, Robert John. Moses and the Law in a Century of Criticism
    since Graf. Leiden: E. J. Brill, 1970.

Tosato, Angelo. "The Literary Structure of the First Two Poems of
    Balaam." VT 29 (1979): 98-106.

Tunyogi, Andrew C. "The Rebellions of Israel." JBL 81 (1962):
    385-390.

_____. The Rebellions of Israel. Richmond, Virginia: John
    Knox Press, 1969.

Ubach, Bonaventura. Els Nombres-El Deuteronomi, Lu Biblia, III.
    Montserrat: Monestir, 1928.

Valvekens, J. B. Het Boek Numeri. Brugge: Beyaert, 1935.

Vanhoye, A. "Longue Marche ou Accèss Tout Proche? Le Context de
    Hebreux 3,7-4,11." Bib 49 (1968): 9-26.

Van Seters, John. "Recent Studies on the Pentateuch: A Crisis in
    Method." JAOS 99 (1979): 663-672.

_____. "Tradition and Social Change in Ancient Israel."
    Perspectives in Religious Studies 7 (1980): 96-113.

Vaulx, J. de. Les Nombres. Paris: J. Gabalda, 1972.

Vaux, Roland de. Ancient Israel, Social Institutions. New York:
    McGraw-Hill, Inc., 1965. Volume 1.

_____. "Ark of the Covenant and Tent of Reunion." The Bible
    and the Ancient Near East. Translated by Damian McHugh.
    Garden City, New York: Doubleday, 1971. Pp. 136-151.

_____. The Early History of Israel. Translated by David Smith.
    Philadelphia: Westminster Press, 1978.

_____. "L'Itinéraire des Israéliens de Cadès aux Plaines de
    Moab." Hommages à André Dupont-Sommer. Paris: Librairie
    d'Amerique et d'Orient, 1971. Pp. 331-342.

_____. "Reflections on the Present State of Pentateuchal
    Criticism." The Bible and the Ancient Near East. Translated
    by Damian McHugh. Garden City, New York: Doubleday, 1971.
    Pp. 31-48.

Vermes, Geza. "The Story of Balaam, The Scriptural Origin of
    Haggadah." Scripture and Tradition in Judaism. Leiden:
    E. J. Brill, 1955. Pp. 127-177.

Vetter, Dieter. Seherspruch und Segensschilderung: Ausdrucks-
    absichten und Sprachliche Verwirklungen in den Bileam-Sprüchen
    von Numeri 23 und 24. Stuttgart: Calwer, 1974.

Wagner, S. "Die Kundschaftergeschichten im Alten Testament." ZAW
    76 (1964): 255-269.

Walsh, Jerome T. "From Egypt to Moab: A Source Critical Analysis
    of the Wilderness Itinerary." CBQ 39 (1977): 20-33.

Watson, Robert A. Leviticus-Numbers, The Expositor's Bible. Edited
    by W. Robertson Nicoll. New York: A. C. Armstrong and Son,
    1903.

Weingreen, J. "Case of the Woodgatherer; Numbers XV:32-36." VT
    16 (1966): 361-364.

_____. "Case of the Daughters of Zelophehad (Numbers 27:1-11)."
    VT 16 (1966): 361-364.

Weippert, Manfred. The Settlement of the Israelite Tribes in
    Palestine. Naperville, Illinois: Alec R. Allenson, Inc., 1971.

Wellhausen, Julius. Prolegomena to the History of Ancient Israel.
    Gloucester, Massachusetts: Peter Smith, 1883, reprinted 1973.

Wenham, Gordon J. Numbers, An Introduction and Commentary.
    Downers Grove, Illinois: Inter-Varsity Press, 1981.

Wenham, J. W. "Large Numbers in the Old Testament." Tyndale
    Bulletin 18 (1967): 19-53.

Wharton, J. A. "Command to Bless; An Exposition of Numbers 22."
    Int 13 (1959): 37-48.

Wilson, Robert R. "Between 'Azel' and 'Azel,' Interpreting the
    Biblical Genealogies." BA 42 (1979): 11-22.

_____. "The Old Testament Genealogies in Recent Research."
    JBL 94 (1975): 169-189.

_____. Genealogy and History in the Biblical World. New Haven:
    Yale University Press, 1977.

_____. Prophecy and Society in Ancient Israel. Philadelphia:
    Fortress Press, 1980.

Wiseman, J. D. The Alalakh Texts. London: n. p., 1953.

Zannoi, Arthur E. "Balaam: International Seer/Wizard Prophet."
    The St. Luke's Journal of Theology 22 (1978): 5-19.

Zenger, E. "Funktion und Sinn der Ältesten Herausführungsformel."
    ZDMG, Supplement 1 (1969): 334-342.

INDEX OF BIBLICAL REFERENCES